the Big House Party

While all reasonable care has been taken in the preparation of this book, we cannot accept responsibility for any consequences arising from the use of the information provided herein.

First published in Great Britain in October 2005
by Pendant Press
48 The Paragon, Searles Road, London SE1 4YL

ISBN 0-9549321-0-2

A CIP catalogue record for this book is
available from the British Library.

Design by em Creative
Printed and bound in the UK by Butler & Tanner

10 9 8 7 6 5 4 3 2 1

Contents

It all started when we were trying to find a suitable venue for a mutual friend's 40th birthday bash. Given that we are both travel journalists, we thought it would be relatively easy. But after hours of frustrating searches on the internet, scouring numerous guidebooks and leafing through cottage holiday brochures, we realised it wasn't so simple. There wasn't a book offering good-quality venues that could accommodate large groups. So we set out to write one.

Ten years ago most of us would have been content with hiring a pub or local restaurant to celebrate a landmark birthday or other special occasion. Today we're more likely to make it an even bigger event by going away for a weekend or even longer. It seems that house parties, once a key part of the social calendar for the upper classes, have come back into fashion, even if the traditional dinner gowns and pearls are no longer obligatory.

It took us months of exhaustive research to come up with a shortlist. Then we visited the properties, inspecting each one carefully and chatting to their owners to make sure they had that essential house-party feel. When potential properties didn't measure up, we didn't include them. And if we liked them but they weren't perfect, we thought it was worth saying so. The result is this warts and all guide to 80 properties which

between them offer more than 100 places to stay with family and friends throughout Great Britain.

We have found some fantastic venues – not just castles and manor houses but also cottages, converted barns and farmhouses. Some are really different, with everything from their own bowling alley or vineyard to Daleks in the bathroom and antique arcade games.

There's something for everyone – from the quintessential English country manor where you can go boating on the lake, to houses with ultra-hip interiors, designer furniture and sleek modern bathrooms and kitchens.

And they won't necessarily cost an arm and a leg to hire. Although we feature some very posh places to stay, some of the properties cost as little as £20 per person per night – and that's for the run of a mansion on a country estate.

We've fallen in love with many of the places we've visited, shortlisting them for our not-too-distant 40th birthday bashes.

We hope you enjoy using this guide as much as we enjoyed writing it.

*Jane Knight &
Liz Bird*

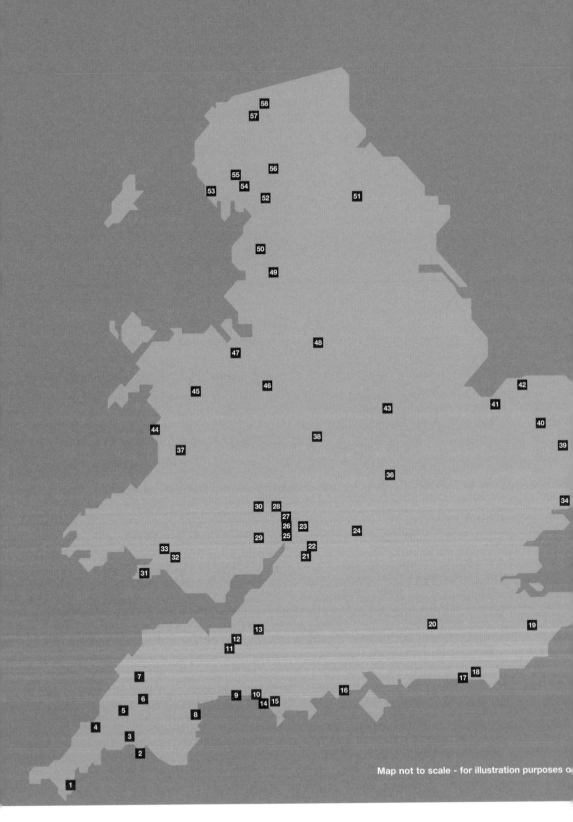

Map not to scale - for illustration purposes o

BIG HOUSE PARTY LOCATIONS
at a glance

at a glance

England and Wales

THE BIG HOUSE PARTY

Map not to scale - for illustration purposes or

Scotland

Castles

Augill Castle, Cumbria

There's a laid-back atmosphere that makes you feel immediately at home in this wonderfully over-the-top Victorian vision of a medieval castle

The Victorians had their own view about what a medieval castle should look like, and this folly is the result – a wonderfully over-the-top stone composition with lots of turrets, Gothic windows and a crenelated roof. Completed in 1841 to give John Bagot Pearson a weekend retreat to play at medieval banqueting with his friends, Augill has an imposing exterior.

Inside, though, an easy-going atmosphere reigns. Polly the labrador and Sooty the cat form the welcoming committee in the hall with its stunning Tudor panelling. Here, instead of a reception desk, you'll find leather sofas made for sinking into, walls bedecked with copper warming pans and stags' heads, and the mesmerising tick of a clock.

Owners Simon and Wendy Bennett do everything they can to make staying at Augill like spending a weekend with friends. This is a real home to relax in – the 15 acres of grounds aren't manicured to perfection and you won't feel obliged to pick up your book every time you get up from a quiet read. Return from a walk in the country – and Augill, in the Eden Valley, is surrounded by Britain at its scenic best – and you can kick off your wellies by the door without causing a scandal.

The heart of the castle and the place to gather after a long day exploring is the enormous music room, with its wood floor, oak panelling, brick fireplace, piano, and more than enough chairs for everyone. It's one of four magnificent public rooms, all large and opulent, with old books scattered around, open fireplaces or wood-burning stoves, and lots of antiques and artefacts in nooks and crannies. There's also another drawing room, more Georgian in style than the music room, where you'll find the honesty bar.

Perhaps the most striking decor is in the dining room, with its blue-panelled ceiling and

long wooden table that seats 24. In the evening, this is tarted up with tablecloths and candelabra for a five-course meal that's big on locally sourced modern British food. Breakfast, which rarely starts before nine and continues until the last person struggles downstairs, sees the table groaning with homemade bread, the best Cumberland bacon, local oak-smoked salmon and free-range eggs from the farm next door.

Upstairs, eight magnificent bedrooms are filled with antique furniture and furnishings to match – expect four-poster beds, wood panelling and carved fireplaces, with wardrobes in turrets. The bathrooms mostly have roll-top baths (one even has a four-poster canopy) with the taps considerately placed in the middle so two can share.

Another two rooms on the ground floor can only be accessed from outside. Done up with modern furnishings, they don't have the same wow factor as the castle rooms – one is quite small and set behind a large walk-through conservatory that together with the bedroom forms a kind of suite – but they are ideal for elderly guests wanting a bit of a breather from the house-party atmosphere.

For groups larger than 20, there is a duplex cottage sleeping four adjacent to the folly. Simply furnished and with bedrooms much smaller than those in the main building, it's nonetheless ideal for families, with a large living space and kitchen.

For the real castle experience and a taste of the high life, you can't really go wrong at Augill. It's a far cry from the castle's previous incarnations – as well as being a boarding school, a nursing home, and a correction facility for boys, Augill has housed some colourful residents, including a surgeon general to Queen Victoria and a suspect in the Jack the Ripper case.

But you can rest easy in your four-posters – none of them has returned to haunt the castle.

AUGILL CASTLE

at a glance

Simon and Wendy Bennett
Near Kirkby Stephen, Cumbria CA17 4DE
01768 341937, www.augillcastle.co.uk

Sleeps: 20-24 plus four children in nine ensuite doubles (two can be double/twins), one twin and one two-bedroom cottage.

Dining: 24 at one table. Rented on a half-board basis. A typical dinner might include griddled Eden Vale brown trout with avocado salsa, fillet of Cumbrian beef with sun-dried tomato and black olive tapenade followed by fallen chocolate soufflé with armagnac parfait. Additional dinners for non residents £40pp for five courses. Augill can sometimes be hired on a self-catering basis for a minimum of four nights – price on application.

Other facilities: tennis court and bicycles.

Children: cots, highchairs, children's menu at high tea. There is a pond in the garden.

Wedding licence: in any of the four magnificent public rooms. Meals for up to 40 seated and 60 buffet style. Marquees for up to 120 can be used in the grounds. No facility fee.

Local attractions/things to do: walking – the Pennine Way and Coast-to-Coast footpaths pass close by. The Yorkshire Dales are a ten-minute drive and the Lake District is 30 minutes away.

Transport: trains leaving London King's Cross take four and a half hours to Kirkby Stephen, three miles from Augill; the Bennetts will pick up guests at the station. Driving takes the same time.

Price: minimum two-night hire. Two nights' half board is £7,800 for 24.

Note: no smoking.

Glenapp Castle, Ayrshire

Beautifully tended gardens, stunning coastal views and delicious food are all

on the menu at this Relais & Châteaux property on Scotland's west coast

There's an air of romance hanging over Glenapp Castle, with its Rapunzelesque towers, a walled garden to rival the one in *The Secret Garden* and a four-poster complete with mini chandelier dangling from its canopy. Even the setting is idyllic – just a mile up the road from Ballantrae of Robert Louis Stevenson fame, this hideaway castle is in one of the less-discovered corners of Scotland, unsignposted and closed off from the world by security gates.

You get there along a stunning coastal route, all crags and open sea, that'll have your eyes straying from the road if you're not careful. But wait a little longer and you'll be able to gaze at the same view perfectly framed by the windows in many of the castle's rooms. The granite island of Ailsa Craig rises dramatically out of the Irish Sea, and on a clear day, you can see the Isles of Arran and Bute and the Mull of Kintyre.

It's the view that determined the castle's position when it was built in 1870, its sandstone battlements with turrets and towers a striking example of

Scottish Baronial architecture. Though a private home for many years, it was falling into disrepair when in 1994 country vet Graham Cowan moved in with his wife, Fay, and started renovations.

Neither has any qualifications in interior design, but they have done a superb job; opulent fabrics are interspersed with antiques they spent six years buying at auction, where they bid for every wooden sideboard and old chamber pot until they were satisfied. Everything works beautifully together, from the drawing room in gold and blue with its highly ornate relief work, to the claret-coloured dining room and the snug library.

In the bedrooms, four-posters, half-testers and canopied beds abound, while some of the bathrooms are original marble. Every room has a talking point – whether it be the view from those on the higher floors or a piece of furniture such as an enormous mahogany wardrobe, an unusual daybed, or a carved trunk. All rooms are spacious and impeccably finished, even the smallest in the house. There's not one but two master bedrooms,

Graham and Fay Cowan
Ballantrae, Ayrshire, Scotland KA26 ONZ
01465 831212, www.glenappcastle.com

Sleeps: 34 plus children in 17 rooms (eight doubles, nine double/twins), all ensuite.

Dining: seats 40 in one room at three tables (there is a second dining room), 28 at a single table. Guests stay half board, with a six-course dinner, for example warm tomato and basil salad, foie gras terrine, breast of free-range chicken, cheddar cheese soup, tarte tatin with nutmeg ice cream and coffee with chocolates. The restaurant has three AA rosettes. Drinks are extra.

Other facilities: tennis and croquet.

Children: cots, highchairs and children's menu. Babysitting can be arranged.

Wedding licence: ceremonies at the nearby Glenapp Church or in the castle and its grounds for a maximum of 34. No extra wedding facility fee.

Local attractions/things to do: golf at championship courses such as Royal Troon and Prestwick, as well as at Turnberry, half an hour away. Shooting and fishing nearby. Clay-pigeon shooting, archery and falconry in the castle grounds. Culzean Castle is close, as are parts of the Robert Burns Heritage Trail. At the castle, cookery demonstrations, whisky and wine tastings, Burns recitals or murder-mystery evenings.

Transport: Prestwick Airport is one hour away, Glasgow is a 90-minute drive.

Price: a mid-week, one-night stay costs about £10,405 including VAT for 34 adults, half-board. Prices vary according to the number of guests and time of year.

Note: the castle is closed in January and February.

one above the other with an interconnecting stairway, both palatial in size, and with high relief cornicing and an air of indulgence.

The feeling of luxury is everywhere you go at Glenapp, and hits you as soon as you walk into the impressive oak-panelled entrance hall.

The food is top notch as well. This member of the prestigious Relais & Châteaux chain serves up beautifully presented six-course meals under chef Tristan Welch, whose CV reads like a menu in itself – he trained under Michel Roux, worked under Gary Rhodes and won the Gordon Ramsay scholarship in 2003. If you're interested, he'll give cookery demonstrations, while castle staff can also organise whisky and wine tastings.

Many guests prefer to just chill out in this Scottish hideaway, exploring the 30 acres of gardens, some woodland, some formal terraces. The highlight of these is the walled garden, where the Gulf Stream helps semi-tropical plants to flourish, and where you'll find a 150ft Victorian greenhouse. It's the perfect secret garden.

Castle Ashby, Northamptonshire

The problem with staying in many stately homes is that you either have to share them with the public during the day, only getting past the silk ropes that section off the rooms after closing, or with the owners who live in them during the evenings. At Castle Ashby, you have neither of these inconveniences – you get the place entirely to yourselves (plus a retinue of very competent staff).

Don't think that because it's closed to the public it's a second-rate stately home either. From the minute you drive through the gates and up the impossibly long drive, the impressive facade with chimneys, turrets and stone inscriptions in Latin coming into view, you know this is going to be really special.

The family seat of the Marquess of Northampton is the real McCoy, dotted with original art, including paintings by Joshua Reynolds and Van Dyck. There are lots of tapestried walls, heavy brocades and antiques from previous generations, plus 200 acres of gardens and parkland designed by Capability Brown.

This Tudor house, which was later extended by Inigo Jones, was built to entertain Elizabeth I, and has been hosting royals ever since, most recently Princess Anne. These days, it also

Architecture by Inigo Jones, parkland by Capability Brown and artwork by Van Dyck all combine to make this an incredibly special place to stay

attracts more than a smattering of celebrities, including Tom Cruise.

With such illustrious guests it's no surprise to hear that Castle Ashby has plenty of rooms in which to entertain. You won't be confined to eat in one dining room, although the magnificent double-heighted Elizabethan Great Hall with its oak panelling, carved fireplace, organ and minstrel's gallery makes the perfect setting for any meal. In fact, there are half a dozen other stunning rooms to eat in, including the Long Gallery, full of columns and ornate ceiling work, and the Reynolds Room, decorated in 16 different shades of blue. There's a wood-panelled armoury for smaller gatherings and the lavish King William Room, with its 18th-century needlepoint. And that's without mentioning the option of breakfast on the terrace, picnics on the island on the lake, or barbecues in the orangery.

With such wonderful settings in which to eat, the food seems almost incidental, which is doing a disservice to the well-presented dishes, of the type you'd eat in a good French restaurant. Should you want a change, though, Castle Ashby can also book a top chef to cater for that special event.

It's just one example of the enormous attention to detail you'll experience here, with everything

tailormade to your requirements. The staff – sometimes so attentive they border on the obsequious – are on duty 24 hours a day to do all those necessary tasks such as pack and unpack, or put your favourite songs on the castle's iPods before you go jogging. Hold a house party here and your guests are automatically given a weblink to adapt their room to their liking – with duvets or blankets, and even their favourite type of tea and nuts – all before their arrival.

The bedrooms are all individually styled with antiques and tapestries. A handful are really special, with either four-posters or half-testers. The Douglas Room has a bed with a history – one Marquess of Northampton promised his wife he wouldn't play billiards any more, but then used the billiards table to make a bed, along with the original bronze pockets and lions' heads. Even the smallest rooms on the second floor have Mulberry fabrics and hand-blocked wallpaper, along with flat-screen TVs and Bose sound systems.

However, the best place to stay is in the State Rooms, a suite originally reserved for visiting royalty, and holding an 18th-century four-poster built for George II. With its floor-to-ceiling wood panelling, Mortlake tapestries and carvings by the Dutch master Grinling Gibbons, it's a real jaw-dropper. And should you tire of all the other places in the castle to eat, you can host a small dinner party here too.

CASTLE ASHBY
at a glance

Olaf Born, general manager
Northampton, Northamptonshire NN7 1LQ
01604 696696, www.castleashby.co.uk

Sleeps: 52 in 26 rooms (16 doubles and ten double/twins) all ensuite.

Dining: there are numerous rooms for different party sizes up to 120. Catered on a full-board basis. A typical menu might include steamed Cornish brill, avocado and coriander sorbet, pan-seared breast of Gressingham duck and a trio of lemon desserts.

Other facilities: billiards room, tennis court, heated swimming pool, gym, croquet and cricket pitch.

Children: cots, highchairs, babysitting plus animal farm and swings in the grounds. However, note that because of the house's antiques, children must be supervised.

Wedding licence: ceremonies in the church in the castle grounds, or in the Great Hall or Long Gallery in the house (maximum 120). Marquees for up to 500. A chapel in the house can be used for blessings. Weddings cost about £28,200 plus VAT with accommodation.

Local attractions/things to do: balloon and horse-carriage rides, sheep-dog displays, archery, shooting, falconry, fishing, quad biking, clay-pigeon shooting and treasure hunts in the grounds.

Transport: London and Heathrow are one hour's drive away, Luton half an hour. A fleet of 12 Mercedes is available to pick guests up at an extra cost.

Price: weekend rates are about £27,000 full board plus VAT for 52 guests. Excludes drinks and activities. A minimum of ten rooms must be hired, although some weekends all 26 rooms need to be taken.

Wedderburn Castle, Berwickshir

Everything at this Georgian castle has been built on a grand scale – from the

magnificent reception rooms with impossibly high ceilings to the bedrooms

There's no need to clear away a corner of the dining room to make a dance floor at Wedderburn – the castle comes with its own ballroom, and a large one at that, with columns, crystal chandeliers, and sprung wooden floor. Just off the oval-shaped morning room (perfect for taking a break from the dancing), it's one of a series of enormous reception rooms in this 18th-century pile, with its grand four-storey crenelated facade. There's also a large covered porch where in bygone days, the occupants of carriages would alight before heading into the flagged entrance hall.

Designed by the Adam brothers, this Georgian castle, which incorporates a much older tower house, has been HQ to the Home family since the early 15th century.

It's definitely more home than hotel – you make your own beds, and don't get flowers or mineral water in your room. But you won't be chivied off to bed at midnight and can pick what time you breakfast in the wonderful old kitchen.

While there are some antiques in the house, it's not bursting at the seams with them, and the decor is more comfortably elegant than ornate, with wooden floors and fires burning in the grates. There is, though, a certain air of grandeur, thanks to the sheer dimensions of the reception rooms, with impossibly high ceilings and huge windows. The curtains alone are five yards long in the drawing room, with its red and green sofas, Oriental screen and baby grand piano.

The dining room boasts a whopping 24-seater oak table in its centre, built within the room in 1897 and never moved since. There's lots of space for additional tables in this room with its splendid Victorian sideboard, chandelier and oil paintings. Here, you can tuck into a traditional locally sourced menu including salmon from the

David Home-Miller
Duns, Berwickshire, Scotland TD11 3LT
01361 882190, www.wedderburn-castle.co.uk

Sleeps: 26-30 (+4). Up to 26 adults plus two children in the castle (four doubles, seven double/twins – two of them with extra single beds – one twin and two singles) with 12 bathrooms. Two cottages are in the grounds, one sleeping two, the other two adults and two children.

Dining: 24 at one table, up to 50 at several. Rented on a catered basis. Three-course menus (£42pp) might include carpaccio of beef with parmesan and truffle oil, grilled sea bass with fine beans and salsa verde followed by brandied chocolate mousse. Two-course informal kitchen dinners £24pp. No corkage but £7.50pp per night for drinks service. If the party size is less than 22 guests, there is a minimum catering fee of £2,500.

Other facilities: billiards, croquet.

Children: cots, highchairs and children's menu. Note that there is a pond and a stream in the gardens.

Wedding licence: for up to 25 in the hall or 92 in the ballroom. Wedding facility fee from £350 to £1,200, depending on numbers.

Local attractions/things to do: clay-pigeon shooting, falconry, archery on site. Nearby is a four-wheel drive school plus golf and the stately home of Manderston.

Transport: Edinburgh is just over an hour away. Trains from London King's Cross take three and a half hours to get to Berwick-upon-Tweed, about 20 minutes away.

Price: two nights for the castle, no meals, from £4,000 midweek, £5,000 weekends. Grooms Cottage from £145 for a two-night short break, Keepers from £155. Breakfasts £11pp.

Note: no pets.

River Tweed, seafood from the fishing port of Eyemouth and Scottish beef and venison.

Next to both these massive rooms are delightfully quaint single bedrooms in the turrets, one with a four-poster, although the rooms are a long way from any of the bathrooms.

The rest of the bedrooms, which are all huge, can seem a little bare as a result of their size but many boast special features – four-posters or half-testers, claw-foot baths and turrets converted into bathrooms or a space for extra beds. One room has even been decked out in tartan.

Two creeper-clad, stone cottages that are ideal for any overspill from the house party are located in the 60-acre grounds. Converted from Georgian stables, they have been done out simply in farmhouse style. And though the rooms aren't small, they do seem snug after the grand dimensions of the castle.

Eastnor Castle, Herefordshire

Pugin's Gothic Drawing Room is the centrepiece of this remarkable castle,

where you eat using the family silver and can even abseil from the turrets

If you want the wow factor for a special occasion, this lakeside castle – built by the first Earl of Somers in 1812 to resemble a medieval Welsh border fortress – really has it.

Certainly you'll get a sensation of awe from the minute you walk through heavy wooden doors past suits of armour guarding the entrance hall to the appropriately named Great Hall with its 60ft ceiling, original stone fireplaces, family portraits and plush furnishings. Somehow this cavernous room, which takes two hours to heat up to a comfortable 20 degrees Celsius, still manages to feel cosy. It's the kind of place you can kick off your shoes and curl up in front of the fire on one of the luxurious sofas.

Every room in this castle is lavishly decorated, none more so than Pugin's Gothic Drawing Room where your eyes are immediately drawn to the elaborate stone-carved fireplace inlaid with the Somers family coat of arms. The huge chandelier is identical to one that hangs in the House of Commons, Pugin's most famous project. Not surprisingly, this is the room that's licensed for civil weddings (TV presenter Davina McCall got married here) and is where most guests like to retire for after-dinner drinks.

Pugin's most complete interior outside the Houses of Parliament hasn't always looked so lovely; the place fell into disrepair after the family moved out at the beginning of the Second World War. It's only been since James Hervey-Bathurst, the first earl's direct descendant, and his wife, Sarah, moved into the castle in 1989 that it's been restored to its former glory.

Nothing has escaped Sarah's keen eye for detail. The lavish decor extends to the 12 individually designed bedrooms heaving with precious antiques. One of the most decadent is the ground floor State Bedroom with its double-height ceilings, elaborately carved Italian four-poster bed, huge oil paintings and embroidered

silk panels hanging from the walls. Next door in the former dressing room is a huge roll-top bath conveniently positioned in front of an open fire.

The 11 other bedrooms are equally impressive. The Queen's Bedroom – used by Queen Mary on her visit to the castle in 1937 – is hung with exquisite 18th-century hand-painted Chinese wallpaper and decorated with 19th-century Chinese-style furniture. And the Red Bedroom has red and gold fleur-de-lys wallpaper, matching curtains and elaborately carved Venetian and French furniture collected by the third earl in the 1860s.

This earl also had a bit of a thing for armour (he called it armouritis) and his collection – the largest in the country – is on display through-out the castle with a large proportion of it, including a life-size knight on horseback, in the Red or Inner Hall.

The other reception rooms in the castle are all special in their own way. In fine weather sip pre-dinner drinks in the Octagon Room with its French windows leading on to the upper

terrace overlooking the lake. Eat using the family silver around the mahogany table in the black and gilt State Dining Room with its crystal chandelier and marble fireplace. And after dinner retire to the Little Library for a game of snooker.

Tear yourself away from all this luxury and there's a 5,000-acre estate to explore. If you get a kick out of high adrenaline activities, you're in the perfect place. Choose from quad-bike safaris across the Deer Park, off-road driving with Land Rover or grass go-karting (which is apparently much harder than doing it on tarmac). You can even abseil from the turrets should you so wish.

Murder-mystery weekends, treasure hunts and dragon-boat racing on the lake can also be organised. If you fancy something a bit more sedate, play croquet on the lawn, try your hand at the maze or wander around the arboretum.

And if you're lucky, James Hervey-Bathurst may even give you a personal tour of his ancestral home.

EASTNOR CASTLE
at a glance

Ledbury, Herefordshire HR8 1RL
01531 633160, www.eastnorcastle.com

Sleeps: 23 plus up to six children in 12 bedrooms (ten doubles, one double/twin and one single). Eight bathrooms (four are ensuite/private, four are shared).

Dining: 22 at main table or up to 80 at separate tables. Catered on a half-board basis, with a typical evening meal consisting of kiln-roasted Scottish salmon with a dill sauce, sirloin of beef with horseradish cream, Yorkshire Pudding and roast potatoes, crème brulée and a selection of English cheeses.

Other facilities: maze, playground, children's assault course, croquet and table tennis.

Children: two cots and two highchairs. Children's entertainers can be arranged.

Wedding licence: up to 80 in Gothic Drawing Room, 80 for dinner in the State Dining Room or 150 in the Great Hall. A £6,750 wedding facility fee is charged (plus VAT).

Local attractions/things to do: clay-pigeon shooting from the ramparts, archery and falconry, quad biking in the Malvern Hills, and off-road driving with Land Rover are all available on the estate. Stratford-upon-Avon and Warwick Castle are within one hour's drive.

Transport: trains from London Paddington take three hours to Ledbury, one and a half miles from the castle. The drive from London takes about two and a half hours.

Price: £225pp per night (double occupancy) or £260 (single occupancy) half board, with a minimum of ten guests. A facility fee starting at £1,700 plus VAT for an evening event is payable for functions of more than 23 people.

Note: the castle is open to day visitors in July and August (except Saturdays) and on Sundays and Bank Holidays between Easter and the first weekend of October. Dogs on leads allowed. No smoking.

Muncaster Castle, Cumbria

Save on the simple but cheap accommodation and splash out on a meal

to remember in this medieval castle in the middle of the Lake District

Weddings are really special at Muncaster, where couples can get married in the timbered church, then stroll through the magnificent gardens with a view of Eskdale for a reception in the castle itself. But you don't have to tie the knot to benefit from the stunning rooms, which can be hired for dinners and private functions. Home to the Pennington family for the past 800 years, this medieval castle is really spectacular, with flagstone floors, huge open fireplaces, stacks of antiques and coats of arms a-plenty.

There are acres of wood-panelled walls and timbered ceilings, particularly in the darkly ornate dining room, whose mahogany table was made from a single tree and where the upper walls are lined with gold-embossed leather. It's a wonderful place for dinner, but then so are the other rooms (in which you can also get married) – including the richly decorated Great Hall with its stained-glass

windows, the octagonal library and the elegant drawing room with its Joshua Reynolds paintings and spectacular barrel-vaulted ceiling.

Upstairs, the bedrooms are just as grand, with ornate four-posters. But you don't get to sleep in the castle. This isn't such a bad thing; the advantage of Muncaster is that you can go to town on a posh backdrop for that special occasion, but don't have to splash out on expensive accommodation. Instead you have two options in the castle grounds – the Coachman's Quarters in the stable yard and a Victorian house, about 20 minutes' walk away. Both are very simply decorated, but then the price reflects this.

The house, which sleeps 20 but can be split into two sleeping eight and 12 respectively, seems the most rustic because of the huge rooms, which contain little more than basic furniture. There is plenty of space for people to sit and eat together,

as well as a walled garden and sea views.

The rooms in the Coachman's Quarters are smarter with pine furniture, but there's still the feel of an upmarket youth hostel, with a simple 'residents' lounge for TV, plus a kitchen and dining area converted from a brick barn. There's also the disadvantage that you're in the centre of a major tourist attraction that attracts 80,000 visitors a year, with the tea and gift shop just below you in the courtyard (if there's a wedding, the castle is closed to other visitors).

On the upside, though, you do get lots of on-site attractions. Muncaster's 77 acres of grounds have a plethora of flowers, plants and trees. As well as woodland walks and a nature trail, children can visit the Owl Centre, with 400 birds, and then try the maze.

And if that's not enough, just outside the castle gates, the whole of the Lake District is beckoning.

MUNCASTER CASTLE
at a glance

Iona Frost Pennington
Ravenglass, Cumbria CA18 1RQ
01229 717614, www.muncaster.co.uk

Sleeps: 12-40. Up to 20 in the Coachman's Quarters at the castle in nine rooms (two doubles, two twins, four twin/doubles plus one apartment for four). Six ensuite bathrooms and three rooms sharing a bathroom. Accommodation for 20 more in a house a short drive through the grounds. The house is split into two: Newtown House sleeps eight (two doubles and two twins) with three bathrooms while Knott View sleeps 12 (two doubles, four twins) with three bathrooms.

Dining: 40 self catering but meals can be arranged in the castle for up to 100. Three-course meals from £55pp might include fresh salmon mousse, roast sirloin of beef, and chocolate and pecan pie.

Other facilities: the grounds include extensive gardens, the World Owl Centre, indoor maze (entrance free if staying at the Coachman's Quarters, £3-£7.50 for those in Newtown House or Knott View) and stables.

Children: cots and highchairs.

Wedding licence: ceremonies can be held in the church and the castle. Buffets for up to 150 or 60 for a sit-down meal. Price of £80-£85pp for a three-course meal (BYO alcohol for a £3pp service charge). Minimum two nights.

Local attractions/things to do: outdoor activities in the Lake District National Park. Steam enthusiasts can ride on the Ravenglass and Eskdale steam railway.

Transport: trains from London Euston to Ravenglass, one mile from Muncaster, take six hours, about the same time as by car.

Price: Coachman's Quarters from £490 per night. Newtown/Knott View from £628-£1,496 for a weekend and £898-£2,138 for a week's self catering.

Note: the castle is open to the public daily from noon to 5pm except Saturdays.

Myres Castle, Fife

A dozen staff will cater to your every need in this plush property, which is run
like a five-star hotel but also manages to have an air of informality about it

The instant the electric gates swing open on to 44 acres of parkland, you can tell it's going to be a swish affair at Myres. Everything runs smoothly at this 16th-century property, which is dedicated to exclusive use – a castle made easy, with carpets and all the necessary mod cons.

A team of 12 staff are on hand to make your stay as comfortable as possible, offering the same standards as a top hotel but without the stuffiness (they pride themselves on remembering your favourite drinks and tailormaking the service to your needs).

Not for Myres the part-time chef who comes and goes at his convenience; here, you get the full-time services of slow food proponent Christopher Potter, who's always on hand should guests want to wander into the kitchen for an impromptu cookery demonstration (formal classes can be arranged too).

Mealtimes are a flexible feast; Christopher has been known to wait until 11.30pm for late arrivals before serving dinner in the formal dining room,

the traditional and locally sourced Scottish fare offset by mahogany and crystal. And breakfast is whenever people stagger down to the atmospheric Victorian kitchen with flagstone floor, leather sofa and an Aga.

Myres is glamorous but you don't get that 'look but don't touch' feel – although it's run like a five-star hotel, it's been given a human touch by owners Jonathan and Jenny White who bought the castle from the Fairlie family in the 1990s.

The Whites have stamped their own personality on a place already filled with memorabilia; five of the nine bedrooms are named after their children, whose pictures feature alongside other framed souvenirs, such as letters from the Royal Family.

Probably the most formal part of the entire castle is the Regency-style drawing room with its Scottish plasterwork ceiling, Steinway baby grand and original Baccarat chandelier. With a distinctive Madeira influence (Captain Fairlie's wife was countess of Madeira), the room also has plenty of

knick knacks and golfing medals on display in glass cabinets, as well as antique furniture. Fold back the rug, and there's a sprung wooden dance floor should you wish to boogie.

The other reception rooms are more casual: a library, in welcoming tones of red and gold, which is also home to a self-service bar; a cosy study with laptop and fax; and a billiards room in the house's chapel, which also has a small minstrel's gallery.

The bedrooms all have unusual features – a dressing table set in a turret here, a priest's hole there, and a staircase from the tower room to the roof, the perfect viewpoint to survey the formal gardens and woodland.

Even the smallest room – Anne's – is still a decent size. Charles' room is a cleverly painted affair that looks like a tent (you have to touch the walls to make sure they're solid), while Tom's holds a lovely oak four-poster that complements the wood panelling.

The bathrooms are just as special, some the size of a bedroom with claw-foot bath, others where you can bathe either on a pedestal or in a sunken bath. There's even an original bath from the Queen Mary ocean liner with a shower cubicle at one end and taps for hard and soft water as well as hot and cold.

The latter goes with the Queen's Room, named because Mary Queen of Scots was reputed to have stayed here (as she is said to have stayed in every posh house in Scotland). It's definitely the most impressive pad in the house, with a magnificent carved double bed, plus a small study in the turret.

Stay here and you really will feel like royalty.

MYRES CASTLE *at a glance*

Lavinia Dowling, general manager
Auchtermuchty, Fife, Scotland KY14 7EW
01337 828350, www.myres.co.uk

Sleeps: 18 in nine ensuite bedrooms (four doubles, five double/twins).

Dining: 18, catered on a full-board basis – full breakfast, light lunch, afternoon tea and a four-course dinner – using local ingredients. Dinner might include twice-baked salmon soufflé, fillet of local beef, poached pear with Myres gooseberry fool followed by a selection of cheeses.

Other facilities: tennis, table tennis, volleyball, billiards, badminton, croquet and mountain bikes. Myres can arrange beauty and massage treatments in the castle and entertainment from ghostly fireside tales to fireworks.

Children: cots, highchairs and children's meals. Note that there is a pond in the garden.

Wedding licence: for up to 30 in the drawing room and 200 in a marquee. Prices from £11,000 for exclusive two-night use of the castle.

Local attractions/things to do: many famous golf courses are within one hour of the castle, including St Andrews and Gleneagles. In the grounds: fly-fishing tuition, clay-pigeon shooting, off-road driving, falconry and archery. Outside the grounds: stalking, shooting and fishing, polo, go-karting and motor racing.

Transport: Edinburgh is a 45-minute drive; Luechars private airport is 15 minutes and Ladybank (for trains from Edinburgh) is five minutes' drive away.

Price: from £295pp per night including all meals and soft drinks. Minimum stay two nights. Minimum of six required for exclusive use.

Note: Myres also has a modern meeting room, seating 14 boardroom style.

Duns Castle, Berwickshire

There's an air of a French château in the Loire about this Scottish castle,

where you eat on Queen Anne chairs in a wood-panelled dining room

There aren't many places where you can sit on Queen Anne chairs for dinner and gaze at paintings that could easily grace the walls of the National Gallery. Duns is the exception, not just a castle, but a home since 1696 to the Hays family, who now share their heirlooms with guests, as well as a story or two about their ancestors. From the moment the butler greets you at the double-doored front entrance, you're made to feel like a very distinguished house guest.

The castle dates back much further than the Hays family's occupancy. Originally a 14th-century tower before being updated into a neo-Gothic pile in the 1820s by architect James Gillespie Graham, its oldest parts are on show in the three-foot-thick walls in the dining room.

This room is undoubtedly Dun's pièce de résistance. It wouldn't look out of place in a château in the Loire, with its intricate wood and plaster ceiling, wood panelling and huge ornate fireplace. It's the perfect setting for long, leisurely dinners of traditional Scottish fare around the large oak table set with silver cutlery, crystal glasses and linen napkins.

After dinner, head out to the bar on the impressive landing, with huge neo-Gothic windows in the stairwell, ornate plasterwork on the ceiling and examples of 15th- and 16th-century Scottish artwork on the walls. There are yet more paintings to admire in the spacious and opulent drawing room, with vaulted ceiling and bow window. You won't find a television here, but you can amuse yourself tinkering on the grand piano, or in the castle's billiards room, which boasts a full-size antique table.

Upstairs in the bedrooms, expect four-posters and antiques – carved wood headboards and wardrobes – with a chintzy backdrop. You get all the trimmings you'd find in a five-star hotel, with luxury toiletries and complimentary water.

Although the Blue Room, which was the original laird's bedroom, is regarded as best in the house, another contender is the huge room at the top of the tower with separate office area, large bathroom and stunning views over the 1,700-acre estate.

Just a five-minute walk from the medieval village of Duns, much of the estate is a nature reserve, offering interesting walks, as well as a variety of other activities, including horse riding and shooting. It also holds several cottages, perfect for any overspill from the castle, including the pretty one-bedroom Pavilion Lodge at the base of a stone archway. The largest, the old dower house of St Mary's, can be combined with the adjacent Coach House to sleep 13.

Fill up the castle and the cottages and you'll have room for 48 people and a pretty good bash. Even though the Hays family still lives in the castle, there's no need to creep around – with so much space, there's plenty of room for everyone.

DUNS CASTLE *at a glance*

Mark Slaney, administrator
Duns, Berwickshire, Scotland TD11 3NW
01361 883211, www.dunscastle.co.uk

Sleeps: 23-48. Up to 23 in the castle in 12 bedrooms (eight doubles, three twins and one single). Five ensuites and four further bathrooms. Four of the doubles have four-posters. Cottages in the castle grounds sleep a further 25 (two in Pavilion Lodge, six in the White House, four in Azalea Cottage, ten in St Mary's House and three in the Coach House).

Dining: 30 at a single table, 60 at separate tables. Half board. Food is traditional Scottish, for example, fresh and smoked local fish fricassée, venison stroganoff and Drambuie ice cream with shortbread. Wine from £15 a bottle or corkage at £10 or £19 for champagne. Hotel rates at bar.

Other facilities: tennis, croquet, snooker.

Children: cots, highchairs, children's menu. Because of the castle's antiques, children need to be supervised.

Wedding licence: for up to 60 seated in the drawing room, or the lower hall. Larger groups can hire a marquee in the grounds but need to arrange their own catering. Facility fees from £500 to £1,750 depending on party size, plus £128pp half board.

Local attractions/things to do: clay-pigeon shooting, quad biking, archery, falconry, paint-ball warfare, shooting, walking on the estate. Sandy beaches are within half an hour's drive.

Transport: Edinburgh is just over an hour away. Trains from London to Berwick take three and a half hours. Berwick is 20 minutes' drive from the castle.

Price: £300 per couple per night half board, including wine, plus a £350 facility fee for parties of 10-17 (no fee for parties over 18).

Leeds Castle, Kent

Walk in the footsteps of England's kings and queens when you stay in what is rightly regarded as one of the loveliest castles in the world

It's hard to believe you can treat one of the most romantic and historic buildings in Great Britain – where England's kings and queens have lived – as your own home, albeit for just a few days. Although it's open to the public, once the day trippers leave, the ropes cordoning off most of the rooms are removed and you have this 900-year-old moated castle all to yourselves.

Listed in the Domesday Book, this spectacular stronghold has had its fair share of politicians and film stars as well as royalty passing through the Norman Gatehouse. A residence for Edward I in the 13th century, it later became one of Henry VIII's palaces. From the 1930s, weekend house parties hosted by the castle's last private owner, Lady Baillie, attracted the likes of Noel Coward, David Niven, Charlie Chaplin and Edward VIII and Mrs Simpson. In recent years, world leaders such as Tony Blair have used it as a venue for peace conferences and international summits.

Today you don't have to be rich or famous to stay at Leeds Castle. Hire a minimum of eight of the 22 bedrooms and you secure exclusive access to the whole place (well, at least from late afternoon). The only no-go areas are Lady Baillie's bedroom and dressing room, which form part of the visitors' tour, and a few very precious pieces of furniture such as a Queen Anne chair dating from 1704.

Sip pre-dinner drinks in the library before dining in the magnificent 73ft Henry VIII Banqueting Hall with its heavily beamed ceiling, unusual ebony floor and stone fireplace: the perfect setting for a celebratory dinner for up to 100 people. Accompany your meal with wine produced at Leeds Castle's own vineyard. For a more intimate setting, the light and airy Castle Dining Room decorated with 18th-century tapestries and a collection of Chinese porcelain

37   **THE BIG HOUSE PARTY** | CASTLES

can seat up to 30 at the polished mahogany table, or 48 for a banquet. You could also opt to dine in the medieval cellars or enjoy a barbecue on the terrace overlooking the floodlit moat. When it gets chilly, retire to one of the elegant drawing rooms for coffee and liqueurs.

Just like the main public rooms, the castle bedrooms – particularly the eight state rooms on the first floor – are full of such glorious antique furniture and objets d'art that it's hard to comprehend you're allowed to sleep in them (be prepared to pay for any breakages: it won't be cheap). One of the loveliest and largest, Walnut, has a four-poster bed covered in a stunning 18th-century silk embroidery, walnut furniture and a Han dynasty vase. The Green Room is also vast with a 17th-century giltwood four-poster, huge paintings and a shower in the bathroom that's big enough for a family of four

(it was made especially for Pavarotti, who sings at open-air concerts in the grounds). Be warned: most of the 'battlement bedrooms' on the top floor have restricted views due to the ramparts.

The only downside to staying at arguably one of the loveliest castles in the world is that during the day you have to share it with hundreds, and sometimes thousands, of visitors (although your bedrooms, along with the Castle Dining Room and library, will be off-limits). During the winter, the hoi poloi will have to leave the castle by 3.30pm, in summer at 5.30pm.

While the day visitors explore the interior, you can head out to the 500 acres of gardens and parkland, play golf on the nine-hole course or try your hand at the maze, safe in the knowledge that on your return you won't have to storm the ramparts to secure this architectural beauty.

LEEDS CASTLE
at a glance

Tim Bartleet, castle general manager
Leeds Castle, Maidstone, Kent ME17 1PL
01622 765400, www.leeds-castle.com

Sleeps: 40-68. Up to 40 in the castle in 22 bedrooms (11 doubles, six double/twins, one twin, four singles). All rooms ensuite apart from four which can be used as family rooms sharing two bathrooms. Extra 14 double rooms on estate.

Dining: 30 at one table in Castle Dining Room (48 at round tables) or up to 100 in the Henry VIII Banqueting Hall. Four-course banquet from £68pp in the castle. Sample menu: fillet of sole with spinach and duchess potato, chicken supreme with foie gras, Panna Cotta and cheese and biscuits. House wine from £13.50 a bottle.

Other facilities: nine-hole golf course, maze, aviary and nature trail.

Children: highchairs and cots. Toddlers' play area.

Wedding licence: for up to 50 in the Castle Dining Room (£4,700 facility fee) or the Gatehouse (£3,700). Receptions up to 100/170 respectively.

Local attractions/things to do: Canterbury Cathedral, the seaside resort of Whitstable and the ancient port of Rye are all within an easy drive. On the estate: hot-air ballooning, archery, clay-pigeon shooting, walking, falconry, golf and croquet.

Transport: trains from London Victoria or Charing Cross to Bearsted, five minutes' drive from the castle, take about an hour. The car journey from London takes about an hour.

Price: double rooms from £275 (single occupancy £200) including breakfast. State rooms from £335 double and £225 single plus a £2,000 facility fee for the castle per 24 hours. A minimum of eight rooms need to be booked.

Note: entertainment such as a string quartet can be arranged. Smoking only in one of the drawing rooms.

Cottages

Bruern Cottages, Oxfordshire

Two storeys, a canopied bed, a dresser, table and chairs and cushioned windowseat… and that's just the Wendy house. Bruern's 12 upmarket cottages, with interiors to rival the Wendy house, really do cater for children.

Dumper trucks and push cars litter the pretty walled garden with its apple trees, colourful flowers and tunnel of wisteria. There's also a heated play cabin with everything from a well-stocked dressing-up box to a dolls' house, Noah's Ark, farm toys and an easel with crayons (there's even a comfy sofa for parents to sit on). It doesn't end there: there's also a climbing frame, child-

sized croquet, cricket and tennis, a heated pool and a separate games room with table tennis, table football, snooker and a piano.

Child safety is paramount – as well as the well-maintained communal walled garden, many of the cottages come with their own enclosed lawns. And parents get what Bruern calls its Peace of Mind Kit, incorporating everything from electricity socket guards to safety locks for cupboard doors. Meanwhile, if you fancy a night out, babysitting can be arranged.

With facilities like these for the kids, you can expect – and get – top-notch conditions for adults.

Plush furnishings, beautiful antiques and toys, toys and more toys make these upmarket properties a hit with both parents and their children

These cottages, built by the Victorians for the horses, carriages and grooms of Bruern Abbey, wouldn't look out of place in the pages of *Country Living*. It's not surprising when you find out that owner, the Honourable Judy Astor (politician Nancy Astor's daughter in law), has been helped by her sister, interior designer Jocasta Innes.

Fabrics by designers such as Nina Campbell, Osborne & Little and Mulberry are the norm, in a plethora of colours and textures, from shimmering silks through to thick tweeds. The result is a country-style decor highlighted by well-placed antiques, as well as marble washbasins from

France and four-posters in the master bedrooms. The little details haven't been forgotten either, with proper lighting for reading, a smattering of games and books and a choice of blankets or duvets on the beds.

You get plenty of extras too – and we're not just talking about the complimentary water and White Company toiletries. Welcome baskets here really are welcoming, with a bottle of champagne and a whole hamper of goodies including home-made bread and cake. And the well-stocked kitchens also contain life's little essentials such as champagne flutes and picnic baskets.

If you'd rather not spoil the sheen on the marble or granite worktops with your own cooking preparations, Bruern has a choice of ready-cooked meals which can be complemented with its own home-grown freshly picked fruit and vegetables, or you can call in a chef to do the cooking.

If there is a downside to all this luxury, it's that guests need to leave at 10am sharp on the day of their departure to ensure that the cottages are sufficiently prepared for their next visitors – which means there's no lingering over breakfast.

Although all the cottages are special in their own right (Saratoga with its galleried bedroom is the perfect romantic hideaway, while the Swedish-influenced Newmarket is equipped for disabled guests), the one best suited to groups is the newest cottage, Weir.

Built with entertaining in mind, it has an enormous open-plan kitchen and dining room leading on to the living area, leaving enough space for a series of adjoining tables to seat up to 30. In warm weather, you can also eat alfresco under the vine-covered pergola on the terrace.

The modern Cotswold stone-floored kitchen comes with not one but two dishwashers, along with an industrial-sized fridge and a food warmer. And there's plenty of space for relaxing, with a library containing a 50-inch plasma television opening on to a beamed seating area with open fire (although Weir also comes with underfloor heating).

All five ensuite bedrooms – three on the ground floor and two upstairs – are as beautifully furnished as the other cottages with lots of rich textiles and antiques. One of the twin rooms has a distinctly French feel with two 19th-century beds and red and white upholstered chairs to match the curtains.

And, of course, children aren't forgotten here, with a dolls' house in the hall along with a selection of wooden toys, dressing-up clothes and a puppet theatre in their own den built under the stairs.

BRUERN COTTAGES
at a glance

Frances Curtin
Red Brick House, Bruern, Chipping Norton,
Oxfordshire OX7 6PY
01993 830415, www.bruern.co.uk

Sleeps: 2-62 in 12 cottages (one sleeping ten, one cottage for eight, three cottages for six, two for five, three for four and two cottages for two). Note that there is only group dining for up to 30.

Dining: for 30 at adjoining tables in Weir (sleeps ten) or a similar number on three tables in Cope (sleeps two). Self catering but frozen meals can be bought – Thai curry for four costs £16 – or catering arranged.

Other facilities: heated outdoor swimming pool available at certain times on week days. Tennis court and bikes.

Children: as well as cots and linen, highchairs, bed guards, stairguards, and baby alarms, cottages come with a kit including safety covers for electrical sockets and safety locks for cupboard doors. Babysitting can be arranged. Many cottages have enclosed gardens and there are plenty of toys, a well-stocked heated play cabin, a games room and a Wendy house.

Wedding licence: no.

Local attractions/things to do: walking in the Cotswolds, Oxford is half an hour away, Blenheim and Woodstock 20 minutes, Stratford-upon-Avon an hour.

Transport: trains from London Paddington to Kingham take one hour 20 minutes. The drive from London takes about the same time.

Prices: four-night midweek break from £2,991 for 30 sharing Weir, Cope and three cottages sleeping six. Three-night weekend from £4,623, one week from £5,440.

Note: good disabled facilities.

Mains of Taymouth Cottages, Perthshire

No expense has been spared in renovating these luxury cottages with saunas and hot tubs in one of Scotland's most scenic corners

Pretty and picturesque are the words that spring to mind here, the former applying to the complex of stone cottages around a courtyard complete with arch and well, and the latter to the scenery at the head of Loch Tay near the quaint village of Kenmore. The only thing marring the picture is the caravan park adjacent to the cottages and run by the same owners, which can be seen from some of the upstairs windows, along with the loch.

But it's a small price to pay for staying in these 19th-century properties, built as the home farm for nearby Taymouth Castle, where Queen Victoria stayed. Irena Menzies and her husband Robin have done an excellent job of doing them up – you know you're in for something special when you see some of the seven cottages have hot tubs in the garden along with wood-burning stoves, pine furniture and modern kitchens.

Although the cottages sleep up to 44, there's only room for 18 people to eat together, so the best bet is to take the two most luxurious properties – Mains Park Court, sleeping ten, and next door's Granary Court, sleeping eight.

The former is the most stunning, and the only one to have a private sauna as well as a hot tub (it also comes with an aromatherapy shower for the full beauty experience). It's very contemporary with underfloor heating and a plasma TV, leather sofas and granite work surfaces. Best of all is the sense of space and light from the huge open-plan living

MAINS OF TAYMOUTH COTTAGES
at a glance

Irena Menzies
Kenmore, Aberfeldy, Perthshire, Scotland PH15 2HN
01887 830226, www.taymouth.co.uk

Sleeps: 18 in two adjacent cottages. Mains Park Court sleeps ten (two doubles, two twins, one single with one Z-bed), all ensuite. Granary Court sleeps eight (two doubles, two twins) with three bathrooms. Note that there are another five cottages in the courtyard, sleeping a further 26, but there is not sufficient dining space for all.

Dining: 18 at separate tables in Mains Park Court. The cottages are self catering. Catering is available at about £35pp for a three-course meal such as smoked salmon, roast breast of duck with gin and lime, and summer pudding. Hampers can be supplied by the on-site shop.

Other facilities: private hot tubs and sauna, on-site nine-hole golf course, snooker room, tennis court and croquet. Restaurant and shop in the adjacent caravan park. A nearby fishing hut can be hired with six sleeping bags, six fishing rods and a BBQ for £250 for three nights or £500 for six nights.

Children: cots, highchairs and stairgates are available.

Wedding licence: no.

Local attractions/things to do: watersports on Loch Tay, fishing, and other country pursuits. There are a number of golf courses nearby – Gleneagles is about 45 minutes away. Other attractions include a tour of Dewar's World of Whisky distillery in Aberfeldy, six miles away.

Transport: Glasgow and Edinburgh are 90 minutes' drive away.

Prices: weekly charges from £2,500-£4,219 for the two cottages, self catering, winter short breaks from £2,300.

Note: stabling and grazing is available for two horses. Pets are allowed in the cottages. No single-sex groups.

and dining area with a mezzanine level up wooden spiral stairs. With some furniture shifting, a large group could happily eat here together.

If Mains Park Court has the ideal group eating area, Granary Court has the perfect sitting room, with a split-level seating area and French doors opening on to the patio with a hot tub.

Tempting as it might be to wallow all day in the water, there are plenty of other things to do, including watersports on the loch and golf, with many courses within an easy drive. Golfers will also find an advantage to being in the same complex as the caravan site – they can use its nine-hole on-site course free during the winter and with reduced green fees at other times.

Barnacre Cottages, Lancashire

Complimentary free-range eggs and friendly animals are just some of the

perks of staying in these four sensitively converted farm buildings

You get a really upmarket farm experience at Barnacre, with everything from beautifully presented interiors to fat, well-cared-for hens that peer through the French doors (and even walk in if you leave them open).

Converted from 18th-century farm buildings, all four cottages are swish, modern and very well maintained, with Italian tiles and parquet floors, leather sofas and pine tables. Everything is top quality from the Villeroy & Boch crockery to the Mark Wilkinson designer kitchens – the kind you'd love to have in your own home. These come with granite work surfaces, American-style fridge freezers with ice and spring water dispensers, and all the other kitchen goodies.

There's also an Aga in The Old Stables, the largest cottage, which sleeps eight. Here the kitchen forms the centrepiece of an enormous 50ft room that's perfect for an informal group supper with a lounge area at one end, and a dining area the other side of the kitchen, which opens on to a conservatory. Although the pine table only seats eight, tables from the other cottages will easily fit in the conservatory to seat up to 23.

Upstairs, as with the adjoining cottages, medium-sized bedrooms and bathrooms sit under the eaves, but with sufficient head room and natural light, thanks to a crop of skylights. As well as pine sleigh beds and built-in cupboards, there are plenty of homely touches such as candles, books and ornaments scattered liberally around.

You might also encounter some hand-painted motifs of mice where you'd least expect them – peeping over a light switch or sliding down the bannisters.

The Old Stables is at the end of a terrace that incorporates Pheasant and Partridge cottages, both of which also come with enclosed gardens ideal for children.

Friendly owners Terry and Sue Sharples live at the other end of the row and do everything they can to make their guests feel at home, particularly the younger ones, who might find a box of toys waiting for them when they arrive at their cottage, and who are encouraged to help feed and pet the animals. The Sharples also try to be flexible on departure times whenever possible.

Standing alone on the other side of their home is the Piggeries, with an impressive wood ceiling rising to an apex and two ground-floor bedrooms. Like the other two smaller cottages, this one has an open-plan kitchen leading on to the dining and sitting area with a wood-burning stove.

With such well-equipped cottages, you might be forgiven for staying in. But it's worth venturing out; Barnacre is in the middle of an Area of Outstanding Natural Beauty, with views over the fields that go on for miles. Don't think of coming here without a car; it's a 40-minute walk to the local village.

Another advantage to staying here is that you can reach either Blackpool or the Lake District in less than an hour but you don't have to be close to all the other tourists. At the end of a busy day's sightseeing, leave the crowds behind and head back to this peaceful farm, where the hens obligingly lay complimentary free-range eggs, and where there are ducks roaming in the garden, a pet lamb in an adjacent field, and the omnipresent Rascal the dog and Tom the cat.

BARNACRE COTTAGES
at a glance

Terry and Sue Sharples
Arkwright Farm, Eidsforth Lane, Barnacre,
Garstang, Lancashire PR3 1GN
01995 600918, www.barnacre-cottages.co.uk

Sleeps: 4-23 in four cottages. The Old Stables sleeps eight (three twins, one double, one bathroom, one ensuite shower room); Partridge Cottage sleeps six (two twins, one double, one bathroom, one shower room); Pheasant Cottage sleeps five (one twin, one double, one single, one bathroom, one shower room); The Piggeries sleeps four (one twin, one double, one shower room).

Dining: space for 23 in The Old Stables, on a self-catering basis, but local catering firms cooking on a modern British theme can supply everything from BBQs and canapés to buffets and three-course dinners.

Other facilities: all-weather tennis court.

Children: very child friendly, with cots, highchairs, stair guards, enclosed gardens, a wooden adventure playground and animals to feed.

Wedding licence: no.

Local attractions/things to do: head off into the countryside – it's a 40-minute walk to the town of Garstang and the nearest village. Day trips can be made to Blackpool, the Lake District and the Yorkshire Dales, all of which are within an hour's drive of the cottages. Lancaster, with its castle and prison, is 20 minutes away.

Transport: stations at Manchester and Liverpool are one hour's drive away; the cottages are almost four hours' drive from London.

Price: from £1,335 for three nights' self catering in the four cottages (Old Stables £440, Partridge £325, Pheasant £300 and Piggeries £270) or from £1,795 per week (£595/£425/£400/£375 in the individual cottages).

Combermere Abbey Cottages, Shropshire

Walking through Combermere's cottages feels like you're leafing through the pages of an interior design magazine, each page turning to reveal yet more impeccably coordinated fabrics, the designs in the wallpaper echoed in the bathroom tiles, and even the position of the hurricane lamps carefully considered.

So it's no surprise to discover that owner Sarah Callander Beckett worked as a sales director for Laura Ashley before taking on the Combermere Abbey estate in a peaceful country corner where Shropshire borders on Cheshire.

That's not to say there's a preponderance of floral prints and bows. In fact, each of the ten cottages is a showcase for designers such as Nina Campbell, Ralph Lauren and Jane Churchill, though it's not immediately obvious which designer inspired which cottage.

Named after individuals from the estate's past, each cottage has a theme – Callander's is, for example, distinctly Scottish: fields of thistles depicted on the curtain poles, mirror surrounds and up the staircase, with a tartan living room and a woollen-checked bedspread.

With furnishings from style gurus such as Nina Campbell and Ralph Lauren, the interiors of these former stables are really swish and luxurious

Don't think for a moment that it's twee – it's very tastefully done with more than a hint of luxury. Cottages don't come much better than these, with open fires surrounded by leather fenders, seagrass matting or wooden floors, original beams, and four-posters or half-testers in the bedrooms.

They have been beautifully restored from a smart red-brick stable block built around a cobbled courtyard in 1837. Where once four sets of grey double doors would swing back to reveal a row of carriages, they now open on to the impressive cottage living areas, with incredibly high ceilings and exposed beams.

With everyone in the same courtyard, Combermere is perfect for a group gathering, although the biggest number that can sit down to eat together is 20. This is in the stunning Beckett cottage with its African decor played out in everything from a chandelier made from antlers to zebra tiles in the bathrooms (there's also a bamboo four-poster and a wonderful galleried bedroom with a tent bed complete with giraffe headboard).

Beckett's cooking space is also more generous than in the other cottages, where the kitchens tend to be on the small, but well-equipped, side (you even get hot-water bottles stashed away in the drawers).

If you want to seat more than 20 for a special occasion, there's the abbey itself, which is more neo-Gothic manor house than Cistercian masterpiece following major adaptations in the 19th century. Here, the marble fireplace and unusual fluted columns of Porters Hall make it an elegant room for a dinner.

Weddings are conducted in the library, with its richly decorated 17th-century ceiling, magnificent stone fireplace and oak panelling. Reached by a dramatic curved staircase, it has wonderful views over the lake, and makes the perfect romantic setting.

As Combermere is on a 1,200-acre working organic farm, there's certainly plenty of outdoors to explore, with woodland trails and an enormous lake covering 143 acres that's ideal for fishing.

Although most cottages have their own patch of garden, you also get the use of a larger area of lawn. This is called, somewhat inexplicably, the Pleasure Garden – there are no fountains or formal areas, but there is a barbecue, children's playhouse equipped with games and mini furniture, and space for outdoor games. There's also a play area with swings, slide and a sunken boat.

The best bit about the grounds, though, is the 18th-century walled garden – all five acres of it, in a series of three different areas, holding an avenue of pleached hornbeams, a tennis court and space for a marquee.

Right at the end, in a part that can only be visited with the head gardener, is a maze made out of fruit trees planted in the shape of an eye, with the greenhouse as the iris.

It looks like even the gardens didn't escape the designer's eye.

COMBERMERE ABBEY COTTAGES
at a glance

Nicola McGrath, administrator
Whitchurch, Shropshire SY13 4AJ
01948 662876, www.combermereabbey.co.uk

Sleeps: 4-49 in ten cottages (six sleeping four; one sleeping five; two sleeping six and one sleeping eight – about half doubles and half twins). Most cottages have two bathrooms but some have one and others have three.

Dining: 20 can dine together in Beckett Cottage, and 16 in Garnock/Malbanc cottages, or for special occasions, the Porters Hall in the abbey seats up to 50 (there is an additional £600 facility fee). The cottages are self catering, but the abbey has a freezer-food menu with, for instance, lasagne for £4pp, and catering can be arranged.

Other facilities: in-cottage masseurs can be booked. Tennis court, croquet, BBQs and a selection of bicycles.

Children: everything from cots to socket guards supplied. There is a wooden playhouse in the garden and a play area with swings, slide and a sunken boat.

Wedding licence: for up to 100 in the Library. Receptions for 40 seated in Porters Hall and 150 in a marquee in the walled garden. Facility fees from £600 to £2,000.

Local attractions/things to do: woodland walks and fishing in the abbey grounds. Chester and Shrewsbury are an easy drive away.

Transport: Combermere is three hours' drive from London; trains take just under two hours from London Euston to Crewe, which is about 11 miles from Combermere.

Price: from £368-£665 for a three-night weekend per cottage or £530-£1,350 per week, self catering.

Note: dogs welcome. The abbey is open for tours (£5) every Wednesday afternoon from April to September.

Dove House, Dorset

There's nothing rustic about the facilities at this rural hideaway with its smart, uncluttered bedrooms, tasteful neutral decor and heated indoor pool

Dove House is one of a new breed of holiday homes that couldn't be further removed from the days when cottages had lots of chintz, mismatched furniture, polyester sheets and six people sharing one bathroom.

Every one of the seven fresh and clutter-free bedrooms (even the single) in this house converted from 19th-century farm buildings has an ensuite bath or shower room. The neutral decor, which should suit most tastes, is complemented by splashes of colour in the coordinated bedspreads, curtains and cushions. And a downstairs double/twin room is ideal for those with limited mobility.

The crowning glory of Dove House is the large, heated indoor pool, ideal for keeping kids entertained on rainy days. When the sun is shining, have an invigorating swim and then spill out of the pool room's French doors on to the south-facing patio for a spot of sunbathing or a barbecue.

Other meals are taken in the large open-plan kitchen/dining room, the focal point of the house, where breakfast inevitably becomes brunch as people naturally congregate around the oak dining table. An extra table can be brought in from the covered portico when Swallows, another property sleeping four, is also rented – there's enough cutlery and crockery for 17 people.

Catering for large numbers isn't too much of a hardship in the modern kitchen with its five-ring gas hob, two electric ovens and a large American-style fridge freezer. It even has two dishwashers, and a separate utility room next door.

However, should you choose not to cook, you can get a caterer in to do the job for you. Some guests even order home-cooked meals to be delivered for the entire duration of their holiday.

After dinner, make your way down the flagstone hallway to the elegant sitting room with a working fireplace, oak floor and antique furniture. There are plenty of entertainment options here, with a

TV/video, CD player and a selection of books, videos and games.

Less than a minute's walk away from Dove, two-bedroom Swallows is ideal for any overspill from the main group and is particularly popular with grandparents when large families take both properties. It is also suitable for people with limited mobility because it's all on one level. Decorated in a contemporary style with wooden floors throughout the living areas and bedrooms, this single-storey cottage has a small kitchen/lounge with French doors leading from both the lounge and double bedroom to an enclosed garden with patio furniture.

The cottages are both in a secluded valley at the end of a mile-long, tree-lined drive on a 1,000-acre estate where the odd walker has been known to get lost. Bring your own bike and take a ride along the cycle paths. Stick closer to home and there's an all-weather tennis court, croquet and badminton to keep you entertained.

DOVE HOUSE *at a glance*

Pippa James
Hampton, Dorchester, Dorset DT2 9DZ
01305 889338, www.dovehousedorset.co.uk

Sleeps: 13-17. Up to 13 in Dove House in seven ensuite bedrooms (one double/twin on ground floor, three twins, two doubles and one single) and four in Swallows (one double and one double/twin, both ensuite).

Dining: seats 14 around kitchen table or 17 with extra table. Self catering but a local caterer will deliver home-cooked food or come and cook for you. Main meals from £7pp, desserts from £2.50pp.

Other facilities: indoor heated pool (restricted to Dove House guests unless Swallows is also taken), all-weather tennis court (available at pre-arranged times – bring own rackets and balls), croquet and badminton.

Children: cots and highchairs available, stairgate, enclosed garden. Babysitting can be arranged.

Wedding licence: no.

Local attractions/things to do: horse riding, sea and river fishing, golf, tennis and sailing. Walks and beaches along the Jurassic Coast. Thomas Hardy's Dorchester, Bridport and Lyme Regis are all within an easy drive. Nearby Abbotsbury has a children's farm and play area.

Transport: trains from London Waterloo to Dorchester, about five miles away, take two and a half hours. London is about three hours' drive.

Price: Dove House from £1,300 for a three-night weekend break in low season and £1,550 for a week. Three-night weekends or four-night mid-week breaks at Swallows cost 75% of the relevant weekly rate, which starts at £320.

Note: no single-sex groups. No dogs in Dove House but one small, well-behaved dog allowed in Swallows.

Upper Rectory Farm Cottages, Warwickshire

Mix and match accommodation to suit the size of your party at these wonderfully versatile country houses with large open-plan living areas

An ingenious system of interconnecting doors at Upper Rectory Farm Cottages means you get an incredibly flexible building-block arrangement of accommodation that allows you to add or take away rooms to suit your party size. The two three-bedroom cottages and one four-bedroom barn can be linked on both upper and lower levels, but if your group size is less than 20, you simply block off some of the bedrooms and reduce the price accordingly.

'We wanted to make it as flexible and functional as possible,' said David Corbett, a farmer who carried out the renovations himself. He's done them beautifully, creating The Granary, The Hayloft and The Barn from the 19th-century buildings of a working farm, three pretty cottages set around a brick courtyard enjoying views over the surrounding countryside.

The whole party can eat together round a large table in The Barn's party room, with its low-beamed ceiling and wooden floor. While there isn't sufficient comfy seating for everyone to congregate after the meal in the adjoining kitchen/sitting room, you can always retire to Granary or Hayloft and shift furniture between the two. As the kitchen/sitting rooms of both cottages interconnect, another possibility for family groups would be to have adults eating on one side and children on the other. In warm weather you can also throw open the French doors for a barbecue on the patio.

All the downstairs open-plan rooms are decorated in a country-cottage style, with lots of oak – tables and cupboards as well as exposed beams – Chinese slate tiles in the kitchen areas and sofas around coal-effect fires. All the usual mod cons are available, from washing machines to videos and CD players.

Wooden staircases lead upstairs to pine-furnished rooms with more beams and floral curtains. There's a lot of light created by some cunningly placed skylights but some of the bathrooms are a bit small. Although the decor is similar in the cottages, each has a special feature – one of the bedrooms in The Granary has old pea sacks arranged artistically in an alcove, while The Hayloft has a third bedroom up a small wooden flight of stairs in the eaves.

Positioned almost slap bang in the middle of England with excellent motorway access, Upper Rectory Farm is a good place for a get-together of people living in different corners of the country. Located in Warwickshire, it's close to the borders of Derbyshire, Staffordshire and Leicestershire as well as a multitude of attractions, from Sherwood Forest to Alton Towers.

Although you reach the cottages via a private road, they're not isolated; the cottage complex has a second courtyard with accommodation for an extra 24 people. That doesn't mean you can take over all of them; while the Corbetts are happy on some occasions to accommodate groups of up to 26 by overflowing into a cottage called The Piggery, the properties around this second courtyard will generally be rented out to other smaller groups of holidaymakers.

The cottages are one of a number of projects being undertaken by the enterprising Corbetts, who live at the farm next door. One of their plans is to open a restaurant that will utilise local produce in a 17th-century pub they bought in the neighbouring village. Cottage residents will be able to enjoy some pub grub or get the same caterers to come and prepare a special dinner.

UPPER RECTORY FARM COTTAGES
at a glance

Jean Corbett
Snarestone Road, Appleby Magna,
Warwickshire DE12 7AJ
01827 880448, www.upperrectoryfarmcottages.co.uk

Sleeps: 12-26. Up to 20 in three cottages (The Granary and The Hayloft with one double and two twins each, and The Barn with two doubles and two twins). All are ensuite except one room. An additional cottage, The Piggery, which sleeps a further six people, is available on request.

Dining: up to 26 in The Barn. Self catering but catering can be arranged. A typical menu might include homemade pheasant paté with apple chutney, local Gressingham duck breast with fresh plum sauce and homemade lemon, apple and syrup tart with hokey pokey ice cream. Three courses from about £25pp.

Other facilities: bicycles. On-site reiki healing and Indian head massage can be arranged. A gym and games room are planned.

Children: cots and highchairs but no enclosed gardens.

Wedding licence: no.

Local attractions/things to do: close by are the National Forest, Twycross Zoo, Bosworth Battlefield and the National Trust's Calke Abbey. Dovedale and Sherwood Forest are both about an hour's drive away, and Alton Towers about 45 minutes.

Transport: trains from London Euston to Nuneaton, about nine miles from the cottages, take just over an hour. The drive from London takes about two hours.

Price: from £1,260 for three nights' self catering for 18 (other rates available for different party sizes and longer stays).

Note: the cottages are non smoking. No pets. The Barn has a shower room for the disabled.

Cotswold Cottages, Gloucestershire

With contemporary kitchens and bathrooms teamed with an eclectic decor, these five cottages couldn't be further removed from a soulless holiday let

Cotswold Cottages owners Linda Camp and James Meyer love to spend time hunting for treasures in nearby Tetbury's antique shops. It's a passion that manifests itself in every square foot of their five properties, all of which are filled with beautiful things.

Having lived at one time in each of the cottages, the couple have left their mark on them all, taking little of their furnishings and accessories when they move on. Even precious drawings of their son Oscar have been left. 'I'm a real magpie,' says Linda, a former interior designer. 'When I've decorated a house and got it just right I find it hard to move things on. For instance, the Dutch samplers I bought for Blandfords (cottage) are so right for the room.'

Rose Cottage, which sleeps ten, is situated in the pretty village of Bisley. The four remaining ones are located in and around the village of Oakridge Lynch.

Two of them, the Old Mill, which sleeps 17, and Blandfords, which sleeps nine, are linked via a footpath through their gardens. The other two, Far Oakridge House, which sleeps 12, and one-bedroom Stable Cottage also sit next door to each other.

Each cottage has its own individual charm.

Once owned by Arts and Crafts architect Norman Jewson – who added the front section of this 18th-century property to create a T-shape –

Far Oakridge House still boasts many of the original features from the era, including beautifully fitted oak drawers underneath the windows, an intricately carved oak staircase and elaborate door furniture.

'We sometimes get Arts and Crafts enthusiasts knocking on the door and drooling over the hinges and latches,' says James.

Recently modernised, the whole place has been kitted out with contemporary bathrooms – including a shower in the ensuite master bedroom with bodyjets that spray you from virtually every angle. A triple-aspect kitchen has all the latest gadgets including a funky red espresso machine and food mixer, a huge fridge/freezer and Neff oven.

Far Oakridge's large dining table means there's room for guests staying at neighbouring Stable, which has more of a traditional cottage feel, to eat with the rest of the group.

There's also plenty of space for 26 people to eat together in The Old Mill's new dining space with its L-shaped table, floor-to-ceiling windows and galleried lounge. Set on a hillside on different levels, the Old Mill feels very higgledy piggledy with lots of stairs leading to numerous reception rooms. The look is very eclectic with gilt mirrors, high-backed sofas and modern art.

A short walk up the hill takes you to another characterful stone cottage, Blandfords, with an inglenook fireplace and mullioned windows. But its best feature is the conservatory dining room leading to a decked area making the most of the lovely views.

You can also enjoy great panoramas from Rose Cottage, which sits on an elevated position overlooking the valley. The 18th-century stone cottage is packed with characterful features including a bread oven in the fireplace, white-panelled walls and mullioned windows. A new wing features a contemporary kitchen and stylish new bedrooms, including one with a roll-top bath.

Linda is happy to organise catering or entertainment for a special occasion at all five properties – part of a very personal touch that goes down well with guests. One group staying at Blandfords showed their appreciation using the alphabet fridge magnets: 'Weekend was fab, thank you. Love us.'

COTSWOLD COTTAGES
at a glance

Linda Camp and James Meyer
Penn House, Oakridge Lynch,
Gloucestershire GL6 7NU
01285 760135, www.cotswoldcottagesonline.com

Sleeps: 2-26. Far Oakridge House sleeps 12 (+2) in five bedrooms (one double with single bed, a further triple and three double/twins). Four bathrooms. Sofa bed. Stable Cottage sleeps two (+2) in one bedroom (one double/twin) with two bathrooms and a sofa bed. The Old Mill sleeps 17 (+2) in eight bedrooms (seven double/twins – one with extra single – and one double). Sofa bed. Seven bathrooms. Blandfords sleeps nine in four bedrooms (four double/twins – one with an extra single bed and trundle underneath). Three bathrooms. Rose Cottage sleeps ten (+2) in five bedrooms (two double, three double/twins) and four bathrooms. Sofa bed.

Dining: The Old Mill has a table large enough to seat 26 people, allowing a large group to take over Blandfords and The Old Mill. Far Oakridge House also has enough seating to accommodate neighbouring Stable Cottage. Self catering. Three-course meals from £17.50pp.

Other facilities: BBQ, Boules and Swing Ball in each.

Children: cots/highchairs in all properties. Toys, games, books, DVDs, videos for all ages in each cottage.

Weddings: no. But receptions in a marquee for up to 80 in Far Oakridge House, The Old Mill and Blandfords.

Local attractions/things to do: hunting, fishing, shooting, walking, horse riding, gliding and antique hunting.

Transport: trains depart London Paddington to Kemble (an hour and 40 minutes journey time) or Stroud (one hour and 20 minutes), both 15 minutes away. London is about a two-hour drive.

Price: Far Oakridge House from £1,700 for a weekend break, £2,268 for a week; Stable Cottage £252/£336; The Old Mill £1,308/£1,745; Blandfords £708/£945 and Rose Cottage £1,054/£1,405.

White Heron Cottages, Herefordshire

You might want to holiday with a large group of family or friends but you don't necessarily want to be living under the same roof all week. With eight units sleeping between four and 16 people, many of which have large communal dining spaces, you can be as sociable or unsociable as you like during your stay at this 700-acre farmed estate on the Welsh borders.

Most of the accommodation is located in and around the newly converted Victorian stables, now called The Colloquy, which sleeps up to 16 adults and six children across four apartments. Next door is one-bedroom

Forge and Gardener's sleeping six. The other two – Sherriffs, sleeping 14, and Field, sleeping four – are in secluded settings within a ten-minute walk of the stables.

The Colloquy offers the most flexible option for a large group of family or friends with interconnecting doors between the four apartments. Open the doors and you can dine together in two of the large open-plan living spaces, close them and you can retreat to your own apartment and cook in a separate kitchen. You can also push back the furniture in one of the living areas to create enough

dining space for up to 40 people. Arrange for a local caterer to cook a special meal for you, or order some cordon-bleu freezer food to be delivered.

Modelled on chic country retreat Babington House in Somerset, The Colloquy features huge glass facades overlooking a central courtyard, underfloor heating beneath rustic oak floorboards and sleek contemporary kitchens and bathrooms – some with roll-top baths. One of the living spaces doubles as a mini-cinema and there's a separate room with a 43-inch TV screen.

In fine weather, eat alfresco on a large terrace in the garden or take a dip in the outdoor heated pool. There's also a squash court, sauna and Jacuzzi.

Another newly converted farm building, Forge, is equally swish with a 60ftx40ft open-plan living space featuring oak flooring, funky wall radiators and a spiral staircase leading to a mezzanine level with an extra double bed. A roll-top bath in the main bedroom makes it a big hit with romantic couples. Italian black slate worktops and modern appliances in the kitchen complete the contemporary look.

You'll find a more traditional cottage interior at Gardener's. It's nicely furnished with an ornate Indian carved wood sofa and a wood-burning stove in the lounge, white-painted floorboards covered by rugs in the dining room, and a large wet room. It also has its own enclosed garden next door to a red-bricked walled garden where you can erect a marquee for a party or wedding.

You could also put a marquee on the large expanse of lawn in front of Sherriffs. The elegant facade of this light-filled Queen Anne grade-II listed house certainly makes the perfect backdrop for a special occasion.

Step inside the three-storey house though, and it has no delusions of grandeur. One sitting room is very cosy with sofas surrounding a huge stone fireplace, a TV, video and collection of books and games; the other is more formal with an ornate fireplace and window seats overlooking the lawn.

Eating together isn't a problem. The dining table comfortably seats 14, or up to 24 rather snugly along two adjacent tables if two other properties, usually Field and Gardener's cottages, are also rented. A large farmhouse table in the kitchen is ideal for breakfast.

Upstairs, all of the six spacious, light-filled bedrooms have a Scandinavian feel to them with neutral tones and pale carpet. One of the best is a double with an iron bed and a rather swanky ensuite wet room with a huge shower rose and blue mosaic tiles. The other ensuite double has a chic camel-coloured suede bed and a large contemporary bathroom with twin sinks.

A ten-minute walk away is two-bedroom Field Cottage, surrounded by apple orchards and blackcurrant bushes with its interior designed by Penny Morrison (whose other projects include the Bath Priory Hotel). Field's best feature is a large neutrally decorated open-plan living and dining room leading on to a decked terrace with garden furniture and a barbecue. It's the perfect place to chill out and escape from the rest of your group.

WHITE HERON COTTAGES
at a glance

Jo Hilditch
Whittern Farms Ltd, Lyonshall, Herefordshire HR5 3JA
01544 340241, www.whiteheronproperties.com

Sleeps: 4-44 (plus seven children) in eight cottages, which sleep between four and 16 people. The Colloquy sleeps 16 across four apartments (one for eight+5 – two of the four doubles are family rooms with mezzanines; another for four in two doubles; a third for two (+1) in one double plus mezzanine and a fourth sleeping two). Sherriffs sleeps 14 (four doubles, one twin and one four-bedded room); Gardener's Cottage sleeps six (two doubles, one twin); The Forge sleeps four (two in a double and two on a mezzanine in the lounge); Field Cottage sleeps four plus one child (one double, one twin and a Z-bed).

Dining: 24 at two tables at Sherriffs; 22 at a long table in Forge and 24 at two of the four apartments, one of which can also seat up to 40. Self catering but three-course meals from about £22pp can be arranged or cordon bleu freezer food can be delivered.

Other facilities: table tennis at Sherriffs. The Colloquy has an outdoor heated pool (May to September), squash court, sauna, Jacuzzi and grass badminton court. There's also a mini cinema in one of The Colloquy's apartments.

Children: cots and highchairs. No babies at The Forge.

Weddings: no. But receptions for up to 150 in a marquee or 50 buffet style in Sherriffs and The Colloquy.

Local attractions/things to do: walking, mountain biking, golf, horse riding, canoeing on the River Wye.

Transport: nearest mainline station at Leominster, a 20-minute drive. London Paddington or Euston takes three hours via Newport. London is about three hours' drive.

Price: Sherriffs from £900 for the weekend or £1,500 for a week. Gardener's £250/£480, Field £230/£400, Forge £230/£400, The Colloquy £1,300/£2,000.

Town Houses

The Old Neptune Inn, Suffolk

Stylish bedrooms, great entertaining spaces and a beautiful inner courtyard

make this 15th-century former hostelry a cracking house-party venue

This medieval merchant's house feels a bit like a riad, a traditional Moroccan abode with an unassuming exterior giving little indication of the spectacle within. Beyond the front door, in true riad style, it has a pretty courtyard with a tinkling fountain – the focal point and one of the many features that makes it such a great venue for a house party.

Socialising is what this place is all about. The baronial-style dining hall with its double-height timbered ceiling and full-height leaded windows overlooking the courtyard has played host to numerous medieval-themed parties. After dinner, push back the table to make space for dancing using a fully integrated sound system complete with DJ decks.

Next door, the beamed living room is dominated by a huge stone fireplace, which takes up nearly an entire wall and packs a powerful punch when it's lit. There's an interesting mix of the old and new with leather sofas, wide-screen television with DVD and Sky Plus alongside an Indian marriage bed fashioned into a coffee table. Wood panelling and some original decorative plasterwork on the ceiling complete the look.

The modern but traditional feel extends to the 11 exquisitely designed bedrooms, the most unusual of which has to be the Galleon. Reached via a spiral staircase, it has one sloping wall of leaded windows and beams overlooking the courtyard, the other three panelled with a 19th-century carved wooden printer's block. Together with the sound of water from the courtyard fountain and the cries of seagulls from the

neighbouring marina, you could almost believe you were on a ship.

Every bedroom becomes a talking point in this house, built in 1490 for a wealthy wool merchant and later converted into a hostelry that Charles Dickens is reputed to have stayed in. The master bedroom, Il Palazzo, certainly has the wow factor, decked out with an Indonesian teak four-poster bed, huge maroon velvet sofa and oak floors. The original 15th-century timber ceiling and leaded windows overlook the courtyard.

After all this good taste it's refreshing to come across something that isn't: a wonderfully over-the-top ensuite bathroom with mirrored walls and steps up to a gold-coloured bath with room for two. Owners Peter Cannon and Luisa Seccatore affectionately refer to it as the Elvis bathroom.

While all the bedrooms have their individual charms, the two smallest ones in the attic are not ideal for tall people and don't have immediate access to bathrooms.

Like the other rooms, they do though have Egyptian cotton duvets, while the bathrooms have White Company toiletries, all carefully chosen by Luisa, who is responsible for the interior design and has an eye for detail.

It's her influence you can see in the farmhouse-style kitchen laid with York stone flooring and kitted out with all the mod cons including a huge fridge/freezer, double oven, dishwasher, food processor, coffee maker and smart white crockery. There's even a bread maker. Next door is a secondary kitchen with another fridge used to store drinks.

THE OLD NEPTUNE INN
at a glance

Peter Cannon and Luisa Seccatore
86-88 Fore Street, Ipswich, Suffolk IP4 1LB
01473 251110, www.theoldneptune.co.uk

Sleeps: 22 adults and up to five children in 11 double bedrooms. Six ensuite plus two further bathrooms.

Dining: 22 at one table. Self catering but local caterers can arrange anything from a Jamaican BBQ to a medieval banquet. Prices start at £15pp.

Other facilities: sauna, three-burner gas BBQ, small pool table. Beauticians and complementary therapists can give treatments at the inn. Live bands and murder-mystery weekends can also be arranged.

Children: one highchair but no cots. There is also a dressing-up box. The courtyard is enclosed and has a fountain.

Wedding licence: no but receptions up to 36.

Local attractions/things to do: Constable country is within a short drive; beaches at Felixstowe, Aldeburgh and Southwold – with its brightly coloured beach huts – are all within an easy drive; medieval town of Lavenham. Charter a yacht or take a cruise up the River Orwell from the marina. Golf, go-karting, sailing and clay-pigeon shooting are available nearby.

Transport: one hour from London Liverpool Street by train to Ipswich, a five-minute taxi ride. One hour's drive from the M25.

Price: set rate of £2,600 for a three-night self-catering weekend for the property, £3,600 for a week (Friday to Friday). Two-nights midweek at £1,450 and three nights £1,750.

Note: no stag parties. No smoking in bedrooms.

While dinner is cooking, spill out into the spacious Italianate courtyard for aperitifs. This is also the perfect spot for a barbecue. You won't be confined to using it in the summer months either, thanks to a log-burning chimenea.

While the grown ups chatter, there's plenty to amuse the kids; a games room off the living room is home to a small pool table, board games and a dressing-up box that's often raided by the adults.

Although Ipswich might not be everyone's first choice for a break, the Old Neptune is slap bang next to the marina with its luxury yachts and numerous bars and restaurants. It's also only one hour from the M25, making it an ideal weekend destination for Londoners. Some guests don't even bother going out, but with such a lovely place to stay in, who can blame them?

Pelham House, East Sussex

Boutique hotel meets country retreat at this 16th-century property within a short walk of Lewes' buzzing High Street and only 10 minutes from Brighton

It's hard to believe that this stylish hotel was previously the headquarters of East Sussex County Council. Today, Pelham House couldn't feel less like a place where debates about planning applications and dustbin collection were waged, despite some remnants of its immediate past that have been cleverly recycled.

The bar has been fashioned from one of the curved desks used in the circular council chamber, now home to a 120-capacity ballroom. The former finance director's office has become a quirky bedroom where two walls are still lined with glass-fronted cabinets. And a wonderfully rich tapestry from the chamber hangs in the library with its double-height ceilings, wooden floors, leather sofas and crystal chandeliers.

The interior of this 16th-century house extended in the 19th century has the look and feel of a boutique hotel decked out with chocolate brown leather sofas, contemporary bathrooms and neutral decor. Lots of original features such as the window shutters and fireplaces also give it plenty of character. This is most evident in the 16th-century wood-panelled room with its intricately carved gargoyles and ornate fireplace.

Upstairs, all the bedrooms have been kitted out with locally crafted oak furniture and the very latest bathrooms. Everything is top notch, from the Egyptian cotton bed linen and Neutrogena toiletries to luxurious throws and cushions complementing the Farrow & Ball-painted walls in muted mauves, greens and blues.

A swanky bathroom in the bridal suite has wooden floors, fireplace, a shower with a gargantuan shower rose and a contemporary roll-top bath that sits in the middle of the room – perfectly positioned for gazing at the lovely views of the South Downs.

The location is one of the beauties of Pelham House. While the South Downs with its picturesque villages and great walking are on the doorstep, you're only 10 minutes from Brighton. Not that you need to venture beyond Lewes for a good time. This county town has its fair share of boutiques, bookshops, galleries and restaurants. One of the best places to eat is Circa Brasserie, Pelham House's own restaurant, which is closed to the public when the whole property is taken.

There's a real arty feel to the place – throughout the 23 bedrooms and living areas are contemporary paintings and sculptures by local artists. Julian Bell, grandson of Virginia Woolf's sister, painted the ceiling mural in the grand entrance hall of the adjoining Manor House with its stone floors. And if you're a fan of the Bloomsbury set you can always visit Woolf's house at Rodmell or Charleston House, which are nearby.

PELHAM HOUSE *at a glance*

Jacqueline Head and Diane Rand, managers
St Andrew's Lane, Lewes, East Sussex BN7 1UW
01273 488600, www.pelhamhouse.com

Sleeps: 43 in 23 rooms (15 double/twins, five doubles and three singles). All rooms are ensuite. It's possible to hire half the hotel (the Manor House with 11 rooms) and get exclusive use of selected rooms such as the Panelled Room where you can have dinner.

Dining: 24 in the Panelled Room at one table, 43 at several tables in the dining room or up to 120 for dinner in the ballroom. Catered on a half-board basis. A typical menu might include chickpea feta fritters with vodka cucumber, crab linguine and chocolate tart. From £25pp.

Other facilities: BBQ, croquet and table tennis.

Children: one cot and highchair plus three Z-beds. Babysitting can be arranged.

Wedding licence: for up to 40 in the Panelled Room or 65 in the Terrace Room. Receptions for up to 80 in the Terrace Room and 180 in the ballroom.

Local attractions/things to do: beaches, shops and nightlife in Brighton, ten minutes away. Charleston House – once home to the Bloomsbury set – and Virginia Woolf's house at Rodmell are an easy drive away, as is Glyndebourne Opera House. Anne of Cleves' house and Lewes Castle are both within walking distance.

Transport: two minutes' walk from Lewes station with regular services to London Victoria (70 minutes). One hour's drive from London.

Price: whole house from £3,000 for one night midweek B&B, £6,000 for one night at the weekend and £9,000 for a two-night weekend.

Note: one room for the disabled on the ground floor.

Blanch House, East Sussex

Uniquely decorated rooms, a funky cocktail bar and a minimalist dining room

make this boutique hotel near Brighton beach a big hit with the party set

You can tell Blanch House isn't your run-of-the-mill seaside hotel just by looking at a list of the room names, which include Decadence, Boogie Nights and Snowstorm. Hidden behind the facade of an ordinary-looking Georgian town house in one of Brighton's side streets a short walk from the pier, Blanch is cool and very hip.

Each of the 12 uniquely decorated bedrooms has been carefully thought through with incredible attention to detail, from the telephone to the light fittings. Seventies fans will love Boogie Nights with its orange walls, a matching retro phone and a

leopard-motif loo seat – the only thing that's missing is the shag-pile carpet. And in Snowstorm, you'll find a mobile of falling snowflakes tumbling down over a lime-green bedspread while glass cabinets lining the walls contain a vast collection of the children's snowstorm toy. If you prefer a more opulent look, try deep purple Renaissance with its elaborate gilt mirror and plush red furnishings, or Perrier Jouet with velvet-covered walls, a high-backed velvet sofa and a Victorian roll-top bath at the end of a huge bed.

There really is a room for everyone, which makes it enormous fun choosing who will sleep where. Bunched in clusters on different half landings, they are ideal for allowing smaller groups of the party to be together, although the large number of stairs (there isn't a lift) means that older guests might find the layout less entrancing.

As befits a good boutique hotel, all the rooms have extras such as complimentary mineral water and handmade Belgian chocolates, while most also have flat-screen TVs and DVD players. You'll also find goose and duck-down duvets, power showers and posh toiletries.

There is, though, a drawback if you're shy – many of the ensuite bathrooms (which are in fact shower rooms) only have curtains rather than doors separating them from the bedrooms. But even this element has been carefully integrated into the decor. For instance, the India room (inspired by the owners' daughter India) has a curtain made from strings of colourful fake flowers.

The funky interior is the work of designer Amanda Blanch and her husband Chris Edwardes, who used to manage the bars in London's legendary Groucho Club and Damien Hirst's The Pharmacy before creating his own Seventies cocktail heaven at Blanch House. Here you can choose from a list of shooters and other deadly concoctions as long as your arm from the comfort of your suede pouffe or a funky tangerine bar stool.

Make sure you leave room for dinner. Blanch House is now becoming renowned as much for its food as for its carefully shaken cocktails. The modern British fare served up in the minimalist white dining room makes the most of locally sourced produce, especially fish. There's also an Asian influence in dishes such as bream on saffron mash potato with spiced lentils and coconut sauce.

Small wonder that Blanch House has attracted more than its fair share of celebs; fans include the Gallagher brothers and Gwyneth Paltrow. She checked into Decadence, complete with a huge roll-top bath in the bedroom set off by gilt mirrors, deep red walls and a throne of a chair.

BLANCH HOUSE
at a glance

Chris Edwardes and Amanda Blanch
17, Atlingworth Street, Brighton BN2 1PL
01273 603504, www.blanchhouse.co.uk

Sleeps: 24 in 12 doubles, all ensuite.

Dining: catered on a B&B basis, with seating for 28
at individual tables. Modern British fare includes loin
of rabbit with terrine of leg and bacon, wild sea bass
with tomato tartare and herbed goats cheese tortellini
and chocolate delice with caramelised milk ice cream.
Dinner from £30pp.

Other facilities: in-room treatments such as reflexology,
Indian head massage, facials and manicures can be
arranged. A cruise boat can also be chartered.

Children: cots, highchairs and baby-listening devices.

Wedding licence: for up to 40 in the dining room. A
screen can be hired that can project the ceremony into
the bar area for a further 30 guests. Receptions for up to
80. No facility fee for exclusive use.

Local attractions/things to do: Brighton with its beach,
pier, shops and restaurants is on the doorstep. Walking
on the South Downs with pretty villages such as Alfriston
with its small zoo and adventure playground. Charleston
House, home to the Bloomsbury set, is also within an
easy drive.

Transport: trains from London Victoria or London Bridge
to Brighton take about 50 minutes. Just over an hour
from London by car.

Price: £1,910 B&B for the property per night.

Note: there is no lift in this five-storey building.

Berkeley House, Gloucestershire

This ultra-chic Regency home has been decked out in black and white by its interior-designer owner and comes with all the latest high-tech gadgets

On the outside, this archetypal Regency town house couldn't look more traditional, set on the old square of Tetbury with its antique shops and tea rooms. But step inside Berkeley House and you'll see a Scandinavian-style chic interior in a piano-key arrangement of black and white.

Shoes come off at the front door to protect the floorboards, which like just about every other surface have been painted in Dulux Brilliant White. It's all offset by black furnishings – oversized sofas and giant bean bags in the sitting room, and black tiling in the kitchen – trimmed with accessories ranging from gilt-rimmed mirrors and crystal chandeliers to antique lace curtains.

There's a lot of Swedish owner Lena Proudlock in Berkeley House. She works as a portrait photographer (her work can be seen on the walls) and runs a fabric company, Denim in Style, selling more than 50 different colours of the material and using her black denim throughout the house.

The whole place is like a showcase for her work. 'Everything you see here I designed,' she says, standing in the spacious sitting room, with its open fireplace and wood stacked in an adjacent alcove. 'I sell the bean bags and people keep asking me about the furniture, especially the sofas.'

She calls the style 'shabby chic', though contemporary comfort is more like it. Certainly there's nothing shabby about the electrical goodies – the house has everything from Broadband WiFi access to a Bosch fridge freezer and Miele washing machine and tumble dryer. As well as a 42-inch plasma screen TV in the sitting room, all of the seven bedrooms have flatscreen TVs, DVD players and Sky Plus. There's also a television in the kitchen and one in the ensuite bathroom belonging to the master bedroom.

If there is a downside to Berkeley House, it's that this enormous bedroom is far superior to the others; with floor-to-ceiling windows, it holds a capacious modern white four-poster (another of Lena's creations). The other bedrooms are still large and elegant, though – the room that Lena's son, Oliver, uses when he is at home also has a black leather sofa bed for extra guests. Otherwise, the rooms are all decked out in white, with duvets, Ikea rugs and hanging rails for clothes. There are plenty of extras, too, such as candles and dressing gowns, toiletries and lots of fresh flowers.

Lena's thoughtful little touches also extend downstairs. Although Berkeley House is self catering, she makes sure the large table that seats up to 16 in the dining room, with its tartan carpet and French doors opening on to a large walled garden, is laid with white china when guests arrive, as well as flowers, fruit and chocolates.

In fact, Lena is so accommodating that she'll often take last-minute bookings and turn the house around in 24 hours, decamping across the square to the two-bedroom flat she also owns. Should the group want to overflow into this property too, that's not a problem. The flat is perfect for grandparents or families wanting their own space away from the others and is decorated in a similar style to Berkeley House.

With the same black and white colour scheme, but this time with the addition of grey, the flat's interior looks every bit like a New York apartment but still retains its quaint Cotswolds exterior.

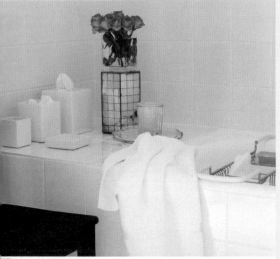

BERKELEY HOUSE
at a glance

Lena Proudlock
16, The Chipping, Tetbury, Gloucestershire GL8 8ET
01666 500051, www.lenaproudlock.com

Sleeps: 14-20. Seven rooms in the main house (four doubles, three twins plus two on a sofa bed). Four extra in Bay Tree Court over the square (one double, one twin). Two ensuites and one further bathroom in the main house, one in the flat. An extra two (+2 on a sofabed) can be accommodated in the Coach House at the end of Berkeley House's garden from spring 2006. One bathroom.

Dining: 16 can sit around the dining table. Self catering. A cook can be organised and there are several take-aways and good restaurants and gastro pubs in and around Tetbury.

Other facilities: BBQ on the terrace with garden furniture.

Children: several camp beds available for children plus a cot. The garden is enclosed.

Wedding licence: no. Small receptions in house or larger ones in a marquee in the garden. Price on application.

Local attractions/things to do: as well as walking in the Cotswolds and visiting local villages, there are many historic houses to see within a ten-mile radius, including the Elizabethan manor Chavenage House. Cirencester with its Roman amphitheatre is nearby.

Transport: trains from London Paddington to Kemble, which is four miles from Tetbury, take about one hour 20 minutes. The same journey by car takes about two hours 20 minutes.

Price: Berkeley House: three-night self-catering weekends £1,440, one week from £2,650. Bay Tree Court: three-night weekends £500, one week £800.

Fell House, Cumbria

There's a great sense of light and space in this converted Victorian warehouse located near some of England's finest walking country

If you like the countryside but don't want to stay in its midst, Fell House is the perfect compromise. Located in the market town of Sedbergh, this self-catering house just off the M6 is an easy drive from both the Lake District and the Yorkshire Dales. The pretty stone building with its arched porch is just a stroll away from the butchers, bakers and supermarket to get provisions for supper. But it's also only 100 yards up the road to reach the foot of the Howgill Fells and some great walking country.

Converted from a Victorian grain warehouse, Fell House has lots of room for socialising (but not wild partying – remember there are neighbours). With the whole of the ground floor open plan, you get an enormous amount of space. And because there is a central enclosed stairwell, this area can be cleverly sub-divided –

the reading zone with its bookcases and games can be blocked off to create an extra bedroom.

Despite its size, the living area feels very homely – if a little scruffy in places – with low-beamed ceilings, plenty of sofas, a flagstoned entrance area perfect for leaving muddy walking boots and a large stone and slate fireplace, albeit with a gas effect rather than a real log fire. There's even an original safe complete with key built into the wall, which try as you might, you just can't unlock. And if you want to watch a video, there's a video-hire shop about 20 yards from the front door.

The same easy ambience is prevalent upstairs in the large open-plan kitchen/diner, with its pitched ceiling, original beams and lots of light streaming in through strategically placed skylights. A large modern table sits in the middle

FELL HOUSE
at a glance

Steve Wickham
Howgill Lane, Sedbergh, Cumbria LA10 5DE
01277 652746, www.higround.co.uk

Sleeps: 10-14 in the house and self-contained flat beneath it (one double, three double/twins, one of which has an extra futon, two sofa beds in different sitting room areas). There are four bathrooms. Another four people can sleep in an adjoining holiday let that can be arranged by Fell House.

Dining: self catering, with room for 14 around the kitchen table. There are good pubs and takeaways just a short walk away in the town. The gastronomic restaurant of L'Enclume is 30 miles away.

Other facilities: there is parking for two cars. Note that there is no garden.

Children: cots, highchairs and stairguard are provided.

Wedding licence: no.

Local attractions/things to do: Fell House is one hour's drive from Windermere in the Lake District and 20 minutes from the major shops of Kendal. The Yorkshire Dales are virtually on your doorstep. The Howgill Fells are accessible directly from the house and offer good walking and bridleways for the mountain biker.

Transport: Oxenholme station is eight miles away; trains from London Euston take about three and a half hours. By car, the same journey takes an hour longer.

Price: one week's self catering for the house and the flat costs from £770-£1,180. At the weekend, deduct £80 from the price.

Note: neither smoking nor pets are allowed.

of this well-equipped room. If you don't fancy cooking, though, there are several good pubs and takeaways in the town.

Three double bedrooms lie off the kitchen, all simply furnished and with dedicated bathrooms. There's more sleeping space two floors down in a self-contained flat. Accessed by the central stairwell, it has its own kitchenette and sitting room (which doubles up as an extra bedroom) as well as a bedroom which also contains a futon for children. If that's not enough space, the owners of Fell House can arrange to take an adjoining separate holiday let sleeping another four people.

Perhaps the major disadvantage of Fell House is the lack of a garden. But with some stunning countryside on your doorstep, that just might not be a problem.

Barns &
Farmhouses

Cliff Barns, Norfolk

With a name taken from the TV character in legendary soap *Dallas*, Cliff Barns obviously isn't going to be your average converted barn.

Interior designer Shaun Clarkson and set designer Russell Hall have created a luxury ranch-style interior with some quirky twists on the theme.

As well as stag heads, riding saddles and cowhide chairs, you'll find specially commissioned wagon-wheel chandeliers and wall lights fashioned from horseshoes and gnarled olive-tree roots. The odd splash of vintage floral wallpaper, glass chandeliers and Venetian mirrors add a few surprising flourishes to this eclectic interior.

You can tell that Hall and Clarkson (who has styled many of London's trendiest bars and restaurants, including the Atlantic Bar & Grill and Denim) had great fun sourcing the pieces for this single-storey, stone barn.

The quirkiness extends to the eight individually designed bedrooms that wouldn't look out of place in a boutique hotel. The Seventies Room, for instance, is decked out with thick purple

Half dude ranch, half hacienda, this quirky but luxurious 19th-century pad is a chic palace of fun and frivolity and comes with its own hot tub and sauna

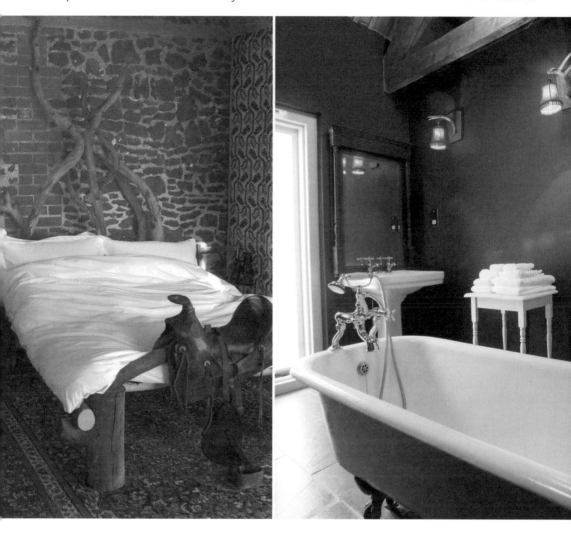

carpet, a psychedelic headboard, period sideboard and original table lamps. If you prefer a more rustic style, the ultra-kitsch Frontier Room has a four-poster bed fashioned from silver birch, chintzy curtains, Alsatian dog figurines and German beer tankards. The whole place is beautifully finished with underfloor heating, contemporary bathrooms and some thoughtful extras such as handmade Norfolk soap and fluffy white bathrobes.

This is the ultimate all-weather party house.

On warm days, pull back the floor-to-ceiling foldaway doors in the 36ft lounge overlooking the central courtyard with its Spanish fountain, or chill out on one of the sun loungers and blast your favourite tunes from the stereo (the barn is set in a three-acre plot, so you won't have to worry about upsetting the neighbours). When it gets a bit chilly, take an invigorating dip in the hot tub or build up a sweat in the sauna.

If you want a change of scene, you can always adjourn to the barn's beach hut in fashionable Old

Hunstanton, a 35-minute drive away, for a bracing walk or dip in the sea.

The north Norfolk Coast is renowned for its sandy beaches and nature reserves including a long stretch at Holkham where *Shakespeare in Love* was filmed. And if you get hungry after all that sea air you can head to one of the numerous gastro pubs along the coast to feast on delicious local seafood including Brancaster oysters and Cromer crab.

The barn works equally well as a weekend retreat for groups of friends or family. Even the four bunk beds in the appropriately named Bunk Room are large enough for adults. The enclosed courtyard – great for young children – has a table-tennis table while the lawns surrounding the property are ideal for ball games.

Cliff Barns also has the large entertaining spaces that you would expect when staying in a barn. Along with the 36ft lounge there's an equally long dining hall that has a table seating up to 18 people, although the room could easily accommodate up to 70 for a party.

Both the lounge and dining hall have 10ft-high stone fireplaces, which create a great focal point with their roaring fires on cold evenings.

Even the kitchen with its floor-to-ceiling windows overlooking the grounds is the kind of place you won't mind spending time in. It has all the equipment you need to cater for large groups, such as a six-hob double oven, American-size fridge and industrial dishwasher.

If you'd prefer to let someone else do the cooking, all kinds of catering can be arranged, from barbecue packs and cold buffets to brunches, Sunday roasts and dinner parties. You can even have a hog roast.

Cliff Barns can also organise wedding receptions – you can get married in either of the large living rooms – including all the catering and entertainment.

Some guests arrange ranch-themed parties and get into character with cowboy hats and toy guns from the dressing-up box. They've even been known to hire a Bucking Bronco.

At Cliff Barns, anything goes.

CLIFF BARNS
at a glance

Russell Hall
Narford Road, Narborough, Norfolk PE32 1HZ
01366 328342, www.cliffbarns.com

Sleeps: 18 in eight rooms (five doubles, one double/twin, one bunk room with four adult-size bunk beds and an adjoining double/twin room). All have ensuite bathrooms with the exception of two rooms, which share a bathroom.

Dining: 18 at a single table but the dining hall can seat up to 70 for a special occasion. Self catering but everything from breakfast and BBQ packs to hog roasts, cold buffets, Sunday roasts and dinner parties can be arranged. You can have a meal waiting for you on the first night, such as fish pie from £12.50pp including French bread, potatoes and green salad. Three-course menus start at £29pp.

Other facilities: outdoor hot tub, sauna, table tennis, and use of beach hut in Old Hunstanton. On-site beauty treatments, holistic massages and yoga classes can also be arranged.

Children: no highchairs or cots.

Wedding licence: for ceremonies in one of the two living rooms. No fee. Marquees for up to 120 (yurts, tipis, Moroccan tents also available).

Local attractions/things to do: waterskiing and trout fishing at nearby Pentney Lakes, clay-pigeon shooting, horse riding at Downham Market – nine miles away – golf, hot-air ballooning, walks at Thetford Forest ten miles away, sandy beaches and nature reserves on the North Norfolk coast, 30 minutes' drive away.

Transport: trains from London's King's Cross take one and a half hours to Downham Market train station, nine miles away. London is a two-hour drive.

Price: minimum three-night weekend breaks start at £2,550-£2,750 self catering for the whole property. A week from £3,750.

Note: no stag parties.

Willows and Beeches, Powys

No expense has been spared in converting these cosy medieval barns into top-class holiday accommodation that you just won't want to leave

Many of the rooms in these two beautifully converted medieval barns in the grounds of Bettws Hall could easily grace the pages of *Country Living* magazine. Richly coloured velvety sofas, antique oak dressers, handmade Indian rugs, oil paintings and a wood-burning stove or open fire create a lovely homely feel in the generously proportioned reception rooms.

A wealth of handcrafted Welsh oak sourced from the owners' 500-acre estate is used to great effect on floors, low-beamed ceilings and grand staircases in these solidly built barns. The local blacksmith also made the wrought-iron bedsteads for some of the uncluttered ensuite bedrooms, while others feature oak four-posters.

Most of the double beds are king size or super king-sized; even the single beds in the two twin rooms aren't really singles – they're three-quarter size. As you'd expect, all of the bedrooms have ensuite bathrooms or shower rooms, a few with cast iron roll-top baths and huge shower roses.

The only downside to Willows and Beeches, which sleep 16 people each, is that the country-style kitchens aren't so well proportioned, making cooking for large groups a bit of a challenge. Of the two, Beeches' kitchen is slightly larger with a breakfast table seating up to eight. Both come with all the mod cons such as a five- or six-hob double oven, fridge/freezers, dishwashers and microwaves.

But you don't need to do any serious cooking if you stay here. The in-house chef, used to catering for shooting parties, can tailor a delicious four-course menu for a special occasion. And, if you take both properties, the 60ft living/dining room in Willows is large enough to allow 32 people to eat together.

If you want a more informal meal, step out of the door and you're right next to the village pub, which serves bar meals as well as traditional ales.

Before dinner, rest your weary bones in the Jacuzzi and sauna shared by both lodges; the perfect way to relax after a hard day's sightseeing, walking or game shooting. On warm summer evenings have a barbecue or picnic by the ornamental lake, or on the banks of the River Bechan in the three-acre grounds.

Between October and January Bettws Hall can arrange game shoots on four local estates while in summer the focus switches to fishing on the River Dovey and its tributary, the River Cleifion.

You get a magnificent backdrop for outdoor activities: Bettws Hall is in the heart of picture-postcard Wales with rolling hills in which to go horse riding or walking. The picturesque Snowdonia National Park and the coast are also within one hour's drive.

There's lots of culture nearby too. Visit the market town of Montgomery with its canal, cobbled streets and Georgian houses below the ruins of a 13th-century castle. The National Trust's Powis Castle and gardens, the Welshpool and Llanfair Light Railway and Glansevern Hall gardens are all within 15 minutes' drive.

Built primarily as shooting lodges, Willows and Beeches can only be rented on a self-catering basis – and then only for week-long stays – between February and September. During the shooting season they are only let for half-board short breaks.

With a week's rental starting at about £100 per person and rising to less than £150, they really do offer great value for money for accommodation of this calibre.

WILLOWS AND BEECHES
at a glance

Ann Evans
Bettws Hall, Bettws Cedewain, Powys
Wales SYI6 3DS
01686 650628, www.bettwshall.com

Sleeps: 16 in each or 32 if both lodges taken (each with six doubles and two twins, all ensuite). Two ground-floor bedrooms in Willows, three in Beeches.

Dining: enough space in Willows for 32 to eat together, or 16 in each. Self catering outside the shooting season, when rental is on a half-board basis. The in-house chef can prepare four-course menus from £28.50pp. A typical meal might include garlic prawn piri-piri with red onion marmalade, brochette of lamb, sticky toffee pudding with hot fudge sauce, and cheese. Wine from £18.50 a bottle.

Other facilities: Jacuzzi and sauna in separate lodge. Picnic tables and a BBQ in the grounds.

Children: cots and highchairs available. Babysitting can be arranged. Lake and river in the grounds.

Wedding licence: no but up to 150 for a reception in a marquee.

Local attractions/things to do: shooting, fishing, clay-pigeon shooting, horse riding, walking and golf. Snowdonia National Park and coast within an hour's drive; Montgomery Canal, Glansevern Hall gardens and the National Trust's Powis Castle are all within a short drive.

Transport: Newtown, just over four miles away, is the nearest train station. Trains from London Euston take about three and a half hours, the same time as by car.

Price: self-catering holidays between February 1 and October 1 start at £1,550 per lodge per week. Dinner, bed and breakfast and bar drinks during the shooting season (October to January) start at £220 plus VAT per night for a double room.

Note: maid service can be arranged. Two dogs allowed in each property. No smoking in bedrooms.

Llwynin Farmhouse, Powys

Whatever the Welsh weather throws at you isn't a problem because the fallback is retreating to this cosy little hideaway in the Brecon Beacons

With lots of higgledy-piggledy rooms, this 18th-century farmhouse and converted barn is the kind of place where you can let the children run riot and hardly notice they're there. If you do, you can always banish them to the rough-and-ready games barn across the yard, where they can play table football, table tennis and darts and shout to their hearts' content.

When they get bored of indoor pursuits, there's two and a half acres of gardens to roam in, complete with picnic tables, rope swings, a paddock, rose garden and a stream, which dries up in summer. It's just how holidays used to be spent before Game Boys and DVDs were invented.

Set in a secluded location in the Brecon Beacons National Park, Llwynin (pronounced Cloy-nin) is ideal for large families and groups of friends looking for good value for money – it's an absolute bargain from about £43 per head for a weekend.

You'll need to share bathrooms though as only one of the nine bedrooms (some of which are quite small) is ensuite.

But there's space where it counts in the two tastefully decorated reception rooms, with a dining room that can seat 20. The attractive kitchen is also large and well equipped, and comes with a range in traditional fireplace surround and a central island with an overhead hanging pan rack.

The welcoming lounge – some of which dates back to 1620 – is full of character with a large stone fireplace and wood-burning stove, oak cruck-beamed ceiling and window seat plus exposed stone walls. Just off this room is a vine-

LLWYNIN FARMHOUSE
at a glance

Bookable through Brecon Beacons Holiday Cottages
Crai, Brecon, Powys, Wales LD3 8TT
01874 676446, www.breconcottages.com

Sleeps: 22 in two interconnecting properties. The farmhouse sleeps 13 (one ensuite double with a single bed, family room with a double and single, one double, one twin and an attic room with three singles). Family bathroom. The barn sleeps 9-10 (one room with four singles, one single with further pull-out bed to make a double and two small doubles). One bathroom and one shower room.

Dining: seats 20. The property is self catering but a local caterer can stock your freezer or cook for you. Prices start at £12 a head for a simple meal such as soup/lasagne/apple crumble and rise to about £30pp for a cordon bleu four-course meal.

Other facilities: a games barn has table football, table tennis, a small trampoline, dartboard and toys. Picnic table with BBQ.

Children: one cot and one highchair.

Wedding licence: no but receptions for up to 40 or a marquee could be erected in the paddock.

Local attractions/things to do: walking, mountain biking, sailing, hang gliding, fishing and canoeing on the River Usk or Wye and pony trekking nearby. Visit second-hand bookshops at Hay-on-Wye and the Gower Peninsula, both within an hour's drive.

Transport: trains from London Paddington to Abergavenny – about an hour's drive away – take about two hours 40 minutes. London is about three and a half hours' drive.

Price: three-night weekends in total from £950 self catering or week-long holidays from £1,600.

filled conservatory that could do with a bit of sprucing up.

All the bedrooms, even the small ones, are wonderfully light and bright: freshly whitewashed walls with cotton duvets in contemporary florals – an Ikea take on Cath Kidston. The huge master bedroom also has a wealth of exposed beams along with an ensuite bathroom.

There's an interconnecting door from the farmhouse to the barn, with its tastefully furnished living room and a rather dark, dated kitchen.

If you'd rather not cook during your stay, there are plenty of local caterers to call on. And this is a great place to go out for a meal; now renowned for its food as well as for its adventure sports, the Brecon Beacons has some superb gastro pubs and restaurants.

Lower Farm Barns, Norfolk

Loft-style chic has arrived in rural Norfolk with these five stylish converted barns, blending the best of traditional local materials with contemporary design

The interiors of these newly converted barns have the look and feel of city loft apartments with open-plan living areas, exposed brickwork and designer furniture.

The only thing that gives away the fact that you're not staying in a chic urban pad is the view: a lush green valley nestled deep in the north Norfolk countryside.

Award-winning architect Anthony Hudson has designed the barns to maximise the living space while maintaining lots of original features such as walls built from rustic-looking flint and a local chalk building material known as clunch. 'We wanted to make the most of the space and light but keep the bold agricultural look,' he says.

No expense has been spared in kitting out all ve barns. Anthony's interior designer wife,

Jenny, has sourced a harmonious mix of old and new furniture and accessories – from Philippe Starck polycarbonate Louis Ghost chairs to antique French chandeliers and Indian carved wood shutters – all teamed with sleek modern kitchens and bathrooms.

Each of the barns has been individually designed, with influences from Morocco, Scandinavia and France. Of the five, only two sleep more than 12, but because they all have open-plan living areas, you can bring in extra tables to seat larger groups when you rent more than one property.

Great East Barn is the largest of the lot, sleeping 14, and is the most loft-like with an open-plan living space on the first floor. In this former 19th-century granary, you can sit on long pale blue sofas with orange scatter cushions

and gaze at wonderful views towards a fording place on the river. An unusual resin and marble pebble floor covers the whole of the seating and dining area with its Italian designer chairs, oak table and trendy silver and orange ceiling lights.

The barn is often taken with Long Meadow, an early 18th-century milking parlour transformed into a Provençal-style interior, creating room for a total of 22 guests. Here, there's a funky Kelly Hoppen Chinese lacquer-red kitchen with a French-look enamelled stove and Philippe Starck Perspex Baroque lights. French doors from the dining room open on to a terrace that's great for alfresco dining.

In Morocco-inspired High Barsham (sleeps 12) lots of rich, earthy colours – blood red, deep purples and aubergines – are complemented by terracotta-tiled floors. There's a luxurious feel to the furnishings with fat sofas and embroidered velvet cushions while silver lanterns or brass and copper lights hang from the ceilings. A galleried mezzanine makes a great playroom for children.

Also popular with children is the Scandinavian-style Grey's Court across the courtyard. One bedroom has loft beds reached by a tiny staircase and a miniature window to peep through in the inner wall. From this little hideaway, kids can watch the rest of the family eating round a long table in the tongue-and-groove-panelled open-plan dining/living area. Another bedroom in this former stables has original saddle racks and a small hay cart.

Next door, single-storey Little Barsham – the smallest of the barns, sleeping four – still feels contemporary but has much more of a cottagey feel.

Located in two massive buildings, all of the barns still manage to feel very private, thanks to their own enclosed courtyard or garden. You can also pre-book times for your whole party at the spa and steam room.

One of the big draws of the barns is their location in uncharacteristically undulating north Norfolk countryside just five miles from the coast with its wonderful sandy beaches.

After a day at the seaside, it's nice to know that you can retire to your very own designer pad in the country.

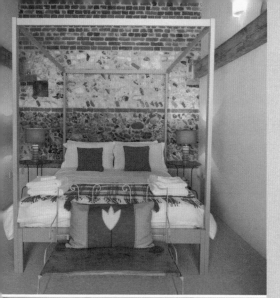

LOWER FARM BARNS
at a glance

Bookable through Rural Retreats
North Barsham, Walsingham, Norfolk MR22 6AP
01386 701177, www.ruralretreats.co.uk

Sleeps: 4-48 in up to five barns. Little Barsham sleeps four (two doubles), Long Meadow sleeps eight (three doubles and one bunk-bed room), Grey's Court sleeps ten (four doubles, one twin), High Barsham sleeps 12 (four doubles, one twin and one double/twin) and Great East Barn sleeps 14 (four doubles, two double/twins and one twin). Most rooms have ensuite facilities. The best combination for larger groups is Great East Barn and Long Meadow (22), High Barsham with Long Meadow (20), or Grey's Court and Little Barsham (14).

Dining: extra tables can be added for communal dining for up to 22 when more than one property is taken. Self catering but a local caterer can deliver pre-cooked meals such as local venison sausages with a mushroom and port sauce from £11.50 for a family-size portion.

Other facilities: games room with table tennis, table football, darts; badminton sets and boules; spa and steam room (booking times for each barn).

Children: cots and highchairs.

Wedding licence: no.

Local attractions/things to do: the north Norfolk coast with its wonderful sandy beaches is five miles away.

Transport: trains from London King's Cross take one and a half hours to King's Lynn, about 30 minutes from the barns. The drive from London takes three hours.

Price: Little Barsham costs from £357 for two nights' self catering, £797 a week; Long Meadow from £751 for three nights, £1,234 a week; Grey's Court £997/£1,684; High Barsham £1,227/£1,989; Great East Barn £1,341/£2,504.

Note: no dogs or smokers. No hen or stag parties. Only seven-night stays in July and August.

Wintonhill Farmhouse, East Lothian

Enjoy some of the perks associated with staying in the grounds of a beautiful stately home when you rent this house on a working farm near Edinburgh

The joy of staying in this modernised 19th-century farmhouse is that as well as being able to relax completely in a home away from home, you can also lord it up when you please by taking advantage of all the benefits of its setting in the extensive grounds of a stately home.

When you fancy seeing how the other half lives, stroll down to the Jacobean Winton House, one of the most important architectural works in Scotland with its carved twisted chimneys created by James VI's master mason, William Wallace.

Farmhouse guests get a free tour of the luxurious interior with its intricate plaster ceilings and fascinating history. For that special dinner, you can also hire the magnificent dining room and eat among Van Dycks and oils by Scottish artists Allan Ramsay and Sir Henry Raeburn.

Now the home of the down-to-earth and friendly Sir Francis and Lady Ogilvy, Winton House also has bedrooms for overflow guests from the farmhouse, some of which are four-poster, and every bit as elegant as the reception rooms.

Sated by the high life, return to relax in front of your own log fire at the cosier stone farmhouse, previously the factor's house. This is more of a kick off your shoes and put your feet on the sofa kind of place. But there are elements of grandeur in the original Victorian tiles in the hallway and in particular, the atmospheric dining room with its round table, leather-back chairs and claret walls.

Though the house is self catering, you don't have to conjure up your own meals or even your own entertainment. Staff at Winton House are used to organising corporate events and can arrange anything from a chef to pipers and a whisky tasting at the farmhouse.

But should cooking be your thing, the farmhouse-style kitchen with its long pine table has all the gear, including a Rayburn. There's also an ante-room stuffed full of green wellies for walkers, a separate utility room for drying out wet clothes and storing golf bags and even a games room with a ping-pong table.

The main downside to staying here is that you'll have to share bathrooms, although all the six bedrooms up the pitch-pine stairway do have bathrobes for you to wear when wandering the corridors.

It's also not the kind of place where ornaments and knick knacks are scattered, so the rooms – particularly the bedrooms – can look a bit bare because of their size, but do provide plenty of space for your own things.

Some of them also boast wonderful views over the surrounding Scottish hills – the Lammermuirs to the South and the Pentlands to the West. There are scenic walks to be had in this stunning countryside as well as plenty of outdoor activities. Again, estate staff can organise whatever you want to do, be it hot-air ballooning or paintball warfare.

The Lammermuir hills also provide the pure clear water for the famous Edinburgh malt produced at the nearby Glenkinckie Whisky Distillery in Pencaitland, where you can see the distillers at work before stocking up on the tipple. And golfers will be spoilt for choice with 20 courses – including ten per cent of the world's links courses – within 30 minutes' drive.

Should you tire of the countryside, Edinburgh, with all its culture and its shops, is less than half an hour's drive away.

WINTONHILL FARMHOUSE
at a glance

Robert Steadman, events and marketing manager
Pencaitland, East Lothian, Scotland EH41 5AT
01875 340222, www.wintonhouse.co.uk

Sleeps: 12-24. Up to 14 in the farmhouse in six bedrooms (three doubles, three double/twins. One room is a family room and can sleep four). There are four bathrooms. Possibility of another five bedrooms in the main house, sleeping ten.

Dining: 12-14 in the farmhouse, which is self catering, although chefs can cook a three-course meal for about £30 a head. Up to 72 can eat at round tables in Winton House for £75pp plus VAT but including alcohol 'within reason'. Sample meals might include haggis and walnut filo parcels with spicy plum sauce, duck breast with blackberry sauce and chilled chocolate cups with Tia Maria. A stone turret in the grounds can also be hired for a self-catering BBQ at £100.

Other facilities: table tennis, practice golf bunker.

Children: cots, highchairs, walled garden. Note that the farmhouse is on a working farm.

Wedding licence: for up to 72 in the dining room of the main house or up to 300 in a marquee in the grounds.

Local attractions/things to do: hill walking, shooting and horse riding on the estate, fishing, golf.

Transport: Edinburgh is 20 minutes' drive away.

Price: from £900-£1,200 for a three-night self-catering weekend in the farmhouse to £1,400-£2,000 a week. Main house £150pp per night B&B for exclusive use.

Note: stag and hen parties are welcome in the farmhouse.

Tregawne, Cornwall

The owners of this characterful farmhouse in the idyllic Ruthern Valley

excel at making their house guests feel relaxed and very much at home

The atmosphere that pervades in this 18th-century farmhouse tucked in a lush green valley can best be described in one word: relaxed. Ex-restaurateur David Jackson and Peta Lady Linlithgow, a trained cook, both love entertaining and have a very laid-back attitude towards their house guests. 'If they want to stay up until five in the morning drinking port they can and, unlike a hotel, they really are free to make as much noise as they want,' says David.

The easy-going atmosphere extends to breakfast time, a flexible affair when a hot plate loaded with freshly cooked bacon and eggs and all the trimmings is laid out, and to the honesty bar, from which guests are encouraged to help themselves.

Sip your pre-dinner drinks in the elegant but relaxed drawing room with its open fire, ethnic rugs, comfy sofas and family photos. The food

is good, honest British fare: perhaps a Caesar salad to start followed by rack of lamb or fillet of beef, finished off with treacle tart or cheesecake. In the summer months, you can eat alfresco on the terrace next to the heated outdoor swimming pool (open from June to September).

There are two ensuite bedrooms in the main house, both decorated in traditional country-house style with antique furniture and matching floral headboards and curtains. The rest of the house-party guests stay in three cottages overlooking the original farm courtyard at the back of the house.

Here you can enjoy all the advantages of a hotel (no cooking or clearing up – there's a daily maid service) along with some of the flexibility of self-catering (your own lounge and kitchen to make drinks and snacks).

Decorated in a contemporary style,

David Jackson
Tregawne, Withiel, Wadebridge, Cornwall PL30 5NR
01208 831552, www.tregawne.com

Sleeps: 16. Two ensuite doubles in main house, Clove and Mill cottages both have two double ensuite rooms while Damson cottage has one double and one twin sharing a bathroom.

Dining: best for 12 but can do 16. Catered on a half-board basis, with three-course dinners such as Caesar salad, filet of beef and cheesecake. Wine from £12.50 a bottle.

Other facilities: heated outdoor swimming pool (June to September), croquet and BBQ.

Children: cots, highchairs, high tea and babysitting can be arranged.

Wedding licence: no.

Local attractions/things to do: The Eden Project is 20 minutes away and swimming and surfing beaches are at Newquay, with deep-sea fishing, windsurfing and waterskiing at Rock. There are two golf courses at Trevose and St Enodoc, both nearby. Numerous historic houses and gardens including the Lost Gardens of Heligan and Trebah – a magical ravine garden with its own private beach – are within an hour's drive, as is St Ives, with its Tate gallery.

Transport: nearest mainline stations at Bodmin and Newquay, both about 20 minutes' drive away (London Paddington is four hours and 15 minutes). The journey by car takes about the same time.

Price: from £65-£75pp per night, half board.

Note: dogs welcome.

the cottages have open fires and outdoor seating areas overlooking the grassed courtyard with its pretty hanging baskets and troughs of flowers.

Tregawne has played host to numerous shooting and golf parties – there are two excellent courses at St Enodoc and Trevose – as well as politicians, national newspaper editors and famous comedians.

It's not just about golf either; the farmhouse is perfectly positioned for some of Cornwall's top attractions. The Eden Project is only 20 minutes' drive away, while the Camel Trail cycle path, fishing village of Padstow – home to Rick Stein's foodie empire – and the UK's surf capital of Newquay are all within an easy drive.

If you stay closer to home you can have a dip in the pool, play croquet on the lawn or wander through the nine-acre meadow with the River Ruthern running at the bottom of it. You might even spot an otter.

White Lodge Farm, Norfolk

Gaze out at wonderful views of open fields from the floor-to-ceiling windows

of this converted barn and adjoining cottages in the heart of rural Norfolk

A barn and two other converted farm buildings set around an enclosed courtyard make up the holiday accommodation here, near the pretty Georgian village of Hingham.

All recently converted – the last was completed in summer 2005 – they're finished to a very high standard with underfloor heating beneath ceramic tiles or reclaimed pine, contemporary bathrooms and kitchens complete with all the mod cons. What's more, they have wonderful views over farmland from their own enclosed gardens. So it's no surprise that two of the properties – the Barn and Dairy Cottage – are proud recipients of the coveted five-star rating from tourist board VisitBritain.

The spacious Barn, which works well for either a large group of friends or family holidaying together, is the biggest of the three, sleeping 12. Large properties often don't have enough seating in the lounge for the whole group, but this isn't a problem in the Barn. The huge upstairs living room, decorated with contemporary photographs of beach huts and the Norfolk countryside, has five three-seater sofas (including a sofa bed that can accommodate an extra two people) as well as a large screen TV, DVD and video.

There's also plenty of room for the whole group to eat together around two farmhouse tables in the open-plan kitchen/dining room that leads on to a patio where you can sit and admire the views. When it gets chilly, retreat through the French doors to a small lounge area with a wood-burning stove.

The Barn isn't short on bathrooms either – two of the six bedrooms have ensuite facilities and there are a further three large bathrooms, including a wet room, with power showers.

There's great attention to detail in all of the generously proportioned bedrooms equipped

with hairdryers and black-out lined curtains – an essential if you want to prevent your kids getting up at some unearthly hour – although the modern pine furniture might not be to everyone's taste. Two of the double rooms have ample space for a cot.

Cooking won't seem too much of a chore in the well-equipped kitchen with an eight-ring gas hob, double oven and a large fridge/freezer. There's also a separate utility room for laundry.

If your group is larger than 12 you can overflow into one of the two adjoining cottages, Stable or Dairy, which sleep six each, as there's room for 18 to dine together in the Barn.

Dairy's pièce de résistance is a conservatory where you can sit and eat while gazing out at wonderful views over the countryside. There's also another dining table in the kitchen/dining area and a double-height lounge complete with oak beams and a large feature fireplace with wood burner.

Stable Cottage actually feels more loft-like than the Barn with a stunning double-height, open-plan kitchen/dining area and mezzanine level offering an additional lounge space (and single futon).

There's plenty to do in the surrounding area if you do tire of the numerous country walks and the shared games room, with its table tennis and table football.

White Lodge has negotiated discounted green fees at some of the 12 golf courses located within 12 miles' drive of the farm. There are also plenty of family attractions within an easy drive including Banham Zoo and the Dinosaur Adventure Park.

And after a hard day's sightseeing you can arrange for a local therapist to come and give you an on-site massage. Perfect.

WHITE LODGE FARM
at a glance

Helen and Tony Richardson
Hardingham Road, Hingham, Norfolk NR9 4LY
01953 850435, www.whitelodgefarmcottages.co.uk

Sleeps: 12-18. The Barn sleeps 12 (+2) (four doubles, two twins, one sofa bed) with five bathrooms. Combine with either Stable Cottage sleeping six (+1) (two doubles, one twin and one single futon in the hayloft) with one ensuite and one further bathroom or Dairy Cottage, which sleeps six (two doubles, one twin – all ensuite).

Dining: the Barn seats up to 18. Self catering but meals can be arranged – anything from lasagne, salad, French bread and fruit salad from £8.50pp to cold buffets (from £10pp) and three-course meals from £12.50 a head.

Other facilities: games room with table tennis and table football. DVD, book and video loans.

Children: two cots (bedding not provided), two highchairs and a steam steriliser. Enclosed gardens.

Wedding licence: no.

Local attractions/things to do: walking, mountain biking and horse riding at nearby Thetford Forest – the largest lowland pine forest in Great Britain with a high-level assault course; Norwich (30 minutes' drive); golf (12 courses within 12 miles). Nearby children's attractions include Banham Zoo and the Dinosaur Adventure Park.

Transport: trains from London Liverpool Street to Norwich or Diss, 30 minutes' drive from the farm, take two hours to Norwich, one hour 40 minutes to Diss. London is two and a half hours' drive by car.

Price: four-night mid-week breaks from £600 for the Barn, £300 for Dairy and £270 for Stable, self catering. Three-night weekend breaks from £750/£300/£270 and week-long stays from £1,000/£430/£380.

Note: no smoking. One well-behaved dog allowed. No single-sex groups.

Halls & Houses

Maunsel House, Somerset

Sir Ben Slade, the owner of this medieval manor house set in 90 acres of parkland, can give you a personal tour when you stay at his family home

Going round Maunsel House with its owner, Sir Benjamin Slade, is rather like a fascinating history lesson, which is what you'd expect from someone who can trace his ancestors back to Charles II on his mother's side. There are lots of colourful characters from the family's past: the lady who was so distraught at finding a wrinkle, she locked herself away and was never seen again; the ancestor who built Nelson's flagship, the Victory; and Sir John Slade, aka Black Jack – 'probably the worst general in the army' who

danced with Marie-Antoinette. Their portraits, including some of Sir Ben himself – a talkative, amiable man very far from what you'd imagine a lord of the manor to be – are among those hung on almost every available wall of Maunsel's public rooms.

It was Sir Ben's foresight that helped save Maunsel House from financial ruin. When, in 1986, he took over from Uncle Alfred 'the Rake' and Aunt Freda 'the Bleeder' who had spent what was left of the family fortune, Maunsel was

in a general state of disrepair, riddled with dry rot. Raising cash to renovate the house by charging visitors 50p a visit, Sir Ben has created a wonderful venue for an old-fashioned house party.

Instead of overstated elegance, this is a family home that's been lived in, where the carpets might be slightly frayed around the edges, but where you'll find plenty of ambience, with suits of armour and swords on the walls along with some excellent hospitality (Sir Ben and his partner, Kirsten, can be as present or as absent as you want). There are some quirky additions too; the house has one of the oldest loos in Somerset, and there's a room above Sir Ben's flat that can only be reached via a ceiling panel.

The house dates back much further than the Slade family, who moved in relatively recently in 1771; it's mentioned in the Domesday book and was visited by Chaucer. Spend an evening here,

and you can move through the ages, the various rooms added at different times during Maunsel's history. Start in the bar, with flagstones, timber roof and wood settles, where a Saxon thane named Brictwold was lord of the manor before being removed by a Norman baron.

Then pass through the Norman entrance hall with its Tudor ceiling to the Victorian side of the house, with its elegant pale green dining room, its long wooden table surrounded by leather chairs and life-size carvings of Africans on either side of the fire. After dinner, sink into one of the sofas in front of the fire in the pine-panelled library or dance in the ballroom, empty 'since Aunt Freda sold all the furniture', but perfect for a knees up or a wedding.

Upstairs, there's plenty of furniture, particularly in the bathrooms, which are often as big as the bedrooms and include dressing tables, sofas and even a drinks cabinet in the shape of a globe. They also hold some spectacular baths

North Newton, Nr Bridgwater, Somerset TA4 OBU
01278 661076, www.maunselhouse.co.uk

including a 'coffin bath' in wood, where the lid comes down, and one of the few remaining combined Victorian shower and baths.

The bedrooms are well furnished, most with four-posters and plenty of antiques, including beautiful examples of marquetry and an ornate 200-year-old Florentine mirror. However, one of the attic rooms does have a particularly low ceiling.

When you're not marvelling at Maunsel's stunning interior you can wander around the grounds that are filled with wildlife including a peacock, guinea fowl, and a herd of unusual looking White Park rare-breed cattle.

But the undisputed lord of the manor in Maunsel's animal kingdom is a cross-bred black Labrador/Doberman called Jasper, who inherited £50,000 and was the subject of a bitter custody battle.

At Maunsel, even the dogs are a little bit different.

Sleeps: 18 in nine rooms (eight doubles, one twin). There are eight ensuite bathrooms.

Dining: up to 22 at one long table (space for more to be added) or 84 in the ballroom. Let on a B&B basis although caterers can be arranged and self-catering is possible. Three-course buffets from £25 a head, and sit-down meals from about £35. House wine £15 a bottle, or BYO for £5pp corkage.

Other facilities: beauticians can be arranged to visit the house.

Children: children's meals, but no cots or highchairs.

Wedding licence: in the ballroom for up to 80 or a marquee in the grounds for larger numbers. £3,500 plus VAT for hire of the venue and one night's B&B.

Local attractions/things to do: plenty of walks nearby and a loch for longboat hire. Glastonbury is about 15 minutes' drive away, Wells is about half an hour and Street, with its outlet stores, 15 minutes away. Numerous events can be organised, from a music festival and pig roast in the grounds to shooting nearby.

Transport: Maunsel is just under three hours' drive from London, and one hour 45 minutes by train from London Paddington to Taunton, which is 15 minutes away.

Price: from £1,000 per night plus VAT for B&B plus a flat rate of £2,500 plus VAT to use the house.

Note: smoking is only allowed in the bar.

Toft Hall, Staffordshire

This quirky, family-friendly house on the edge of the Peak District is packed with so much entertainment that some weekend guests don't even go out

Eight years ago, 17th-century Toft Hall was derelict. The chimney had fallen through the roof into one of the bedrooms and dry rot was rife. But it was love at first sight for Sue Moore who fell for this 'wonderful mad house' – one of the few oak-cruck frame buildings in Staffordshire – and its stunning location on the edge of the Peak District. She has lovingly restored Toft Hall to create a cosy bolthole with all the modern conveniences of home and a few quirky features that will provide plenty of talking points during your stay.

Don't forget to duck when you walk into the four bedrooms on the top floor of this grade-I listed building, once home to the High Sheriff of the county; the doors are only 4ft 6 high. While the kids will love darting in and out of these rooms, the low door frames aren't ideal for the elderly – although once inside the ceilings revert to normal height. Another great addition is a 19th-century upright, seat-shaped bath called a Sitz. Sue was planning to install a shower in the small top floor bathroom but couldn't resist this unusual space saver. You'll also be able to admire some of the original wattle and daub protected by glass panels in one of the bedrooms and the snug.

The latter room is for kids with its Xbox games console. If they tire of that – and lots don't – there's a games room with table tennis, darts, table football and air hockey.

Sue hasn't forgotten the youngest children, who will love playing with the dressing-up box and dolls' house under the stairs in the hall. There's also a playhouse in the south-facing garden, its fenced-off pond teaming with frogs' spawn in the spring, and with great views over unspoilt countryside.

Adults haven't been neglected either. The music room is a very grown-up zone with its cream carpet, gold silk curtains and limited edition artwork. It's also a great party space where you can put on one of the party-mix CDs and crank up the volume – with 2ft 6 stone walls, you won't disturb the neighbours (they're only sheep, anyway).

The reception rooms are so numerous in this house that there's plenty of room for everyone to spread out. When you do want to get together, the living room with its original quarry tiled floors, wood-burning stove and four leather sofas is large enough to accommodate the whole group of more than 20 people. There's a large TV with DVD to goggle at plus walls lined with books.

Everyone can be seated round a large table in the dining room too, on the contemporary leather chairs that provide an interesting contrast to the richly coloured brocaded curtains. The room makes an atmospheric venue for a special meal with its original stone fireplace, 'Eating Room Red' Farrow & Ball-painted walls, parquet flooring and lots of candles.

Sue can recommend a great local chef who not only brings staff to serve you champagne and canapés but also gives you a choice of starters, main courses and desserts on the night – just like in a restaurant.

Not that cooking will be too much of a chore at Toft Hall. A handmade wood and stone Smallbone kitchen comes complete with lots of smart gadgets such as a Dualit toaster, juicer, bread maker, American fridge freezer and a Neff oven with an induction hob. There's even a second kitchen next door with a small table that's great for serving up breakfast and high tea for the kids.

At the end of a hard day enjoying yourselves you can retire to exemplary bedrooms – some with the original shutters, oak doors and beams – and more heavy curtains framing the rolling hills beyond.

TOFT HALL *at a glance*

Sue Moore
Heaton, Staffordshire SK11 OSJ
01260 226609, www.tofthall.co.uk

Sleeps: 23 in ten bedrooms (four doubles, two twins, one double/twin, one single and two family rooms sleeping up to four each). Two rooms are ensuite and there are three other bathrooms.

Dining: table seats 21. Self catering but a local chef can stock your freezer or prepare everything from a buffet or BBQ to a celebration dinner with waiting staff (from £23 per head).

Other facilities: games room with table football, table tennis, air hockey and darts. Xbox console, dressing-up box and Wendy house. BBQ, football and badminton nets. Holistic in-house beauty treatments can be arranged.

Children: one cot (bedding not supplied). Babysitting can be arranged.

Wedding licence: no but small receptions for 21.

Local attractions/things to do: wonderful walks from just outside the front door and horse riding at Flash, England's highest village. There are numerous gardens nearby such as Biddulph Grange and Tatton Park as well as Wedgwood and Royal Doulton tours. Alton Towers theme park is less than a 30-minute drive. Pretty towns of Buxton, Ashbourne and Bakewell are all nearby.

Transport: trains from London Euston take two hours to Stoke, a 30-minute drive from the hall. The drive from London takes more than three hours.

Price: three-night self-catering weekends from £1,650 for the property, four-night midweek breaks from £850 and week-long holidays from £1,950.

Note: no pets. No smoking. Maid service can be arranged.

Peek House, Devon

Kids and parents alike will love the games room and mini cinema in this immaculately presented, spacious mansion on the Devon/Dorset border

It's hard to fault Peek House. This newly converted Victorian mansion built for Sir Henry Peek on a private estate near Lyme Regis has superb facilities. With nearly 11,000 square feet arranged over four floors, it is huge, allowing large groups of people plenty of room to spread out without disturbing each other.

The basement of this immaculate house is devoted to entertainment. Kiddie heaven comes in the form of a dedicated room with Sega video games, air hockey, table football and a pool table. Next door is a mini-cinema, DVD library and state-of-the-art surround sound. If you fancy a bit of pampering, a local therapist can come and perform a soothing massage or facial in the treatment room. Even mundane matters such as laundry are taken care of with a room housing a washing machine and tumble dryer.

While the kids can make as much noise as they like in the basement, adults can have a game of cards over the teak table in the library upstairs or chill out in the spacious lounge with its high-beamed ceilings, wooden floors and wood-burning stove. When the whole group wants to get together, there's enough space for everyone to sit down on three gigantic sofas, which is not

something that can be said for many holiday homes catering for large parties.

Even cooking won't seem like a chore in the oak-crafted contemporary kitchen with its granite worktops, breakfast bar, Belfast sink, American style fridge/freezer, white crockery and Dualit toaster. Bang the gong before supper in the dining room, the perfect venue for a posh dinner party with its fireplace, dark green walls and window seats overlooking the courtyard.

If you don't fancy cooking, caterers specialising in local, seasonal produce can organise anything from a Mediterranean buffet to a five-course extravaganza with champagne and canapés.

Everything's done out in the best possible taste throughout this house, where even the artwork has been chosen to coordinate with the decor. Such attention to detail also extends to the landings, one of which doubles as a second lounge with a chic little grey sofa, suede pouffe and quaint fireplace.

Among some unusual touches is an ironwork column entwined with ivy and contemporary lights that runs up the four-storey exposed brickwork staircase. Owner Judith Ellard, who commissioned

if from nearby Branscombe Forge, says it reminds her of Jack and the Beanstalk.

Seven stylish, individually decorated bedrooms – five of which have ensuite bathrooms – are filled with a mix of contemporary and antique furniture. The huge master bedroom has a modern teak four-poster while another room has a Japanese feel to it with a low bed, black and white curtains and coordinating flowery wallpaper.

If there is a downside to Peek House it's that there's no enclosed garden. There is a lawn at the front of the house with mature copper beech trees, garden furniture and a gas-fired barbecue but as it's next to a small car park, it isn't very private.

However, there are plenty of other solitary places on the 350-acre estate surrounding Peek House, including a private beach a half-hour's walk away – one of many pebbly beaches dotted along this spectacular coastline now dubbed the Jurassic Coast, England's first natural World Heritage Site.

Visit the fishing port of Lyme Regis with its sandy beaches and world famous Cobb harbour just two miles down the road, buy fresh fish off the beach at Beer or go walking along the South West Coast Path, which runs through the estate. Exeter, with its cathedral and historic quay, is about an hour's drive. Take the kids to numerous family attractions such as Crealy Adventure Park near Exeter and a go-karting track at Budleigh Salterton.

That's if you can tear them away from the games room and mini cinema.

PEEK HOUSE
at a glance

Judith Ellard
Rousdon Estate, Nr Lyme Regis, Devon DT7 3XR
01297 444734, www.peekhouse.co.uk

Sleeps: 14 in seven bedrooms (five doubles and two double/twins), five of which are ensuite. One further bathroom.

Dining: dining room comfortably seats up to 14. Self catering but catering can be arranged. One local caterer specialising in local produce can organise anything from a Mediterranean buffet from £12pp to a four-course meal with champagne and canapés from £35pp.

Other facilities: games room with table football, air hockey and Sega video games as well as a pool room and DVD mini-cinema. There is a beauty treatment room, three bikes and a BBQ.

Children: travel cot.

Wedding licence: no.

Local attractions/things to do: walking along the South West Coast Path, fishing and horse riding. Seaside resort of Lyme Regis, fishing village of Beer and Branscombe – reputed to be the longest village in England – are all within an easy drive. The cathedral city of Exeter is within an hour's drive. Kids' attractions include the theme park Crealy Adventure Park near Exeter and go-karting track near Budleigh Salterton.

Transport: Axminster, six miles away, is the closest railway station (journey time from London Waterloo: two hours 40 minutes). Three hours' drive from London.

Price: self-catering weekends from £1,800 in total from October to March. Week-long stays from £2,250.

Note: no smoking. Up to two well-behaved dogs allowed.

Glenmorangie House, Ross-shire

Decanters of whisky are just one of the perks of staying in this characterful

seaside retreat owned by one of Scotland's most famous malt houses

The house bears more than a passing resemblance to the whisky: mellow and lingering, making you want to kick off your shoes and curl up on a sofa; and even lightly smoked, with the smell of open fires hanging in the air. There are also tasteful reminders that you are staying in a building owned by one of Scotland's most famous malt houses – a whisky barrel in the stairwell, part of the distillation unit in the hallway, and a welcome 'wee dram' in a decanter for each bedroom.

It's not just the details that have been carefully thought through at this 16th-century house on Scotland's east coast – the whole renovation has been carried out with panache. Even the 1970s addition of the morning room and dining room has been done sympathetically, the former with plump sofas, modern bookshelves and wood-panelled walls, and the latter just the right size to hold the long table where evening meals are served. Big on traditional Scottish fare, dinners include a Haggis course with neaps, tatties, and whisky to wash it down – although less adventurous guests can have soup instead.

There's also an atmospheric second dining room for smaller groups in the oldest part of the house. Next door is the dimly-lit Buffalo Room, with its low ceiling, stone fireplace and a grandfather clock counting out the rhythm of life in this rural corner of Scotland. There are also some wonderful coastal views from the windows.

The most spectacular panoramas, though, can be seen from some of the six bedrooms upstairs, particularly from one of two master bedrooms, which is decked out with a maroon bedspread and curtains, a tartan carpet, and matching low-backed chairs. The other bedrooms might not be as spacious, but they are just as well decorated and all come with flat-screened TVs, Molton Brown toiletries, complimentary water, chocolates and, of course, whisky.

As well as the six ensuite bedrooms in the main house, there are three cottages in the grounds. Unlike some properties, Glenmorangie's cottages don't come as second best to staying in the main house; just over the lawn, strung out in a long, low line, they are stylishly contemporary with modern four-posters and a separate sitting room with sofa bed (probably more suitable for one adult).

As far as activities go, there's a lot more of the whisky world to discover – as well as a free tour of the distillery a few miles down the road, guests can enjoy a malt tasting in the evening and even have a whole whisky-themed weekend.

For those who aren't so moved by the spirit, there's a range of outdoor activities, including husky sledging in all weathers down the gravel drive, fishing, falconry and boat trips to see dolphins. Back at the house there are plenty of board games along with a giant chess set in the garden, and a library filled with books about Scotland including the History of Curling and the life of Mary Queen of Scots.

At the end of the day it's nice to know you can retire to your seaside retreat, sink into a sofa and enjoy a tipple or two. There's a huge selection on offer, including more than 50 varieties of whisky.

But whatever you do, just don't ask for a Glenfiddich.

GLENMORANGIE HOUSE
at a glance

Maggie McQuillan, office administrator
Cadboll, by Tain, Ross-shire, Scotland IV20 1XP
01862 871671, www.glenmorangieplc.com

Sleeps: 18 (+3). Six ensuite double/twin rooms in the house plus three cottages, each with a double bedroom and a sofa bed – suitable for one adult – in the sitting room.

Dining: 22 at a single table. Catered on a half-board basis. Traditional Scottish food such as roast red snapper, Haggis or cream of carrot and mussel soup, loin of lamb and Drambuie and vanilla Panna Cotta. Alcohol is extra or BYO for £5 per bottle corkage.

Other facilities: complimentary visit to Glenmorangie distillery a few miles down the road.

Children: cots, highchairs, children's meals and an enclosed garden.

Wedding licence: for up to 60 in the house or outside in a marquee.

Local attractions/things to do: clay-pigeon shooting, husky sledging, archery and falconry in the grounds. All kinds of evening entertainment can be arranged in the house from whisky tastings to ceilidhs. Nearby, salmon and trout fishing, pony trekking, shooting, and golf at the Royal Dornoch Golf Club. Boat trips can be arranged to see dolphins.

Transport: Inverness airport is about an hour's drive away.

Price: from £2,500 per night, half board, for the whole house.

Note: closed in January.

Grove House, Gloucestershire

Get dressed for dinner by the glowing light of a log fire before sipping aperitifs in the stylish drawing room of this quintessentially English country home

Grove House is warm and cosseting. From Henry, the portly and friendly Jack Russell, greeting you at the door, to the comforting tick of the grandfather clock in the hall and delicious home-cooked food, this 14th-century house has a lovely ambience.

With more than 22 years operating as an upmarket B&B (it's one of the original Wolsey Lodges where guests often have dinner as well as breakfast), it's also a home that owners Michael and Ellen Ross are happy to share.

As award-winning ex-restaurateurs, the couple love entertaining and are dab hands in the kitchen. Ellen makes her own bread and

uses fruit and vegetables from the garden. In the evening, she might cook smoked salmon and prawn parcels with a salad of mixed leaves, roast duck with apple sauce and stuffing, followed by chocolate tart and praline ice cream.

On warm summer evenings many guests dine on the patio. The rest of the time there's no better place than the atmospheric 18th-century wood-panelled dining room bathed in candlelight and the warmth of a log fire, the table decorated with one of Ellen's extravagant floral displays.

In the morning, admire the views of the

ornamental lake as you tuck into another gourmet treat. The hot buffet might include kedgeree, smoked haddock or fishcakes along with the usual 'full English' fare. Eggs are cooked to order whenever guests heave themselves out of bed.

The loveliest room in Grove House is a spacious light-filled drawing room with cream furnishings, corniced ceilings, and a crystal chandelier. It's a great place to meet for tea and homemade cake after a day's sightseeing or walking, particularly as it gets the late afternoon sun. It's also an ideal rendezvous for pre-dinner drinks where you can help yourself from the honesty bar; there's no standing on ceremony here.

All seven bedrooms in the main house are decorated in traditional country-house style, two with four-posters and lovely views of the ornamental lake. Rooms in the oldest part of the house have a more higgledy-piggledy feel to

them with original beams and sloping floors.

Larger groups can also take one of the cottages in the 13-acre grounds. Two-bedroom Garden Cottage has a super king-size four-poster room with a spacious ensuite shower room. A charming lounge – complete with another fireplace – can seat 12 for dinner if you fancy cooking supper for yourselves one night. Next door are two bedrooms in separate annexes. Another cottage, Summerhouse, sleeps two.

Grove House's idyllic lakeside setting makes it a big hit for wedding receptions, which are held in the converted 18th-century hay barn with candle chandeliers and log fire. In warm weather the party often spills out on to the croquet lawn where marquees can be erected. The barn also makes a great hen and stag party venue, where you can make as much noise as you like and won't have to worry if you drop red wine on the purple carpet.

GROVE HOUSE
at a glance

Michael and Ellen Ross
Bromesberrow Heath, Ledbury,
Gloucestershire HR8 1PE
01531 650584, www.the-grovehouse.com

Sleeps: 12-23. Up to 12 (+1) in the main house in seven rooms (three twins, three doubles, and one small single room with an adult-size bed). Four ensuite and the rest share one bathroom. A further ten people can be accommodated in cottages in the grounds. Garden Cottage has one double bed, one twin. Two annexes have one double and one twin. Summerhouse Cottage has one double.

Dining: 23 in the house at one table. Catered on a B&B basis but dinner can be arranged from £25pp. A typical meal might start with smoked salmon and prawn parcels, then move on to roast duck and chocolate tart with praline ice cream. Larger groups can be catered for in the barn.

Other facilities: tennis court, table tennis, snooker, croquet and use of neighbour's unheated outdoor pool.

Children: one highchair, three cots. There is an unfenced ornamental lake in the grounds. High tea and babysitting can be arranged.

Wedding licence: no but an 18th-century converted hay barn can be hired for receptions up to 100 for £850.

Local attractions/things to do: Ledbury, Hereford, Gloucester, Worcester and the Severn Valley Railway are all within an easy drive. Walking in the Malvern Hills, Welsh hills, Forest of Dean and the Cotswolds.

Transport: nearest train station is four miles away at Ledbury (trains from London Paddington take nearly three hours). London is about a two-hour drive.

Price: from £39.50pp per night B&B.
A minimum of eight people secures exclusive use.

Note: no smoking in bedrooms. Dogs allowed in cottages.

Plas Glansevin, Dyfed

It's hard to find large self-catering houses as big or as versatile as this

Georgian mansion, set in the western foothills of the Brecon Beacons

Few large properties offer such flexible group accommodation as this sprawling Georgian mansion and Coach House. Here, you can mix and match the properties to suit house parties as small as 17, to as large as 62. With the Coach House sleeping up to 23 and Glansevin Mansion accommodating 39, you can rent either one, both, or even take the main house and part of the Coach House.

The mansion itself is made up of two very different halves. In the 'posh part' just through the covered portico with its Doric columns, you'll find refined reception rooms befitting a Georgian country house. The imposing entrance hall alone has a listed Nash staircase, ornate fireplace and wooden floors covered with Persian rugs. Then there's the 35ft drawing room – complete with its own bar area – with deep red walls, plush sofas and another feature fireplace. Huge sash windows overlook the front lawn dominated by an 800-year-old oak tree.

But head towards the back of the house past the TV and games room and the decor gets a little scruffy in the nicest possible way. You won't need to worry too much about spilling a drink or two on the flagstone floor in the 60ft oak-beamed dining room with its inglenook fireplace and adjoining caterer's kitchen. That's one of the great things about Plas Glansevin: it's not too precious. 'We want people to relax and not worry if they've left a few drink stains on the table – there are probably some there already – or feel they need to keep a constant eye on the kids,' says house manager Mandy Isaacs.

Upstairs, the 19 simply furnished bedrooms are all a good size and come with dark wood furniture, patterned duvets, framed Indonesian textiles and original Georgian shutters and sash windows. Many have their original fireplaces.

There's also a newly converted ensuite bedroom on the ground floor that has been kitted out for the disabled.

The mansion's warren of rooms makes it a great place for games of hide and seek. There's table football and table tennis inside, plus ball games, putting or croquet outdoors. In summer the outdoor unheated pool will no doubt be the main attraction, while when it's cooler, the recent addition of a wood-fired sauna will make for some fun Scandinavian-style dashes between the two.

Neither the pool nor the sauna are open to guests staying at the Coach House, which is just 50 yards away from the mansion, unless they form part of the same party.

However, this property has other attractions for teenagers, including its own den in the woods that comes with table football and table tennis. The house, furnished in a contemporary style, also has a mezzanine, with sofas and a TV, that's accessed by a pull-down ladder, the ideal teenagers' pad.

This forms part of the open-plan kitchen/living area that's reminiscent of a trendy loft apartment with double-height ceilings, and a breakfast bar in the black marble-topped kitchen. It's not a huge space for a house sleeping up to 23, but some of the party can move into the adjoining dining room, with its unusual arched wooden ceiling and sliding glass doors leading on to the lawn.

The four best bedrooms – including a master room with a swanky contemporary sandstone bathroom holding a whirlpool bath – are in the main part of the house. Eight others are located in the rather appropriately named Accommodation Block and look a bit like the rooms in a budget hotel: clean and functional but not overbrimming with character.

PLAS GLANSEVIN
at a glance

Harvey Peters
Llangadog, Dyfed, Wales SA19 9HY
01550 777121, www.glansevin.com

Sleeps: 17 to 62 in various configurations. Hire the Coach House for 17 or 23 in 12 rooms (five doubles, four of which are ensuite, six ensuite single/twins and one single). Or take Glansevin Mansion, which sleeps 39 in 20 rooms (four triples, 11 doubles and five singles). Some 12 rooms are ensuite and there is a room for the disabled. The mansion can also be hired for 24, 34 and 37 people. Or take the mansion and the Coach House's Accommodation Block for 54.

Dining: 23 in the Coach House or 62 in the mansion. Self catering but caterers are available, with prices from £12pp for soup/lasagne/apple crumble to about £30pp for four courses.

Other facilities: Glansevin Mansion: outdoor unheated pool, wood-fired sauna, croquet, mini-putting range, BBQ, volleyball net, table tennis, table football. Coach House: den in woods with table football and table tennis.

Children: cots and highchairs in both properties. Babysitting can be arranged.

Wedding licence: no but up to 70 for a reception.

Local attractions/things to do: plenty of outdoor activities in the rugged mountains and coastal areas nearby including golf (five courses within 45 minutes).

Transport: trains from London Paddington via Swansea take four and a half hours to Llangadog station, five miles away. The drive from London is about four hours.

Price: Coach House: three-nights' self catering from £1,480, one-week stays from £2,260. Mansion: from £2,970/£4,360 for 24; £3,260/£4,930 for 34 (add an extra £80 short break or £100 for a week if 37 and an extra £80/£100 for 39). Mansion and Coach House Accommodation Block (up to 54): £4,180/£6,310. Mansion and Coach House (up to 62): £4,740/£7,190.

Trevor Hall, Denbighshire

A Dalek in the bathroom, Space Invaders games in the smoking room and a bedroom called Twin Peaks can all be found in this magnificent property

Eccentric is probably the best way to describe the interior of Trevor Hall. Walk around this magnificent grade-I listed, red-brick building, and you'll find a Dalek in the bathroom, a 1950s jukebox alongside the more traditional stag heads in the medieval dining hall, and antique arcade games – some of which still work. It's a sign of the quirky tastes of Trevor Hall's owner, music agent Louise Parker, and those of her late husband Louis (whose family owns an amusement arcade business).

The Dalek was used in a music video for one of the Parkers' clients, The Prodigy, and there are numerous other bits of pop memorabilia dotted around the house. The walls of the Regency drawing room are lined with accolades for best-selling records from All Saints, Steps, Blue and Boyzone, many of whom have stayed at the hall.

This place is all about fun. Kids – and big kids – will love playing on one of the original Space Invaders in the wood-panelled smoking room or trying their luck on the 10p grabber or other working arcade games. There's a games room with a pool table, and the opulently furnished drawing room also serves as a cinema with a pull-down 6ftx5ft screen and surround sound system for DVDs and videos.

There are some superb entertaining spaces that don't come much grander than the medieval-style dining hall with its floor-to-ceiling stone fireplace, 14ft oak dining table and Victorian geometric floor tiles (bizarrely this beautiful floor was preserved by animal droppings after a farmer, who bought the hall following a devastating fire in 1963, used it as a livestock shelter).

As well as entertainment, Trevor Hall also provides some great places to chill out. Get cosy on one of the sofas and watch a video in the snug or tinkle the ivories on the baby grand piano in the Italianate music room with its

whitewashed wooden floors, neo-classical columns and Venetian mirror. There's even an electric guitar (and you won't have to worry about disturbing the neighbours on this 85-acre private estate).

For all its grandeur, this wonderful house feels incredibly relaxed. That's probably because all of the original furniture and ornaments – even the family photographs – stayed behind when Louise and her family moved into the Coach House next door.

Upstairs, all seven bedrooms are individually designed and beautifully decorated. The Moroccan- and Indian-themed rooms are painted in earthy colours and adorned with rich textiles. There's also a more traditional four-poster room and the charming Blue Room with its tiny fireplace, white iron bed and window seats. In the room appropriately named Twin Peaks, you'll find antique wooden single beds, and a huge bathroom with roll-top bath.

From the upstairs windows, you can see the Italian garden that sits alongside a restored Victorian greenhouse housing original vines, and a barbecue and seating area with panoramic views over the Vale of Llangollen.

There's also a children's playground, plus a menagerie of pets, with a cow, sheep and rabbit that will keep the kids entranced for hours. You can even bring your own horse to ride along the estate's network of bridleways.

TREVOR HALL
at a glance

Louise Parker or June Jones
Trevor Hall Rd, Llangollen, Denbighshire,
Wales LL20 7UP
01978 810505, www.trevorhall.com

Sleeps: 12/14 adults and up to four young children in six doubles and one twin. Three rooms have ensuite bath and/or shower rooms and there are four further bathrooms.

Dining: 14 comfortably around one table. Self catering but local caterers can prepare anything from buffets starting at £15.50pp to three-course dinners from £22.50pp. Alternatively, a local cook can prepare all your meals.

Other facilities: pool room, cinema room with all satellite channels, DVDs and videos (library of both available on request), baby grand piano, children's playground, stabling and paddocks for up to two horses (at extra cost). In-house holistic treatments can be arranged.

Children: one travel cot and highchair, children's playground.

Wedding licence: no. Small receptions for up to 30.

Local attractions/things to do: walking, horse riding, and horse-drawn canal boat trips along the Vale of Llangollen, crossing the world's biggest aqueduct at Llangollen, three miles away. The house and gardens at Plas Newydd are also nearby, as are Ruthin Castle and the medieval town of Chester.

Transport: trains from London Euston take three and a half hours to Ruabon station, two miles from the hall. The drive from London takes about the same time.

Price: from £2,250 for a three-night self-catering weekend or mid-week break (Monday to Thursday) and £2,750 for a week's self catering, based on 12 people (an extra £200 for the remaining double room). A welcome hamper and toiletries are included in the price.

Note: smoking is only allowed in the smoking room. Up to two dogs permitted, but not in the bedrooms. Separate kennel also available.

Skipton Hall, Yorkshire

One of the biggest attractions of this grade-II listed Georgian house is its superb location – just 20 minutes from the picturesque Yorkshire Dales

Comfort rather than grandeur is what it's all about at Skipton Hall, a Georgian grade-II listed house built by wealthy cattle drovers in a small Yorkshire village. Staying here is rather like visiting a great aunt's house in the country with antiques, such as the grandfather clock in the grand hallway, and lots of floral furnishings.

Two interconnecting sitting rooms – one cream, one claret – have china tucked away in cabinets and chandelier lights, but are also full of plump sofas, knick knacks, books and open fires that add to the relaxed feel.

You'll find the kind of facilities here that you want in a home from home – a small office tucked under the stairs and a simple vaulted basement, which is great for discos but also doubles up as a games room and a small gym.

A former retirement home where catering for large groups was the norm, Skipton Hall has an extremely well-equipped kitchen with two dishwashers, a coffee machine large enough for 24, two sets of china and a fridge freezer and separate fridge in the larder. The kitchen is also very spacious and attractive with an Aga, breakfast table and Shaker-style cupboards.

Should you prefer to have a special meal prepared for you, caterers can serve up dinner-party food in the dining room, which with its high-backed chairs and slate-green walls has a more contemporary look than the rest of the house. It's a lovely room, with enormous candlesticks on the table and a large bow window overlooking the garden.

A small television room on the ground floor can be converted into a downstairs bedroom (the double bed is stashed away in the wardrobe), ideal for those with limited mobility who might also benefit from a private bathroom down the corridor

Audrey Skipsey
Skipton on Swale, Thirsk, North Yorkshire YO7 4SB
01845 567037, www.hireskiptonhall.co.uk

Sleeps: 24 in 11 bedrooms (six doubles, five twins) plus the morning room (with a double 'wardrobe' bed). Five bedrooms are ensuite, with four further bath/shower rooms.

Dining: 24. Skipton Hall is self catering but caterers can be called in for buffets, dinners or BBQs from about £20pp including waitress service for a three-course dinner. A typical menu might include fish terrine with fresh mayonnaise, beef Provençal with olives, tomatoes and white wine followed by toffee cheesecake.

Other facilities: small gym, table-tennis and darts board. There is a BBQ in the garden.

Wedding licence: no.

Children: cot, highchair, toys and enclosed garden.

Local attractions/things to do: the scenic Yorkshire Dales are just 20 minutes away and the cathedral city of York can be reached in less than an hour. Thirsk and Ripon race courses are close by – transport can be arranged. The World of James Herriot Centre, with its living quarters from the 1940s and 50s and sets from the TV series, is 10 minutes' drive away.

Transport: trains from London King's Cross to North Allerton, 20 minutes from Skipton Hall, take between two and a half and three hours. The same journey by car is about three and a half hours.

Price: three-night self-catering weekends for the property from £2,990 and £4,200 for a week.

Note: the house is completely non smoking. Pets are allowed but only in the kitchen area. There is a bathroom for the disabled on the ground floor.

that's been adapted for disabled use.

Upstairs, 11 bedrooms are spread over the first and second floors, two with four-posters and some filled with antique furniture. In keeping with the downstairs decor, the homely feel prevails, with blankets rather than duvets and simple bathrooms. Some rooms boast views over the gardens, the River Swale and the surrounding lush green landscape.

The countryside is one of the main reasons people come here, with the scenic Yorkshire Dales just a 20-minute drive away, although you can also be in York within an hour.

While it is possible to get to Skipton Hall by train and taxi, you really do need a car; it might be in a village but there isn't a pub or corner shop. The bonus for drivers, though, is that it's very accessible by road, being just a few miles away from the A1.

Drumkilbo House, Perthshire

This historic manor has had its fair share of royalty passing through its

doors in the last 700 years - from Robert the Bruce to Queen Elizabeth II

It looks like a series of simple terraced cottages with its white facade and slate-tiled roof, but this manor house has more royal connections than many Scottish residences.

The first recorded owner of the original fortified tower was Scottish king Robert the Bruce. Fast forward to the last century, when a cousin of the royal family, Lord Elphinstone, acquired the estate, and the connections are more modern; in the drawing room is an ornate marble fireplace, a present from the late Queen Mother. Her daughter, Queen Elizabeth II, stayed at Drumkilbo. Lord Elphinstone even built a new wing in the 1960s designed to provide the kind of entertainment facilities that would suit his royal cousins.

The rest of the house mostly dates back to Victorian times, when Scottish architect Sir Robert Lorimer substantially enlarged it, adding intricate plasterwork on the drawing-room ceiling. The elegant interior reflects these additions although a 13th-century spiral staircase with its tartan carpet is still at Drumkilbo's core.

Rooms are large with high ceilings, wooden floors, ornate fireplaces, artistically draped curtains and plenty of ornaments. There's also a more modern television room and a billiards room complete with its 100-year-old table. And although dancing isn't allowed in the house, the separate Carriage House is ideal for a ceilidh or a disco.

One of the best things about Drumkilbo is the flexibility it offers on how you rent it. Take it fully staffed and enjoy three-course meals featuring Scotland's best produce – local game such as venison, grouse and partridge or wild Tay salmon with organic fruit and vegetables from the garden (the asparagus is renowned locally). Staff can also organise everything from a Burns supper or Scottish banquet to Celtic music, or even a private theatre production.

Alternatively, take the place on a self-catering basis, using the large kitchen with its Aga and all the necessary equipment that you'd need to cook for a large group.

Either way, you get to eat in the genteel dining room with a Regency table, china-filled cabinets and an impressive marble fire surround moved from Lord Elphinstone's previous home at Carberry Tower.

The room has scenic views of the 16-acre grounds, which feature walled gardens, manicured lawns, rhododendrons, azaleas, and plenty of mature trees. Most of the bedrooms also have views of the grounds and the surrounding countryside (although there is one downstairs room). There's also a cottage in the grounds, which sleeps four, for any overspill from the house.

This is a wonderful place to be in summer, particularly as Drumkilbo has something that's a rarity in Scotland – an outdoor pool (although you'll have to pay extra for it to be heated).

There's plenty to do outside the grounds, too, with shooting, salmon fishing in the River Tay and golf – there are 60 golf courses within an hour's drive of the house.

If you're keen to pursue yet more history, head for the Moot Hill at Scone, which was the ancient crowning place for the Kings of Scotland, or Glamis Castle, featured in Shakespeare's Macbeth and childhood home to the late Queen Mother.

At Drumkilbo, one of the rooms has been named the Glamis room in honour of this link, and comes with its four-poster draped in tartan and with a separate dressing room.

Not surprisingly, this is where Queen Elizabeth II slept when she stayed there – just across the way is the lady-in-waiting's room. Even if you're not royalty, this really is a great place to play laird of the manor.

DRUMKILBO HOUSE
at a glance

Denise Webster, marketing manager
Meigle, Blairgowrie, Perthshire, Scotland PH12 8QS
01828 640445, www.drumkilbo.co.uk

Sleeps: 23-27. Up to 23 in the house in eight rooms and two suites (three doubles, five twins, and two suites, one with a double and two single rooms, another with a double and one single). There are ten bathrooms. Braveheart Cottage in the grounds has one double and one twin, sharing one bathroom.

Dining: 28 seated at several tables. Catered on a half-board basis. A typical meal might include carrot and courgette soup, roast rack of Scottish lamb and duo of white and dark chocolate torte.

Other facilities: outdoor swimming pool (available between June and September and heated at extra charge), billiards, croquet.

Children: cots, highchairs and baby alarms. There is an enclosed garden plus a swing, slide and seesaw.

Wedding licence: for up to 28 seated in the dining room and 45 for a buffet in the main house or up to 100 in a marquee on the lawn.

Local attractions/things to do: Glamis Castle, childhood home to the Queen Mother and featured in Shakespeare's Macbeth, is five minutes away. Also nearby is Scone Palace – the Moot Hill at Scone was the ancient crowning place for the Kings of Scotland. There are plenty of highland activities, including shooting, salmon fishing in the River Tay, hill walking and golf — there are 60 golf courses within an hour's drive of Drumkilbo.

Transport: Edinburgh is one hour away, Dundee airport is 12 miles.

Price: half board from £90pp per day for a minimum of eight people. One week's self catering costs from £3,500 for the whole house.

Tresillian House, Cornwall

You know you've hit the jackpot as soon as you sweep up the gravel drive of this immaculate house, set in beautiful gardens just five miles from Newquay

With nearly 40 windows – albeit two of them trompe l'oeil – an octagonal skylight in the hallway and neutral decor, this Regency mansion has a light and airy feel so often missing in period properties.

Built in 1801 and extended in 1848, the house is large enough to hold 15 people without feeling crowded. Even the large hallway with its impressive oak staircase and hardwearing wooden floors is big enough to double up as a playroom for the kids. Keep an eye on them from the comfort of the plush sofas and an ottoman in the south-facing drawing room with its marble fireplace and double-height corniced ceilings.

You'll find the same good taste in the library and in the smart Regency-green dining room replete with a mahogany table, ornate cornicing and crystal chandelier that's perfect for a special occasion dinner.

The only room that could do with being a bit bigger is the kitchen, where too many cooks would definitely spoil the broth. Despite this, it's modern and well equipped with a large fridge/freezer, four-oven, oil-fired Aga, microwave, dishwasher and small breakfast table. And at least you don't have to worry about doing your laundry here; a utility room housing a commercial-sized washing machine and dryer is found at the side of the house (although you have to walk out of the front door to get to it).

Up the oak staircase is a balustraded balcony leading to eight uncluttered, stylish bedrooms with antique furniture and great views of the gardens. These include an ensuite four-poster room and a lovely south-facing ensuite twin overlooking the ornamental lake. The other rooms share two bathrooms, one with a Victorian roll-top bath and enough space to swing several cats. With cream carpeting throughout the whole of the first floor and plenty of sunlight flooding through all those windows, it feels wonderfully light.

The friendly head gardener, John Harris, who has worked on the estate for more than 20 years, generally shows guests around the house when they arrive and is on hand if they have any questions. He will also give tours of the 22-acre grounds, which are home to an Elizabethan barn used as a film location for *Twelfth Night* and a 200-year-old walled vegetable garden.

As well as supplying guests with a selection of home-grown organic fruit and vegetables during their stay, John is a dab hand at flower arranging. A qualified florist, he decorates the house twice a week with beautiful blooms from the garden.

On one guest's birthday, he produced a display of 350 of her favourite pink sweet peas and he really goes to town at Christmas when the house is made to look very festive – decked out in traditional Victorian style with swags over the fireplaces and a large decorated tree in the hall. John has even written a book about moon gardening and is often interviewed on the subject for local radio.

If you're interested in all things horticultural, there are numerous other gardens to visit in Cornwall, including The Eden Project, Trebah – a wonderful ravine garden with a private cove – and the Lost Gardens of Heligan as well as National Trust properties (the Trust's Trerice is just down the road).

There's plenty more to keep you amused too, including great beaches for swimming and surfing at Newquay, miles of rugged coastline to explore on the South West Coast Path, and the fishing village of Padstow, home of chef Rick Stein's food empire. There's also arty St Ives, with the Tate gallery, sandy beaches and great cafes and restaurants.

Kids' attractions are numerous and include Flambards theme park near Helston, the Seal Sanctuary at Gweek and themed attraction Dairyland, which is only a few minutes' walk down the road from this extremely elegant country house.

TRESILLIAN HOUSE *at a glance*

Bookable through Forgotten Houses
Trerice, near Newquay, Cornwall TR8 4PS
01326 340153, www.forgottenhouses.co.uk

Sleeps: 15 in eight bedrooms (two doubles, three twins, two rooms with bunk beds and a single). Two ensuite bathrooms plus two other bathrooms.

Dining: 16 at one long table. Self catering but catering can be arranged. One local caterer offers a Cornish tea with locally smoked fish sandwiches, a platter of local cheeses, jam and scones with clotted cream and saffron buns from £7.50pp. Cold buffets from £10pp and three-course meals from £15pp.

Other facilities: BBQ.

Children: one highchair and one cot.

Wedding licence: no.

Local attractions/things to do: swimming and surfing at Newquay, five miles away. The Eden Project, St Ives and Padstow are all within an easy drive. National Trust properties such as Trerice and Lanhydrock, and numerous gardens such as Trebah and The Lost Gardens of Heligan are nearby. Cycling along the Camel Trail near Wadebridge, about 16 miles away. Numerous kids' attractions include Flambards theme park near Helston, the Seal Sanctuary at Gweek and Dairyland for kids, which is just down the road.

Transport: trains from London Paddington to Newquay, five miles away, take four and a half hours, the same time as the car journey.

Price: from £2,300 per week (flat rate) for the house, self catering. Two-night breaks cost £1,150 and three nights £1,725.

Note: no dogs.

Waterside

The Lodge, Argyll

Views don't get much better than from this stylish lochside retreat where you

can tuck into plentiful local seafood – if you can take your eyes off the vista

The setting is what it's all about at The Lodge. And what an idyllic one it is, right on the loch, with gardens rolling gently down to the water and on the far shore, pine-clad rolling hills forming a dramatic backdrop.

A 63ft twin-masted yacht is moored at the end of the garden, ready to take guests for day trips to the Isle of Bute, and a grown-up treehouse nestles in the branches of a pine tree, its balcony directly over the water.

You could sit and look at the view for hours, which is why you find a telescope almost as soon as you enter The Lodge's front door, and why the iron beds in the front bedrooms face the windows, allowing you to watch the Scottish mist drift down between hill and lake from your pillow. If you tire of gazing at the view you can pack a picnic and set off across the loch in a canoe or rowing boat.

The location was what prompted The Lodge's owner, Iain Hopkins, who runs a production company for photographic shoots, to buy it almost a decade ago. Since then, it's featured in hundreds of fashion shoots for everyone from Marie Claire to Marks & Spencer, and all the supermodels have passed through its doors.

But there's more than the stunning setting to this 1860s Arts and Crafts-style lodge with its gabled roof and duck egg blue and white paintwork. Inside, there's lots of wood – both floors and ceiling – offset by deep red walls and furnishings, with more than a splash of tartan. While you can feast your eyes on the vista outside, in the spectacular dining room you can feast on some of Scotland's best cuisine. Here, in a room with a large inglenook fireplace, original 1860s wallpaper and a stained-glass representation of the original owner's daughters, the table almost groans under the weight of the food and a row of oversized candlesticks.

Naturally, seafood features high on the menu, with a chef who dives for scallops, oysters from nearby Loch Fyne and The Lodge's own home-cured gravadlax of salmon.

When you've eaten your fill, stagger out to one of the three other reception rooms – the snug television room, the more formal hall-cum-drawing room or the bar, with its vast range of malts.

Upstairs, in the seven bedrooms, expect more wooden floors, huge iron bedsteads, roll-top baths and tongue-and-groove panelling. This traditional feel is offset by carefully thought out details – an old typewriter here, ornate angel lights there, and books everywhere.

For the ultimate lochside stay, though, follow model Helena Christensen's lead and check into the summerhouse, a romantic cream and red building right at the water's edge. It may be simply decorated, but it comes with its own deck leading directly down to the water and a bed on the mezzanine level reached by a ladder. It's the perfect place to fall asleep to the sound of water lapping gently outside.

THE LODGE
at a glance

Iain Hopkins
Loch Goil, Argyll, Scotland PA24 8AE
01301 703173, www.thelodge-scotland.com

Sleeps: 16. Seven rooms in the house (four doubles, three double/twins, with five ensuites and two sharing a bathroom) plus the summerhouse for two, with shower room.

Dining: 18 at one table, 30 at round tables. Catered with breakfast, afternoon tea and dinner provided. Three-course dinner plus canapés, cheese and coffee might include seared scallops on a bed of braised leeks with a light basil sauce, pan-fried medallions of Scottish beef, and raspberry and whisky crème brulée.

Other facilities: Canadian canoes and a rowing boat.

Children: as well as a treehouse, there is high tea, cots and highchairs. Note though, that the loch is just at the end of the unfenced garden.

Wedding licence: ceremonies inside or by the loch shore. Marquees for up to 80.

Local attractions/things to do: day trips to Bute onboard The Lodge's 63ft yacht. On dry land, there's an in-house masseur while ceilidhs and casino nights can be arranged. Nearby, you can go quad biking, horse riding, mountain biking, walking, fishing, try falconry or water-sports. Shopping trips to Glasgow, just over an hour's drive away.

Transport: The Lodge is just over an hour from Glasgow and two hours from Edinburgh. Seaplane transfers from Glasgow Airport or private jet charters from London can be arranged.

Price: from £150pp per night including breakfast, afternoon tea and dinner. Minimum eight people required for exclusive use.

The Riverside, Cornwall

Spend hours messing about in boats before returning to this catered

waterside house for a home-cooked meal and unlimited French wine

This whitewashed house on the edge of the Helford River has cracked the magic formula for a relaxing holiday by combining all the perks of a hotel – you don't have to cook, wash up or make your own bed – with the informality of home. All you have to do is sit back and enjoy yourselves while someone else does all the work.

The Riverside also happens to be set in an idyllic location in the picturesque village of Helford. If you're a passionate yachtie or just like messing about in boats, you'll be in heaven. Discover hidden creeks and beaches inaccessible by road in a 19ft motorboat or take out one of two sailing dinghies from the boathouse below the property. Moor at nearby Durgan to explore Glendurgan and Trebah gardens or stop at Port Navas creek to buy some Helford oysters.

Lunch is the only meal of the day you have to make. The rest of the time the easygoing chef, Linda, will serve up – and clear away – a cooked breakfast and three-course evening meal in the small oak-beamed dining room (with the exception of Wednesdays when the staff have the day off).

Unlimited French house wine is available every night before dinner and throughout the meal. On Tuesday evenings Linda prepares a special dinner with champagne, hors d'oeuvres and an extra cheese course. Children can have high tea or eat with the adults.

A typical evening menu might start with crab paté with homemade bread (the housekeeper's fisherman husband catches the fish), and coq au vin followed by a fruit syllabub made with Cornish cider. Linda is happy to vary meal times and encourages guests to be adventurous with their breakfast choices, which means you can have a bit of a lie in before tucking into kedgeree, pancakes or Eggs Benedict.

Special-occasion dinners are Linda's speciality. She once cooked up a red-coloured menu for a Ruby Wedding and, using her knowledge as a food historian, recreated recipes popular during the First World War for a Royal Navy veteran's 90th birthday.

Guests have their own fridge/freezer in the large, well-equipped kitchen where they can store provisions for lunch. In warm weather, the paved

THE RIVERSIDE *at a glance*

Nicol Glyn
Helford, Helston, Cornwall TR12 6JU
01865 400825, www.theriverside-helford.co.uk

Sleeps: 12 adults and five children in six ensuite bedrooms (three doubles, three double/twins). Two have small, separate rooms with bunk beds and there is a small, single room off one of the bedrooms.

Dining: table seats 12. Catered on a half-board basis with wine. On the staff's day off (usually a Wednesday), a continental breakfast will be left and guests can eat out or cook their own meals.

Other facilities: two dinghies (one Wayfarer, one Laser) and a 19ft Cygnus riverboat (plus tender). Wet room. BBQ.

Children: travel cot and three highchairs. Babysitting can be arranged.

Wedding licence: no.

Local attractions/things to do: walking on nearby Lizard Peninsula; numerous gardens to visit including Glendurgan and Trebah; sandy beaches such as Kennack Sands; National Seal Sanctuary at Gweek; Flambards Theme Park near Helston; Mullion Cove; St Ives for the Tate, shopping and beaches; open-air Minack Theatre at Porthcurno; The Eden Project. Golf and fishing.

Transport: nearest mainline train station is at Redruth, about a 50-minute drive (London Paddington to Redruth takes five and a half hours). About five hours' drive from London.

Price: three-night breaks from £175pp half board, four-night breaks from £225pp (both for a minimum of six people) and week-long stays from £295pp. In high season, a minimum of eight guests are needed. Children aged 4-12 pay half price, toddlers pay £95 per week.

Note: smoking only in sitting and dining rooms. No dogs.

front terrace overlooking the water is a great place to eat alfresco.

The waterside views are just as lovely from the three bedrooms in the main house, all of which are well decorated with matching curtains, bedding and cushions along with thoughtful extras such as fresh flowers and White Company toiletries. The largest of the bedrooms also has a small room off the bathroom ideal for a young child.

The remaining three bedrooms can be found up some steps in the wisteria-clad buildings at the back of the house. Two of them also have an adjoining small room housing bunk beds, which are only suitable for children.

But you don't come to The Riverside for the bedrooms, you come for the relaxing waterside setting. Even in the height of summer the village of Helford, which is built around a creek, doesn't feel overrun with tourists, thanks largely to its restricted access to cars. There is just one pub and one shop, as well as a tea garden and a sailing club, where Riverside guests can get temporary membership.

Old Kilmun House, Argyll

Whatever the weather you'll find plenty to keep you entertained – both inside and out – at this 17th-century house located on the edge of Holy Loch

Cupboards and storage rooms aren't just stuffed full of the normal self-catering equipment at Old Kilmun House – there's a whole treasure trove of extras. The garden shed houses a selection of bikes, several sets of golf clubs are lined up in the cellar, and there are half a dozen fishing rods to grab should you fancy a quiet day by the water.

In fact, there's just about everything you'll need to take advantage of the house's scenic position on the shore of Holy Loch, surrounded by some of Scotland's best countryside for outdoor pursuits. Only an hour's drive from Glasgow, the area is breathtakingly beautiful, a picture postcard of lochs, glens and rolling hills.

It's a walkers' paradise, with half a dozen spectacular routes radiating from Old Kilmun itself, including Puck's Glen and the Ardnadam Heritage Trail. The hill climbs aren't too back-breaking for a really enjoyable cycle, and there's both loch and river fishing for rainbow and brown trout.

As for excursions, one of the best is to the Isle of Bute, just 18 miles away, with its plentiful gardens to visit as well as Mount Stuart, home to former racing driver Johnny Dumfries, who is now Marquess of Bute.

Back at Old Kilmun House, there's lots to keep you occupied – the cellar holds a snug with leather sofas and widescreen TV, as well as a games room, decked out in red, with a three-quarter-size billiards table plus table football.

Outside, the two-and-a-half acre garden with path up to the adjacent arboretum boasts everything from croquet and badminton to a trampoline (as well as some fun oversized wooden chairs). There's more than enough to keep a whole family entertained.

That's not to say Old Kilmun isn't suitable for groups of friends – it's a great grown-up

kind of place to stay as well, though you'll have to be prepared to share the bathrooms (there are just two bathrooms and one shower room between 18 people).

There's a traditional feel to the interior of this 17th-century house built by the Duke of Argyll's family, probably created by the large amount of pitch pine. A whole range of wood is on show; in addition to a newly installed sauna, an impressive bannister runs all the way to the second floor, wood-panelled walls frame the lochside view from the bedroom windows, and the splendid dining room has floor, walls and ceiling in wood. Taken together with the heavy brocade curtains and an open fire, it makes the perfect place for a dinner party.

You don't have to cook for yourself either; although Old Kilmun is self catering, three-course dinner parties featuring typical Scottish local produce can be arranged. Sit back and let someone else do the work as you tuck into pan-fried scallops in a lemon and chive butter sauce, rack of lamb, and organic chocolate

brownies with a raspberry coulis. Or take the half-hour drive to the Loch Fyne Oyster Bar for some delicious seafood.

For less formal meals, the large kitchen with its pine table and Aga plus all the electrical mod cons makes a cosy place to gather. The kitchen was a Victorian addition to the original building, as were two flats on the end of the house. Although the work has been carried out sympathetically, the flats are occupied, so you might not get the garden entirely to yourself.

Another tiny negative to the house which may or may not bother you is the rather unattractive (though definitely hard wearing) brown patterned carpet that leads from the hallway up the stairs to the landings.

Carpet apart, the decor is simple and comfortable, particularly in the sitting room, with its cream sofas, flowing curtains, and a well-stocked bar holding remnants from previous house parties plus two complimentary bottles of champagne.

Sit back, pour yourself a drink, and relax.

OLD KILMUN HOUSE
at a glance

John Davies
Kilmun, Argyll, Scotland PA23 8SE
01505 843678, www.oldkilmunhouse.com

Sleeps: 18 in eight rooms (five doubles, one bunk room for two, two triples), sharing two bathrooms, a shower room and one extra toilet.

Dining: 14 in the dining room, 12 in the kitchen. Self catering but meals can be arranged for about £40 a head. A typical menu might feature pan-fried scallops in a lemon and chive butter sauce, rack of lamb, and organic chocolate brownies with a raspberry coulis. Local takeaways and pubs.

Other facilities: golf clubs, eight bikes, fishing rods, trampoline in garden, snooker room, table football, DVDs and videos, sauna and spa bath.

Children: cot and highchair.

Wedding licence: no but you can get married in the church next door. Receptions in the house for up to 40 for a £500 fee.

Local attractions/things to do: there are plenty of outdoor activities in The Trossachs National Park, such as walking, cycling, watersports, golf, deer stalking, quad biking and clay-pigeon shooting. Excursions to the Isle of Bute, 18 miles away, with its numerous gardens as well as Mount Stuart, home to former racing driver Johnny Dumfries.

Transport: Glasgow airport is one hour away, including a 20-minute ferry ride.

Price: one week's self catering £1,295-£1,995 for the house, short breaks of three or four nights, from £995.

Note: cleaning can be arranged at about £8 an hour.

Mansefield House, Argyll

The lochside views and the plentiful hill walking that's all around are what it's a[ll] about at this Victorian residence, which is seemingly in the middle of nowhere

This red-gabled house wouldn't look out of place in a film of *The Railway Children*, except there's a loch, not a railway line, at the bottom of the garden. Flanking the shores of Loch Long are hills the Victorians named the Arrochar Alps, making for a mesmerising setting seemingly in the middle of nowhere (albeit a nowhere with a rather nice village inn just down the road plus a direct rail link to London). Actually, Arrochar is just 45 minutes from Glasgow. And as locations go, it takes some beating.

So it's rather apt that the friendly young couple who own Mansefield House – Fiona and Tom Butcher – found it through Channel 4 TV's *Relocation Relocation*. 'We were actually looking for something in Glasgow but we saw this and fell in love with it,' says Fiona, who now lives with her husband in the old coach house just down the drive.

They've done the property up with care, filling the Victorian interior that still has original cornicing and ceiling roses with modern furnishings. The spacious ground-floor rooms all have dark wood floors and are decorated in neutral tones with beige sofas and pine tables. Although the decor is minimalist in the sitting room and dining room, it's by no means bare, and there are some quaint additions; a hamper in the dining room contains logs for the wood-burning stove, while an old Singer sewing machine on the side pays testament to the nearby factory.

There's more to look at out of the windows, with picturesque loch views from both reception rooms and two of the bedrooms, which are decorated in white with pine beds.

Because Mansefield House is self catering, special attention has been paid to the kitchen, which is large and well equipped. However, if you don't feel like cooking, there are plenty of other food options, from the takeaway curries in the shop just down the road to the original Loch Fyne oyster bar, nine miles away, as well as catered dinner parties.

MANSEFIELD HOUSE
at a glance

Fiona Butcher
Arrochar, Argyll, Scotland G83 7AG
01301 702956, www.mansefieldhouse.com

Sleeps: ten plus two in five bedrooms (four doubles, one twin) and two additional Z-beds. Two ensuite bathrooms, one other bathroom and a separate toilet.

Dining: for 12, self catering, although caterers can supply everything from shepherd's pie with cheese crusted leeks at £6pp to a three-course dinner party at £25 a head.

Children: cot and highchair. There is an enclosed garden.

Wedding licence: no.

Other facilities: masseur can be called to the house, pottery shop in the garden, BBQ.

Local attractions/things to do: all the activities associated with Loch Lomond and The Trossachs National Park, including boat hire five minutes away, seaplane rides on Loch Lomond, walking and fishing. Inveraray Castle is 20 minutes' drive away. Pottery courses and reiki and relaxation weekends can be arranged.

Transport: the sleeper train leaves London Euston in the evening and arrives in Arrochar, just over a mile from Mansefield House, early the next day. Glasgow airport is a 40-minute drive.

Price: minimum two-night rental for the house on a self-catering basis from £550, three nights £650, one week £850-£1,400.

Note: dogs welcome for a £20 supplement each.

Just off the kitchen lies another essential room – a separate laundry/drying room with dehumidifier/heater to ensure that outdoors gear dries out overnight. Considering Mansefield's location in the heart of Loch Lomond and The Trossachs National Park, it's an ideal base for walkers of every ability, starting with the many low-level walks leaving right from the front door, up through to four Munros (mountains higher than 3,000 feet) in the Arrochar Alps.

There's also an endless list of other activities to enjoy, including mountain biking, pony trekking, boating and fishing on both Loch Long and Loch Lomond, which is two miles away.

Nor are the activities over once you get back to the house, where there's a games room with a small snooker table and the possibility of calling in a masseur to ease any aching muscles. And should you feel in need of a bit of retail therapy, just nip up the drive to the shop where Tom sells the ceramics he makes.

Upper Court, Gloucestershire

Play at being Ratty from The Wind in the Willows at this traditional English manor house that comes with its very own boating lake and Dovecote

Country scenes don't get more quintessentially English than the views from this Cotswold stone Georgian manor house. Surrounded by weeping willows, Upper Court's lake comes complete with swans and a boat in which you can spend hours messing about on the water, just like Ratty from *The Wind in the Willows*.

If you'd rather sit and enjoy the view, take tea or have a glass of Pimm's on the lawn, where breakfast and dinner can also be served. Should it get a bit chilly, you can always retreat through the French doors to the dining room with its crystal chandeliers reflected in the polished mahogany table.

Even breakfast doesn't have to be taken in the dining room. You can have it delivered to your bedroom – some with canopied four-posters and views of the lake – which are decked out in traditional English chintz with antique porcelain and needlework. It's quite refreshing that owners Bill and Diana Herford haven't succumbed to the latest craze for country houses to transform their interiors with chocolate brown leather sofas and Venetian mirrors.

One of the original Wolsey Lodges, Upper Court is an upmarket B&B where you can also have dinner, offering a traditional country-house experience that's so successful it's attracted everyone from supermodels to thespians treading the boards at nearby Stratford-upon-Avon. It's a family affair with one son the resident chef, another a potter who can host pottery weekends.

If you'd prefer to enjoy all the facilities of Upper Court – including a heated outdoor pool, tennis court, games room and billiards – in a more informal environment, you can always rent one or more of the cottages in the 15-acre grounds. Groups of up to 24 often take the 18th-century Coach House that sleeps 11 with two other adjoining smaller cottages, Courtyard Cottage and The Stables.

A huge living room in the Coach House is large enough to seat the whole party for dinner along two refectory tables. It's a lovely loft-like space with double-height ceilings, light flooding in from large windows, modern oil paintings and etchings on the walls along with a gas-flame stove that creates a cosy feel.

A further two cottages – a tiny romantic Dovecote and the 18th-century Cotswold stone Watermill Cottage sleeping ten – both have scenic views of the lake.

Up at the manor house, a typical weekend house party might start with tea and cake in the yellow drawing room with its plush drapes and fine antiques. After freshening up in your room, help yourselves to drinks from the honesty bar before taking lanterns to navigate your way up the lane to the village pub for some fine fare (it's very popular so you'll need to book ahead).

On Saturdays, guests often take a hike over Bredon Hill for a pub lunch, go horse riding at nearby Staunton, play golf or go clay-pigeon shooting. Others prefer to laze around the grounds, have a dip in the pool or take the boat out on the lake.

After a day spent enjoying yourselves, you can always book Petra, a Czech masseur, to ease any aching limbs in the comfort of your room before sitting down to enjoy a slap-up meal. That's if you can take your eyes off that fabulous view.

UPPER COURT
at a glance

Bill and Diana Herford
Kemerton, Gloucestershire GL20 7HY
01386 725351, www.uppercourt.co.uk

Sleeps: 10-24. Up to ten in the main house (three doubles, one twin and one double/twin suite – all ensuite). The garden flat sleeps two (double/twin) and can be catered or self-catered. Alternatively, you can hire three of the cottages for 24: The Coach House (sleeps 11), Courtyard Cottage (sleeps eight) and The Stables (sleeps five). Also Watermill Cottage (sleeps ten) and the Dovecote (two+1).

Dining: 24 around dining table in main house. Rented on a B&B basis with the option of dinner at £35pp. Wine from £10 a bottle or £4pp corkage if BYO. Catering available in cottages from £22pp. The Coach House seats 24 at two tables.

Other facilities: outdoor heated pool open from May to August, tennis court, table-tennis and darts, billiards table, croquet and boat for use on lake.

Children: in cottages only. Cots and highchairs. Babysitting can be arranged. Note the pool and lake.

Wedding licence: for up to 30. Receptions for up to 200 in marquee on lawn. Hire of lakeside venue: £1,500.

Local attractions/things to do: numerous castles such as Sudeley and Warwick and historic houses including Blenheim Palace within an hour's drive. Horse riding, fly fishing, clay-pigeon shooting and golf.

Transport: nearest station at Evesham or Cheltenham, both 11 miles away. Trains from London Paddington take two hours. London is two and a half hours' drive.

Price: doubles from £120 B&B per room per night or from £95 per night for a twin. Coach House from £885 per weekend or £1,105 per week, Courtyard Cottage £615/£775, Stables £350/£460.

Westover Hall Hotel, Hampshire

Seaside chic meets Victorian luxury in this unique building with stunning stained-glass windows, where you'll find grandeur but not austerity

You can't help but say 'wow' when you walk into the galleried hall of this Victorian seaside house on the edge of the New Forest. It's decorated top-to-toe in oak – from the floors, panelled walls and staircase to the minstrel's gallery.

Complementing this forest of timber are some beautiful stained-glass windows depicting prep-Raphaelite scenes from *The Enchanted Wood*: knights ride their horses through the trees, while a peacock's tail sweeps down over the door.

The windows date back to the house's first owner, German industrialist Alexander Siemens, whose wife disliked curtains and asked for something different. Totally disregarding cost – a fortune was spent on wood alone – the couple created a house that became one of the most luxurious residences along the south coast.

The seaside location means there's plenty to look at out of the windows as well as marvelling at the flamboyant interiors. Views of The Needles rising out of the Solent can be appreciated from the sunroom, through the enormous bay windows

in the trendy bar, and from the oak-panelled dining room, where contemporary French food is served on tables decorated with huge flower-filled vases.

Fill your lungs with fresh sea air on the terrace, or stroll down the garden to the pebbly beach, where the hotel has its own beach hut. There are low-rise condos on either side of Westover Hall, which means you don't get that away-from-it-all feeling, but the beach is generally quiet.

This Victorian property's seaside location gives it a delightfully unstuffy air – grandeur without austerity – but a lot of that also comes from the fact that it's a family-run affair. Owners Stewart Mechem and Nicola Musetti are siblings, their mother works on the front desk, and their father handles the finance. Even Arthur the cat, who works for model agency Storm when he's not lolling over the desk or at the foot of the stairs, adds to the ambience.

The Mechems also have an art dealer cousin, who has sourced some spectacular furniture for Westover Hall, including a cabinet on the staircase that was designed by Lalique for his house in

WESTOVER HALL HOTEL
at a glance

Stewart Mechem and Nicola Musetti
Park Lane, Milford-on-Sea, Lymington,
Hampshire SO41 OPT
01590 643044, www.westoverhallhotel.com

Paris. Such carefully chosen antiques and knick knacks are interspersed with Stewart's colourful, modern artwork (he holds frequent exhibitions) and black and white fashion photography, creating a great blend of old and new.

'We try to be faithful and sensitive to the feeling of the house but also want to keep it contemporary because when it was built, it was cutting edge for its time,' says Stewart. 'It's a bit like walking a tightrope.'

It works though. Take the formal but comfy lounge with its original green-and-white tiled Arts and Crafts fireplace complemented by matching curtains, well-padded sofas, old suitcases and lots of candlelight in the evening.

Upstairs, the bedrooms have a more contemporary feel, with suede headrests and Mulberry throws plus little extras such as waffle dressing gowns. Half the rooms boast a sea view with two sharing a roof terrace.

However, guests staying in bedrooms without a sea view won't feel too hard done by when there's such a magnificent interior to admire.

Sleeps: 25 in 12 bedrooms (six doubles, four double/twins, one single, one apartment for four), all ensuite.

Dining: up to 50 at either one or several tables. Catered on a B&B basis. Three-course dinner £38.50pp. Food is contemporary French, for example seared scallops with forest asparagus, trio of lamb – rack, saddle fillet and kidney – and coconut vacherin millefeuille with marinated mango.

Other facilities: there is a beach hut on the beach at the bottom of the garden with panoramic sea views; massages can be arranged here or in the hotel.

Children: cots and highchairs. Babysitting can be arranged.

Wedding licence: for up to 50 in the lounge.

Local attractions/things to do: take the ferry to the Isle of Wight and The Needles for the day, charter a yacht for lunch from Lymington, walk on the coast or in the New Forest. The National Motor Museum at Beaulieu is also nearby.

Transport: trains from London Waterloo take almost two hours to New Milton station, ten minutes from the hotel. Driving takes about two and a half hours from London.

Price: £3,250 in total per night during the week to £5,000 on Saturdays, B&B.

Country
Estates

Manderston, Berwickshire

Dance in the opulently decorated ballroom and have afternoon tea in the Chinese-style drawing room at this magnificent Edwardian stately home

You don't just get to play at being Lord of the Manor at Manderston, you get to have dinner with one. Lord Palmer is in his element when, seated at the head of a long mahogany table on a Chippendale chair, he hosts a formal dinner of traditional Scottish fare washed down with generous amounts of wine from his cellar. 'The house was built for entertaining. When it's full, it's full of life,' he says. His ancestors have entertained in the house since the 1860s, so he should know.

You couldn't ask for a better backdrop either – open fire, urns made by architect Robert Adam, oil paintings covering the walls, and a spectacular ceiling relief depicting Mars, god of war, with dancing muses surrounding him. It's one of a series of special ceilings at Manderston that will have you walking around craning your neck to take it all in, from the paintings of Apollo and Venus in the ballroom ceiling panels to the colourful relief work in the drawing room.

Not that there aren't plenty of other things to view at eye level or below at Manderston, which started life as a Georgian mansion but was adapted in the early 20th century. When Sir James Miller, aka Lucky Jim, told his architect that cost 'simply doesn't matter' one of the last great Edwardian houses was created.

You get a taste of the opulence at the stables, which cost £20,000 to build, complete with Doric columns and panels of huntsmen and hounds in high relief. The dairy is pretty special too – decked out in marble, it's shaped like a church cloister.

But the real eye opener is the house, set in 56 acres of formal and informal gardens bursting with rhododendrons and azaleas, with a lake and woodland. Inside the pillared entrance porch is the best craftmanship the Edwardian era had to offer, with inlaid marble floors, large ante-rooms and a silver staircase, the only one of its kind in the world. There are even a couple of secret doors and passageways.

This is a stately home where you aren't just confined behind roped-off sections (although Manderston is open to the public during the day). Just like the participants in Channel 4 TV's *The Edwardian Country House*, which was filmed at Manderston, you can play billiards in the red-wallpapered library, take tea in the Chinese-style tea room, and dance in the ballroom with its silk-embossed velvet walls.

And you don't have to admire the silver staircase from afar – you can leave your fingerprints on it as you climb the cantilevered marble stairs, inspired by the Petit Trianon at Versailles, on your way to bed.

Upstairs, leading off the wide, columned corridor, there are four stunning state rooms with original furniture and bathrooms holding porcelain baths and original Edwardian fittings. Other rooms are in the Bachelor and West wings and while not as elaborate as the state rooms, they are well furnished.

Is there a snag? Only that because Manderston is open to day visitors, there will be crowds. But as their visits are confined to Thursdays and Sundays in the summer months, if you time your visit right you'll get the whole place to yourselves. As long as you don't mind sharing it with Lord Palmer and his family.

MANDERSTON *at a glance*

The Lord Palmer
Duns, Berwickshire, Scotland TD11 3PP
01361 883450, www.manderston.co.uk

Sleeps: 20 in ten rooms (four doubles, six twins), all with ensuite or private bathrooms. Four rooms are state bedrooms, while the rest are more modern.

Dining: 20 at the dining table for a hosted meal with Lord Palmer, although there is room for 40. Guests stay on a half-board arrangement plus tea. All drinks are included, with champagne, wine from the cellar and a well-stocked bar. The three-course dinner is traditional Scottish, using local ingredients. A typical meal might include smoked salmon with papillottes of shrimp, fillet of border lamb and fresh white peach sorbet.

Other facilities: all-weather tennis court, croquet lawn and snooker room.

Children: older, supervised children are welcome.

Wedding licence: small, select weddings of 20-30 people.

Local attractions/things to do: bikes and riding on the estate, shooting, clay-pigeon shooting, falconry and archery can be arranged. Golf courses and fishing nearby.

Transport: Edinburgh airport is a 70-minute drive. Trains from London King's Cross to Berwick-upon-Tweed take three and a half hours. Berwick is 20 minutes away.

Price: £180pp per night half board with alcohol plus an £800 per day facility fee – both exclude VAT. Apply for prices for additional dinner guests.

Note: Manderston is open to the public on Thursdays and Sundays during the summer.

Llanfendigaid, Gwynedd

The same family has lived here for the past 800 years, so it's no wonder that guests feel so much at home in this beautiful corner of the Welsh countryside

An entry in the guest book at this country mansion in Snowdonia National Park says it all: 'We don't feel like we've stayed in a rented house, more like someone's home.' It's not just any old family home either: Llanfendigaid (meaning Parish of the Blessed) has passed down through generations of the same family, the Nanney-Wynns, for more than 800 years.

There are lots of reminders of the past as you walk around this spacious house, which was renovated to its current design in 1742 and is set in a lush valley within half a mile of the sea. The walls are lined with ancestral portraits as well as a family tree charting the history of the Nanney-Wynns, who were once among the Welsh landed gentry.

Current owner Will Nanney-Wynn Garton Jones, who holidays in the house every year, has collected artefacts documenting his ancestors' last 200 years including a portrait of Sir George Everest, one time Surveyor General of India and after whom Mount Everest is named. Another ancestor was Sir William Jones, judge in Lord Clive's India.

Despite its illustrious past, there's nothing pretentious about Llanfendigaid. An ornate entrance hall with beautiful coloured geometric tiles is now home to a full-size pool table. The lounge is a great chill-out zone for kids with its hardy leather sofas, games, large-screen TV, video and DVD. Across the hall, the more refined drawing room feels like an adult-only space with its elegant sofas, panelled walls, gilt mirror, wood-burning stove and the Nanney-Wynn coat of arms over the fireplace.

Think carefully about booking this house if you can't live without an ensuite bathroom or shower: there aren't any. Ten bedrooms share two simple bathrooms – one of which has a roll-top bath –

and a shower room. They're perfectly adequate but not kitted out with the latest suites.

You may also feel the need to fight over the bedrooms. Two of the doubles – one with a sleigh bed, the other with an iron bedstead – really stand out with white wood-panelled walls, antiques and window seats with views out to sea. The other rooms, particularly those on the top floor under the eaves, are more simple and are sparsely furnished.

Downstairs the large kitchen with a separate breakfast area is well equipped with an Aga, electric oven and huge fridge/freezer but feels a bit tired and could do with updating. Next door the dining room has a 12ft elm table and benches with views on to an acre of wooded gardens.

Because of the shared facilities, the house most appeals to large family groups, and often hosts three generations of the same family. Grandparents, though, may opt to stay in the neighbouring three-bedroom property, Ty-fendigaid – probably so they can escape the noise when it all gets too much. Groups of walkers, sailors and golfers are also frequent guests.

Both properties can use the indoor pool, which is just across the lane and is available year round. You can also swim from a nearby sandy and shingle beach, which is accessible via a private path or a short drive down the lane.

If you want more than a beach, there's plenty of stunning countryside around Llanfendigaid. Make use of the house's mountain bikes for an exhilarating ride or head out on foot to tackle Snowdonia's magnificent mountain, Cader Idris.

Stick closer to home and you can roam across the estate's 300 acres of farmland, play croquet on the lawn or just sit and watch the resident peacocks strut their stuff.

LLANFENDIGAID
at a glance

Will Garton-Jones
Rhoslefain, Tywyn, Gwynedd, Wales LL3 9LS
07867 905544, www.llanfendigaid.co.uk

Sleeps: 16-21. Up to 16 in the house in ten rooms (five doubles, three twins and two singles but only 16 of the 18 beds can be used because of insurance). Two bathrooms and one shower room. Neighbouring Ty-fendigaid sleeps an additional five (one double, one twin and one single) sharing one bathroom.

Dining: seats 16. Self catering but one of the house managers can do the catering. Light lunches start at £3.50pp, two-course meals at £10pp. Main meals include Welsh lamb followed by homemade bread and butter pudding.

Other facilities: heated indoor pool available year-round and shared by both properties, pool table, croquet, bikes for hire.

Children: cots and highchairs. The five acres of grounds are walled, fenced and gated but children can get out on to the 300 acres of surrounding farmland.

Wedding licence: no.

Local attractions/things to do: outdoor activities including excellent hill and beach walking, pony trekking, sailing and golf. A sand and shingle beach is within half a mile of the house down a private path. Other beaches at Tywyn, seven miles away, and Aberdovey, ten miles away.

Transport: trains from London Euston take five hours to Tywyn, seven miles away. The drive from London takes about four and a half hours.

Price: five-night (Thursday to Tuesday between November and Easter) breaks from £900 for the house and £100 for Ty-fendigaid if booked at the same time. Week-long holidays from £1,500, self catering.

Note: no pets. Single-sex groups welcome.

Buckland House, Devon

With week-long holidays costing less than £100 per person, this enormous grade-II listed country mansion works out as incredible value for money

There can't be many country houses you can rent – complete with their own lake and church on a 280-acre estate – from less than £50 a head for a weekend.

And you certainly get a lot of house for your money. Originally given by William the Conqueror to one of his loyal soldiers, Buckland was rebuilt following a fire in 1790 to become an enormous grade-II listed Regency mansion that could easily accommodate more than the 26 people allowed.

It's probably quite common to spend time ambling along hallways peering into endless rooms as you try to find the rest of your party. For starters, there are three different places you can eat depending on your mood: around a large farmhouse table in the Victorian kitchen, in the separate oak-panelled breakfast room or at the French polished table in the formal dining room with its antique silver and Royal Worcester china.

Choose between two sitting rooms: a cavernous drawing room with wooden floors, rugs, fireplace, ornate cornicing and a gargantuan brass chandelier or a smaller white-panelled room – the only part of the original house that remained following the fire. Or retreat to the library with its crystal chandeliers, easy chairs, dark wood floors and ornate drapes.

The wow factor has to be reserved for the galleried ballroom with its dome ceiling, marble fireplace, wooden floors and a grand piano, making the house a hit for weddings and other large celebrations. In summer, guests can spill out of the floor-to-ceiling French doors that open on to the lawn.

Buckland House's size also makes it perfect for kids who can play hide and seek in the warren of rooms or amuse themselves by donning the contents of the fancy dress cupboard in the nursery, which is packed with books and games. Teenagers can make a beeline for the table tennis or play snooker in the room next to the ballroom. There's also an outdoor unheated pool.

Up the magnificent oak staircase are 15 traditional country-house bedrooms with wooden floors, antique furniture and copies of *The Field*

BUCKLAND HOUSE *at a glance*

Ralph Nicholson
Buckland Filleigh, Beaworthy, Devon EX21 5JD
01409 281645, www.bucklandhouse.co.uk

Sleeps: 26 in seven doubles, five twins and two singles plus three cots. Five out of the nine bathrooms are ensuite.

Dining: 26 round the main table. The ballroom also takes 70 for dinner and the adjoining sitting room an extra 50. Self catering but local caterers offer anything from buffets to elaborate dinners. A four-course meal plus canapés and handmade chocolates starts at £32pp.

Other facilities: snooker room, table tennis, mini snooker, darts, croquet, BBQ, unheated outdoor pool (May to September), fishing lake and rowing boat.

Children: cots, highchairs. Babysitting can be arranged.

Wedding licence: for up to 120. Ballroom takes around 70 for dinner and the adjoining sitting room an extra 50.

Local attractions/things to do: picturesque fishing village of Clovelly, sandy beaches on the north Devon coast and the cathedral city of Exeter are all within an easy drive. Walking in nearby Dartmoor National Park. The Eden Project is within one and a half hours' drive.

Transport: fast trains from London Paddington to Exeter, just over an hour's drive away, take about two hours. London is around four and a half hours by car.

Price: a week's self catering for the house costs from £2,380. Short breaks available between November 1 and March 31. Two- and three-night breaks are 50% and 70% respectively of the week-long price. Extra nights charged at 10% of the weekly price. Oil central heating costs about £30-£60 per day during winter. Gas by meter reading between October 1 and May 5.

Note: no single-sex groups. Pets welcome (additional charge of £16 per dog, maximum three).

and *Country Life* on the bedside tables. Three rooms – including a charming single with a tiny fireplace and sink – have four-poster beds. Some of the bathrooms are particularly characterful with Victorian roll-top baths and ornate fireplaces.

Several bedrooms still have their old dormitory names from when Buckland was a boarding school. This gives you some idea of their size: many could easily sleep a whole gaggle of children. The four-poster looks almost lost in the huge master bedroom with corniced ceilings, crystal chandeliers and French doors leading on to a balcony with wonderful views over the grounds.

It's not surprising that many guests rarely leave the house, let alone the estate, during their stay. There is, though, plenty to do outside. Explore the acres of private woodland, play croquet on the lawn, try clay-pigeon or pheasant shooting, or go fishing on the lake. Situated on the edge of Dartmoor National Park, Buckland House is also ideally situated for exploring the north and south Devon coasts.

Carnell, Ayrshire

Famous Scots John Knox and William Wallace both played a part in the history

of this impressive house, where the grounds also hold reminders of the past

Even the gardens tell a story at this 16th-century house. Two squares of lime trees just south of the property have been planted with two 'officers' on each side to represent the Scottish contingent at the 1743 Battle of Dettingen in the war of the Austrian succession. It's just one unique feature of this 2,000-acre estate that's also renowned for its walled garden and some of the best herbaceous borders in the country.

The house is just as impressive as the grounds, its origins dating back to a 16th-century tower owned by the family of William Wallace, the Scottish hero who waged guerrilla warfare against the English. Substantial neo-Jacobean additions three centuries later helped create today's rather grand building, which lies at the end of a driveway where pheasants roam.

Descendants of the same family still live here – Michael and Debbie Findlay have a self-contained flat in the house shared with their two children and three dogs. Indeed, Carnell is very much a family home, the emphasis being on comfort rather than stuffy elegance, where guests can feel free to stroll into the large family kitchen and make themselves tea. The downside, though, is that with the family on site, you can't expect to go on partying into the wee small hours.

You can still have a good time, though – discos can be arranged, and there's plenty of room in the house for everyone to spread out, with both a billiards room and a snug television room with lots of books.

The most convivial room is the large entrance hall, which has a welcoming open fire, chairs crying out to be sat in and china-filled cabinets. Large enough to act as a second sitting room, it has the same high ceilings and warm decor that characterise the rest of the reception areas. The even more spacious sitting room is also welcoming, and holds a piano along with plenty of antiques.

There's a choice of two dining rooms – one very traditional with a mahogany table complementing the rose-coloured walls and chairs. The other, smaller room is much quirkier. Converted from an old cow barn and dubbed the John Knox room after the famous visitor, this atmospheric vaulted part of the Peel Tower is decorated with heraldic shields and makes the perfect setting for either a shooting lunch or relaxed breakfast.

Food is a big part of the experience at Carnell with lots of locally sourced produce – including game, lamb, beef and salmon from the estate – and fruit and vegetables from the garden. Tuck into scallops with chilli jam and crème fraiche, Aberdeen Angus fillet of beef en croute with a gratin of wild mushrooms and vanilla cream pots with armagnac and orange apricots.

With such a spread, it's good to know there's plenty to do outside to work off the extra calories, with lots of walks and activities such as clay-pigeon shooting and falconry. Carnell is well placed for golfers too, with Turnberry, Prestwick and Royal Troon golf courses all nearby.

Back at the house, when it's time for bed, climb the wooden staircase or the twisting stone steps of the tower to country-style bedrooms furnished with antiques. Although one room has a four-poster and there's a roll-top bath in a huge bathroom, most bedrooms are less elaborate than the downstairs reception rooms. They are though, very well equipped, with kettles, bathrobes, complimentary water, telephones and plenty of magazines.

For anyone who finds getting upstairs a bit of a challenge, there's even a lift – a welcome, modern addition to this house full of history.

CARNELL
at a glance

Michael Findlay
Hurlford, Ayrshire, Scotland KA1 5JS
01563 884236, www.carnellestates.com

Sleeps: 20 in ten rooms (four doubles and six twins), all with dedicated bathrooms.

Dining: 22 at the single mahogany table or 40 at a series of tables. Catered, on a half-board basis, with a three-course dinner such as scallops with chilli jam and crème fraiche, Aberdeen Angus fillet of beef en croute and vanilla cream pots with armagnac and orange apricots. Bring your own wine or have it delivered from a local shop – there is no corkage charge.

Other facilities: billiards, tennis, croquet, squash, table tennis.

Children: cots, highchairs and children's meals are all provided but note that there is a pond in the grounds.

Wedding licence: for up to 100 people, either in the garden or in the house.

Local attractions/things to do: there is plenty of shooting (notably pheasant), clay-pigeon shooting, falconry, archery and walking. There are golf courses at Prestwick, Turnberry and Royal Troon, all within an easy drive. Other top courses such as Loch Lomond, Muirfield and Gleneagles are slightly further – within an hour and a half's drive.

Transport: Prestwick airport is just 20 minutes away, with Glasgow 40 minutes and Edinburgh 90 minutes.

Price: from £185pp per night half board, based on at least 12 people (£3,700 for 20 people).

Drynachan Lodge,
Inverness-shire

Stuffed birds and stag heads sit alongside shabby-chic furnishings in this remote 1820s hunting lodge owned by a former Vogue fashion editor

Take one former Vogue fashion editor, add an 1820s family hunting lodge, and you end up with Drynachan, a house that exudes the same kind of effortless boho chic as its mistress, Lady Isabella Cawdor. Stuffed birds and stag heads are now complemented by William Morris wallpaper, silk damask chairs and lots of velvets and other rich fabrics to give a shabby-chic feel, with a little more emphasis on the chic.

You probably shouldn't come here if shooting isn't your bag – it's etched into the very walls of the dining room, where 19th-century charcoal drawings depict country pursuits, and carvings on the wood panels around the window bear the names of shooting parties throughout the ages who have stayed at the lodge.

Even the simple but elegant bedrooms haven't escaped the hunting theme, some of them containing the house's original gun racks alongside iron bedsteads and roll-top baths.

The hunting lodge feel is strongest in the Tartan Room, carpeted and curtained in the Cawdor family tartan with wood-panelled walls and ceilings, stag horns over the open fire, and lots of dark wood furniture. It's a great place to relax after dinner, with the added advantage that there's a separate sitting room next door – perfect for children.

Although the dusky pink lodge, added to by successive generations of the family, isn't particularly attractive from the outside, it's more than compensated for by the stunning setting. In one of the more remote corners of the world (you can easily get cut off by snow during the winter) – Drynachan is nestled in a valley by the Findhorn River, surrounded by rolling hills and woodland and reached over scenic moors of Scottish heather.

With such a spectacular location, it's no

surprise that the estate has been the subject of some big-name photographic shoots. Posh and Becks posed for a magazine cover at the lodge and photographers Mario Testino, Annie Leibovitz and Patrick Demarchelier have all worked here. And that's before mentioning all the other celebrity guests, from Sarah Ferguson to TV chef Hugh Fearnley-Whittingstall.

There's plenty to occupy you without leaving this 60,000-acre estate (although it's worth popping into the historic village of Cawdor to visit the 14th-century castle). Trek to one of the numerous picnic bothies, fish in the river, or go shooting; the heather is alive with game, and Drynachan is one of the best shoots in the country for partridge. There's also grouse and pheasant shooting.

There is a clutch of pretty cottages dotted around the estate for any overflow guests from the lodge, with two six-bed cottages (Gardener's and Fisherman's) just next door. They all bear Lady Cawdor's trademark decor, which hits just the right note between simple rustic and cute. She's styled the cottages in the same way she might have approached one of her fashion shoots, teaming high-street labels with designer names. So you'll find Ikea work surfaces and checked lino kitchen floors but they'll be mixed with Brabantia bins and Egyptian cotton sheets.

DRYNACHAN LODGE
at a glance

Cawdor bookings manager
Cawdor Estate Office, Cawdor, Nairn,
Inverness-shire, Scotland IV12 5RE
01667 402402, www.cawdor.com

Sleeps: 22-48. Up to 22 in the lodge in 12 rooms (nine doubles, one twin, two singles) with nine bathrooms. Cottages on the estate sleep a further 26 (three cottages for six, one for four and two cottages sleeping two).

Dining: 30 seated in the dining room. Catered on a full-board basis. Food is traditional Scottish with a modern twist, such as spicy mussel bake, halibut with cream fennel pollen sauce, berries in a tuile basket, and cheese. Alcohol is on a BYO basis.

Other facilities: a masseur can be arranged for the lodge and cottages.

Children: cots, highchairs, stairgates, children's menu. Child care can be arranged.

Wedding licence: outside or in the lodge, for 30 seated or more in a marquee.

Local attractions/things to do: shooting – notably partridge but also grouse and pheasant; river and loch fishing and walking. The 14th-century Cawdor Castle is nearby, as is Culloden – site of the battle of Bonnie Prince Charlie's ill-fated uprising against the English – and Nairn, with its beach and golf course.

Transport: Inverness airport is 35 minutes' drive away.

Price: £155pp per night plus VAT full board, minimum eight guests for three nights. One week for eight costs £6,250 plus VAT, additional guests £105pp per night plus VAT. Children 3-12 years pay £60pp per night plus VAT. Shooting parties: minimum charge £3,040 plus VAT for eight guns for two nights. Additional guns are charged at £190pp plus VAT per night.

Note: no pets in the lodge.

Harburn House, West Lothian

This beautiful Georgian home is set in 3,000 acres of scenic woodlands and lochs but is only half an hour's drive from the culture and sights of Edinburgh

The beauty of Harburn is the flexibility you get when you hire it. One of the few properties of this calibre that can be booked on either a catered or a self-catering basis, this creeper-clad Georgian house can be taken over completely, giving you the run of the commercial kitchen, should you so choose (though you won't get the chef's knives – he makes a point of locking them up).

And if having the house to yourselves isn't enough (it sleeps 16), you can take the whole estate, with three lodges sleeping another 24 set among 3,000 acres of scenic woodlands and lochs. There's room for 40 people to eat together in the main house's dining room, which because Harburn is built on sloping land, you reach by going downstairs, though the room still enjoys views over the grounds.

Lit by candles and a glowing fire at night, this room with its large table is a pleasant place to sit, either devouring your own gastronomic creation, or a five-course meal concocted from locally

sourced, fresh ingredients by chef Mike and his team.

As with the catering arrangements, there's an easy atmosphere throughout the whole of Harburn, which was built on the site of a castle blown up by Oliver Cromwell. The Spurway family, who inherited the property in the 1970s, has given it a relaxed feel – chintzy but not snooty in the least.

The four reception rooms that radiate from the pillared hallway, with rug-strewn flagstones and a spiral staircase, all exhibit this laid-back elegance. Filled with antique furniture, the drawing room is still the kind of place where you could happily put your feet up on the sofa. And you're not constrained by set meal times, either. If you take the catered option, breakfast can be at any time you care to roll out of bed.

Once you are up, there's plenty to do. Harburn benefits from being on the fringes of Edinburgh (and more than one celeb has stayed here when

HARBURN HOUSE *at a glance*

Rozi Spurway
Harburn, West Calder, West Lothian,
Scotland EH55 8RN
01506 461818, www.harburnhouse.com

Sleeps: 16-40. Up to 16 in eight rooms in the house (four doubles, four double/twins) all ensuite or with private bathrooms. Another 24 in three lodges (for ten, nine and five).

Dining: 18 can sit around a single table, up to 40 at several tables. Harburn can be rented on a catered or self-catered basis. Three- to five-course meals cost from £40-£55pp and might include steamed scallops with asparagus and lemongrass butter sauce, roast loin of pork Normandy style and Harburn Scotch trifle. Wine is available at retail rates or £6pp corkage.

Other facilities: billiards, rowing boats on the loch, tennis court (not in great condition).

Children: cots, highchairs and a buggy.

Wedding licence: for up to 80, more in a marquee. Facility fee of £4,000 for the estate for a weekend, plus dinner for £45pp, excluding wine.

Local attractions/things to do: shooting, walking, fishing, archery, rowing on the estate's loch and championship golf courses nearby. Edinburgh is 17 miles away and there are historic sites within an hour's drive, including Linlithgow Palace, birthplace of Mary Queen of Scots, and restored cotton mill town, New Lanark.

Transport: Edinburgh is half an hour away; transfers can be arranged (£30 a car).

Price: from £2,500 plus VAT per day on a full-board basis for the house or £10,000 plus VAT per week self catering for the whole estate sleeping 40.

Note: cleaning can be arranged for self-catering lets at £7.50 per hour.

visiting the city) as well as being in its own rural paradise, where you can row to an island in the loch for a picnic, walk, fish or shoot. Back at the house, there are books to be read in the well-stocked library, and a stylish billiards room, with its hide and oak chairs overlooked by a Raeburn oil painting of Sir David Baird, a family ancestor.

After a day of activity or relaxation, it's up the spiral stairs to the bedrooms – all but one are on the first and second floors – which are spacious, some with four-posters or brass bedsteads, others with large bow windows and ornate cornicing. The lodges, too, are well furnished, particularly Haymains, which sleeps nine and comes with an elegant cream sitting room and farmhouse-style kitchen. Nor will anyone staying there be left to fumble their way blindly through the trees at the end of an evening at the main house; Bill the night attendant is happy to drive people back to their lodge when they're ready to turn in.

Blair, Ayrshire

There's history a-plenty in this 11th-century elegantly furnished house that's been the seat of the same family since Richard the Lionheart's time

The stark but impressive stone exterior of this 11th-century house almost makes you expect to see Jane Eyre standing at the front door as you sweep up the long drive. Instead, it's Caroline Borwick, often accompanied by her troop of dogs, who makes guests feel at home from the moment they arrive. 'We welcome people with a drink and then tell them about the history of the house,' she says.

And what a fascinating history it is. The seat of the same family since Richard the Lionheart's time, Blair is reputed to be the oldest continually inhabited mansion house in Scotland.

Such a rich history makes a wonderful backdrop for special occasions. The base of the three-storey Norman tower is the perfect location for a disco, while the 17th-century servants hall now houses a magnificent snooker table. And the old kitchen with its domed-timbered ceiling is ideal for more intimate lunches with its oak table and doors leading on to formal landscaped gardens where you'll also find an outdoor heated pool and tennis court.

The house is filled with antiques including some Louis XV tapestried furniture in the elegant 52ft drawing room, which is reached via stone spiral stairs, its ceiling an example of early Scottish plasterwork. Old tomes lie in the bookcases while china is arranged in alcoves – no wonder the Borwicks are quite particular about young children not staying here.

But guests don't need to stand on ceremony and are encouraged to make themselves at home. There are comfy sofas to sink into and a cosier television room off the oak-panelled dining room.

The Borwicks are also happy for you to wander into the modern kitchen any time you like to make yourself coffee and tea.

They're just as flexible on catering. Either hire Blair on a B&B basis and eat out at a number of local pubs or restaurants, or include dinner in your package. A typical menu might feature warm salad of monkfish, Parma ham and mushrooms, followed by medallions of venison with port and redcurrant jelly and seasonal organic vegetables. Round it off with raspberry tart in pecan pastry and local cheeses.

After dinner retire upstairs to 14 individually decorated bedrooms. The most splendid is Cecily Blair with its ornate French 18th-century four-poster. Antiques abound throughout the bedrooms of this well-furnished house, with Dutch inlaid pieces in one room and an original Chinese Chippendale bed in another.

One bedroom has even been decked out entirely with Napoleonic memorabilia, including furniture belonging to an officer serving in the Napoleonic Wars as well as a picture of the emperor himself. As Caroline Borwick's ancestor Captain William Blair sailed with Nelson, the room represents another slice of Blair's history.

Some of the bathrooms are equally impressive, many with claw-foot baths and concealed loos in chests.

The Borwicks haven't forgotten all the extra touches that add to the homely feel in the bedrooms. As well as bathrobes, complimentary water and fresh flowers, there's plenty of whisky. You can also call in a masseur to ease any aching limbs or arrange to have some reiki healing in a more modern bedroom that doubles up as a therapy room.

Outside there's a 400-acre estate to explore along with a huge range of activities available nearby including clay-pigeon shooting, falconry and quad biking. There are also numerous excellent golf courses such as Turnberry and Loch Lomond.

BLAIR
at a glance

Caroline and Luke Borwick
Near Dalry, Ayrshire, Scotland KA24 4ER
01294 833100, www.blairestate.com

Sleeps: 25-36. Up to 25 in the main house (six doubles, five twins, three singles, all with private bathrooms, bar one single); five (+2) in the self-catering Stable Cottage (one double and one triple sharing two bathrooms plus a sofa bed in sitting room); and B&B for six in three ensuite rooms in the Carriage House, where the Borwicks live.

Dining: 36 at one table or 60 at individual tables. B&B or half-board basis. A typical menu might include monkfish salad, venison and raspberry tart.

Other facilities: heated outdoor pool, tennis court and snooker. Therapy room for massages or reiki treatments.

Children: only older, well behaved children are welcome; there are lots of valuable antiques in the house.

Wedding licence: up to 150 seated in the drawing room, more in a marquee in the grounds. Up to 60 for dinner and a reception in the house. Weddings plus house for two nights' B&B for up to 25: £7,000.

Local attractions/things to do: horse riding, falconry, clay-pigeon shooting, quad biking, the beach, sailing and power-boat outings all nearby. Famous links golf courses – Blair is 15 minutes' drive from three courses and 40 minutes from Turnberry and Loch Lomond.

Transport: Glasgow Airport is 25 minutes' drive; Prestwick 20 minutes and Edinburgh 90 minutes.

Price: half board including house wine £188pp per night (£4,700 for 25). Minimum six people for exclusive use. B&B £94pp per night. Stable Cottage from £450 for up to three nights, or £650 per week. B&B in Carriage House £80 per double room per night.

Note: Blair is strictly no smoking.

Kentchurch Court, Herefordshire

Look familiar? That's because this beautiful estate, which has been in the same family for more than 1,000 years, was the star of a recent TV series

This grand stately home was painstakingly restored to its former 19th-century glory as part of Channel 4 TV's *Regency House Party* series. It took a team of builders, craftsmen, decorators and scene painters three months to faithfully recreate the era.

Kentchurch's owners, John and Jan Lucas-Scudamore, vacated the property during the makeover in 2003, which also included stripping it of all modern conveniences such as central heating, electric lights and plumbing. Thankfully, all these have been restored, leaving guests to enjoy a spruced up country house with new curtains, carpets and sparkling clean chandeliers (the Lucas-Scudamores are also rather pleased the team managed to fix the fire in the Terrace Room, which no longer smokes).

Ten of the house's 13 bedrooms used for filming are now freshly decorated in traditional country-house style, some with sleigh beds and four-posters. Although only two of the rooms are

ensuite, there shouldn't be much of a queue to use the facilities: there's one bathroom for every two bedrooms.

Two of the most characterful bedrooms are in the tower designed by John Nash. The impressive Owain Glyndwr room (named after the Welsh hero whose daughter married Sir John Scudamore and who reportedly stayed at Kentchurch after his disastrous campaign against the English in 1416) has wood-panelled walls, a four-poster bed and a charming bathroom with roll-top bath and fireplace. And the Painted Room boasts wooden floors, a stone fireplace and a roll-top bath and loo behind a partition.

The three bedrooms that weren't redecorated for the TV series are in the less characterful 1950s extension and are much smaller and more suitable for children.

For all its grandeur, Kentchurch is a very relaxing place to stay, thanks to down-to-earth hostess Jan who has been organising house

KENTCHURCH COURT
at a glance

Jan Lucas-Scudamore
Pontrilas, Herefordshire HR2 0DB
01981 240228, www.kentchurchcourt.co.uk

Sleeps: 24 in 13 bedrooms (six doubles, five twins and two singles). Two are ensuite, one has a private bathroom and the rest share a bathroom between two.

Dining: seats 22. B&B but dinner can be arranged. Three-course dinner from £25pp – menus might include homemade venison sausages with red onion and mushrooms, pheasant with cream, bacon and parsley sauce, and toasted almond and chocolate roulade filled with cherries. BYO wine. Picnic lunches can be arranged.

Other facilities: snooker room, tennis court and croquet.

Children: no cots or highchairs but high tea.

Wedding licence: no but receptions for up to 80 for sit-down meal, 130 for a buffet and up to 200 in a marquee on the lawn. £2,000 facility fee.

Local attractions/things to do: walking and horse riding on the estate or in the nearby Black Mountains. Clay-pigeon shooting, paint balling and archery can be arranged. Pheasant shooting on local estates. Trout fishing on the River Monnow, which runs through the estate, or salmon fishing on the River Wye. Eastnor Castle, Hereford, Ross-on-Wye, Leominster and Hay-on-Wye are all within an easy drive.

Transport: nearest train station at Abergavenny, 12 miles away (London is two and a half hours via Newport). Three hours' drive from London.

Price: from £70pp per night B&B plus £250 fee for exclusive use. Minimum of six people required.

Note: no dogs in house.

parties for more than 15 years. Renowned for her risqué jokes, she makes everyone feel at home and is happy to let children roam freely around this cavernous country house that's been home to the Scudamore family for more than 1,000 years.

She serves up good, honest British fare, including pheasant and venison from the estate, in the elegant dining room with its wall-to-wall family portraits and huge picture windows overlooking the sweeping grounds. Jan's slabs of homemade fudge are also legendary. After gorging yourself on the fine fare, retire to the Terrace Room for coffee and liqueurs or have a game of snooker in the library.

Tucked in a deep valley on the Herefordshire/Welsh border, Kentchurch also scores with its guests because of its physical seclusion, which gives a real feeling of getting away from it all. You don't have to leave the 5,000-acre estate to try clay-pigeon shooting, paint balling, archery and fishing – you can even bring your own horse.

Small Hotels

Ford Abbey, Herefordshire

Enjoy 21st-century comforts in a medieval setting at this upmarket rural

retreat, set in a sheltered valley in the backwaters of unspoilt Herefordshire

The best time to arrive at Ford Abbey is at dusk. Gentle lights twinkle over water as you approach this 15th-century former Benedictine monastery tucked away in a secluded valley. Where monks once went about their spiritual business in spartan austerity, today's visitors can indulge themselves in unadulterated luxury.

Pour yourself a drink from the honesty bar in the oak-beamed sitting room and sink into a sofa next to a roaring fire in the huge inglenook fireplace before tucking into a sumptuous meal. With its timbered ceiling, original bread oven and candlelight reflected in the silver tableware on the heavy oak sideboard, the dining room lends itself to convivial eating. After dinner, retire to the sitting room for coffee and liqueurs placed on a beautifully upholstered gold ottoman in front of the fire. Any musically inclined guests may be tempted to knock out a few tunes on the baby grand piano.

'We want you to feel like you're entertaining at home but with caterers,' says joint manager Everine Van Hassel. This is the kind of hotel where you can turn up late for breakfast and not feel guilty, and where guests are encouraged to prop up the breakfast bar in the kitchen and chat to the chef about the evening menu while he works his culinary magic.

Much of the produce used in the kitchen comes from the property's own organic farm. Tuck into the abbey's sausages, bacon and free-range eggs as part of a traditional English breakfast or opt for a Dutch-style continental spread (Ford's owners, Dr and Mrs Heijn, come from Holland) featuring dried meats, cheeses and deliciously indulgent pastries.

In summer, the place takes on a whole new persona when alfresco dining in the pretty courtyard is the name of the game. Decorated with even more twinkling lights and flowerpots, it's a great place for a disco (set in 320 acres of

farmland you won't have to worry about upsetting the neighbours). If you fancy a barbecue, head for the converted barn overlooking the valley for some of the estate's sizzling Hereford beef steaks. When it gets a bit chilly, you know there's a warming fire waiting for you in the sitting room. There's also an indoor heated pool and fitness centre where you can burn off all those extra calories.

Outdoors, there are plenty of activities to try your hand at, with everything from fishing to horse riding nearby. You can also get some culture by heading to Hereford to see the Mappa Mundi, a vellum map of how scholars viewed the world in the 13th century.

Back at the former monastery, you'll need to watch your head when walking around, particularly upstairs – parts of it date back to the 11th century, when people were a lot shorter. Some of the six suites in the main house have a lovely higgledy-piggledy feel to them with oak

beams and sloping floorboards and walls, but are kitted out with all the latest mod cons. There's a four-poster bed below the Minstrel's Gallery in Lauds while the half-timbered Bee suite has a Victorian spiral staircase leading to the Scribe's Gallery, a large seating area with wonderful views over landscaped gardens. Abbots Suite on the ground floor has excellent disabled access with remote-controlled curtains and electronic sliding doors opening on to a spacious shower room.

In addition to the six suites, there are four contemporary self-catering lodges. Converted from a 15th-century barn and overlooking the landscaped grounds, they have the feel of trendy loft apartments with shower consoles in the middle of the open-plan bedrooms.

Two are suitable for couples, and the other two are large enough for families. But with all that luxury, one thing's for sure: none of them are suitable for monks.

FORD ABBEY *at a glance*

Michael Westenbrink and Everine Van Hassel, managers
Pudleston, Nr Leominster, Herefordshire HR6 ORZ
01568 760 700, www.fordabbey.co.uk

Sleeps: 24 (plus six children on futons) in six double suites and four self-catering lodges, half with two bedrooms and half with one bedroom. One ground-floor suite has disabled access.

Dining: 30 at a long table in the dining room. Catered on a half-board basis. Three-course dinners might include Jerusalem artichoke soup with confit of duck, lamb with parsnip mash and banana crumble. Wine from £16.50 a bottle. The courtyard and covered BBQ area can be used in warmer months for an extra 40 guests.

Other facilities: indoor swimming pool, small fitness area, covered BBQ area. On-site massage.

Children: cots and highchairs. Note the stream and pond in grounds.

Wedding licence: for up to 35 in the dining room and library. Sit-down wedding breakfasts for 30 can be arranged with an extra 40 for a buffet or BBQ.

Local attractions/things to do: visit Hereford's Mappa Mundi, a vellum map of how scholars viewed the world in the 13th century, as well as the cathedral, shops and restaurants at Left Bank Village on the city's River Wye – all within a 40-minute drive. Walking and picnics on the estate or the Welsh Borders. Golf, fishing, horse riding and clay-pigeon shooting.

Transport: trains from London Paddington take three hours to Hereford, a 40-minute drive away. The drive from London takes about three and a half hours.

Price: £4,800 for one night's half board for 24 people including a four-course dinner.

The Well House, Cornwall

Tuck into delicious seafood from the fish market at Looe when you stay at this Victorian house, which prides itself on its informal atmosphere

You won't find any room numbers or names at the Well House, a deliberate move by co-owner Nick Wainford who wants guests to treat it like home.

With just nine bedrooms, this country-house hotel tucked away down a leafy Cornish lane in the Looe valley has an informal, relaxed atmosphere.

Nick left London more than 20 years ago with the intention of running a salmon farm in Scotland or a garden centre. Instead he stumbled across this stone house built by a Victorian tea magnate on the same site as St Keyne's well, where legend has it that the first person in a married couple to drink the water will wear the pants in the relationship.

His passion for good food and wine has helped the Well House achieve numerous awards for its gastronomy. Today the hotel is the proud owner of an AA three-rosette award.

Food is certainly a big part of the experience here. Much is made of locally sourced produce, such as the lobster, sea bass and turbot – all sourced from the famous fish market at Looe – as well as venison and Cornish lamb.

On warm summer evenings, sip pre-dinner drinks on the terrace before tucking into a meal in the restaurant with its contemporary leather chairs, starched white linen tablecloths and bay windows overlooking three acres of tranquil gardens bursting with rhododendrons, camellias and azaleas.

There's also a bar and a drawing room with a marble fireplace, antiques and lots of original art – Nick is a keen art lover – adorning the walls. In any of these rooms, you might meet Nick's affectionate Staffordshire terrier, Buster, 'who thinks he owns the joint'.

All nine ensuite bedrooms are individually

THE WELL HOUSE *at a glance*

Nick Wainford
St Keyne, Liskeard, Cornwall PL14 4RN
01579 342001, www.wellhouse.co.uk

Sleeps: up to 20. Nine ensuite bedrooms (five doubles, three twins and one family suite sleeping up to four).

Dining: one long table seating up to 30. Catered on a half-board basis. Three-course menus including coffee/tea with petit fours cost £35pp. House wine from £12.50 a bottle. AA three-rosette restaurant, twice voted the Good Food Guide's County Restaurant of the Year.

Other facilities: heated outdoor pool (available May to September), tennis court and croquet lawn.

Children: two cots, one Z-bed. High tea can be provided.

Wedding licence: no but receptions in marquees for up to 150. Buffets for up to 150 or 60 for a sit-down meal. Minimum two-night stay.

Local attractions/things to do: numerous beaches on the north coast such as Fistral, Watergate Bay and Rock and on the south coast at Whitsand Bay and Parr. The Eden Project is a 30-minute drive away. The Lost Gardens of Heligan and other gardens are also nearby. There is also pheasant shooting; horse riding; salmon, trout and sea fishing (including shark from Looe) as well as walking on Bodmin Moor. St Mellion and Bindown golf courses are both within 10 miles.

Transport: trains from London to Liskeard, three miles from the Well House, take three and a half to four hours. The drive from London takes the same time.

Price: from £125pp per night B&B for a minimum two nights (negotiable depending on time of year).

Note: dogs welcome (not in restaurant or public rooms).

decorated – some very contemporary, others in more traditional country-house style. Two large garden terrace rooms are the most luxurious, with lounge areas and French windows leading on to a large patio overlooking the gardens and valley beyond. The top floor family suite has a double bedroom with ensuite bathroom, lounge area and a twin room.

The Well House is set in an ideal location to explore the best that Cornwall has to offer. Close to the fishing villages of Looe and Polperro, it is just half an hour's drive from The Eden Project. The hotel can also organise minibus excursions to the Tate at St Ives as well as lots of other activities such as horse riding or fishing.

After a hard day's sightseeing retire to your Cornish retreat, play croquet on the lawn, have a game of tennis on the all-weather court or take a dip in the heated outdoor pool.

Frogg Manor, Cheshire

Eccentricity rules at this elegant Georgian house filled with hundreds of frogs

– from ornaments and toys to the chocolates served after dinner

Heading up the gravel drive towards this Georgian manor house, you get a clue you're about to stumble on something special from the sign on the verge: 'Welcome to Frogg Manor, an oasis of normality. The mad, mad world is now behind.'

Walk through the front door and you'll be greeted by some of the several hundred frogs dotted around this seven-bedroom house: ornaments, pictures, cuddly toys – leaping out of plant foliage and even served in chocolate form after dinner. Presiding over this amphibian army is eccentric owner and chef John Sykes (or 'Chief Frog', as he calls himself), his long hair fringing the beret that sits atop his head as he whistles his way around the manor.

'The place is named after a girlfriend called Froggie I had when I came here 17 years ago,' he says. 'She hopped off but the frogs keep coming – people bring them to me now.'

Surprisingly, having such a huge collection of frogs in the manor doesn't look tacky. In fact, Frogg Manor is full of Georgian and Victorian period pieces and plush furnishings, with tasteful trimmings such as gilt mirrors, parquet floors and lots of art (albeit with the odd frog thrown in for good measure). Corridors are full of interesting paraphernalia – old gramophones perch on windowsills, shelves bulge with books – and there's a feel-at-home messiness about it all.

The bedrooms are all different and even the smallest, Sherlock Holmes, could still be described as spacious, while Churchill has a bathroom the size of a bedroom. They come with some impressive extras; where in other hotels you'd find a few small bottles of toiletries, at Frogg Manor, you get everything from hairspray and aftershave to stockings and nail-varnish remover. Here, kettles come with a whole array of teas, coffee is in jars rather than sachets, and there are lots of delicious nibbles and complimentary sherry. The Lord Nelson suite also has free brandy and rum to be sipped in wing-backed chairs around the fire 'because it's a naval room', says John.

The best room in the house is the Wellington, with a crown-canopied bed from which pink and blue material tumbles to the floor. Within this huge room – which has its own dressing room as well as bathroom – are an eclectic mix of items; a telescope shares the top of an antique roll-top desk with a high-tech radio, and a chess set on the table by the window looks out over a collection of frog statues in the garden.

You could hole up in this room for days quite happily, but it's worth going out, if only to make a surprise entrance to the sitting room via a door in a bookshelf. A peaceful atmosphere reigns in this ochre and brown room with its Regency armchairs, fringed lamps, and music from the 1930s and 1940s playing softly in the background.

It's a great place for an aperitif before heading to the dining room, where the green decor echoes the frog theme without labouring it. The dinner menu – priced in guineas – is extensive, with lots of local lamb and fresh fish, though the house speciality is chicken java masala, a supreme of chicken baked in a freshly made Javanese curry sauce. There's also an excellent vegan and vegetarian selection.

When you've eaten your fill, don't think the night needs to end with coffee and frog-shaped chocolates. Upstairs is a bar where you can sup a shot of real sarsaparilla, dandelion and burdock as well as more conventional drinks. And at the end of the bar is a party room, a converted barn with disco lights, so you can dance the night away. Just don't kiss any frogs – not all of them turn into princes.

FROGG MANOR
at a glance

John Sykes
Nantwich Road, Broxton, Chester, Cheshire CH3 9JH
01829 782629, www.froggmanorhotel.co.uk

Sleeps: 14 in seven rooms (six doubles and one double/twin) all with ensuite bathrooms.

Dining: 12 can sit around a large table in the centre of the restaurant, with larger groups at smaller tables. The dining room holds 45 comfortably and 60 at a push. Catered on a half-board basis. A typical dinner might include black pudding with grain mustard jus and a poached egg, steamed fillet of sea bass and chocolate mousse.

Other facilities: tennis court.

Children: one cot, no highchairs. No children's menu but child-size meals can be prepared.

Wedding licence: for up to 68 in the manor's converted barn or the gazebo.

Local attractions/things to do: visit the nearby medieval city of Chester, which boasts the largest amphitheatre in Great Britain and the racecourse at Roodee, the oldest in Britain. Chester also has great shops and restaurants. Stroll in the grounds of Cholmondeley Castle, or explore the rolling hills and idyllic villages of south west Cheshire – both within an easy drive. The spectacular scenery of north Wales – great for walking and cycling – is also on your doorstep.

Transport: trains from London Euston take almost three hours to Chester, 12 miles away. The drive from London takes just over three hours.

Price: £1,349 per night for seven rooms including dinner and continental breakfast on every night but Saturday, which costs £2,165 (minimum charge for exclusive use). Buffet lunch £25pp.

Crosby Lodge, Cumbria

It's a family affair at this country-house hotel that's filled with beautiful

antiques and is just a few minutes' walk from the Hadrian's Wall footpath

There's a bit of a mother and daughter act going on at Crosby Lodge, just minutes from the border city of Carlisle. While owner Patricia Sedgwick runs the hotel, her wine merchant daughter, Philippa, selects the vintages on the comprehensive wine list and organises tastings. If you like a particular bottle, you can buy a case to take home from her shop in the courtyard.

There's a pleasant family atmosphere inside the 19th-century lodge, which isn't a bit stuffy even though the exterior with its crenellations and Virginia creeper looks quite traditional. Inside it's more of a cross between a gentleman's club that has thrown open its doors to ladies, and something out of *Antiques Roadshow*.

Pieces of period furniture are scattered throughout the public rooms, with a chaise longue here and a cabinet filled with china there – all offset by some stunning flower arrangements.

There are plenty of places to relax – in the light-coloured sitting room with its original Adam brothers' ceiling and pretty window seat, or the more convivial, larger bar with lots of easy chairs, which also opens on to a small room, perfect for smokers. The wood-beamed dining room is particularly atmospheric with an enormous oak fireplace and matching dresser providing a wonderful backdrop for the fine British fare served up, and particularly the sweet trolley and homemade bread and preserves for which Crosby Lodge is locally renowned.

Upstairs, there are four-posters and original half-testers in a few of the bedrooms, such as the honeymoon room, which has a huge wardrobe in

CROSBY LODGE *at a glance*

Patricia Sedgwick
High Crosby, Crosby on Eden, Carlisle,
Cumbria CA6 4QZ
01228 573618, www.crosbylodge.co.uk

Sleeps: 25 in 11 ensuite rooms (five doubles, three double/twins, three triples).

Dining: 50 at individual tables. Catered on a half-board basis. Dinner might include hot crab bake, roast rack of lamb and kidneys in brandy cream, followed by homemade white chocolate ice cream.

Other facilities: wine warehouse in the courtyard.

Children: cots, highchairs, children's menu, a walled garden.

Wedding licence: for up to 65 in the dining room. Dining for 165 in a marquee in the grounds. Facility fee: £200, marquee price on application.

Local attractions/things to do: Hadrian's Wall footpath runs along the lodge's boundary and Birdoswald, one of the best preserved Roman forts along the wall, is six miles away. Fly fishing and clay-pigeon shooting can be arranged. Carlisle, with its 11th-century castle and Tullie House – a museum and art gallery featuring Victorian and pre-Raphaelite work – is four miles away. The Lake District and the abbeys of the Scottish borders are both within an easy drive.

Transport: trains from London Euston to Carlisle, a ten-minute drive away, take four and a half hours. The drive takes five hours; Crosby Lodge is not far from the M6.

Price: from £2,950 per night on a half-board basis for 25 guests.

Note: dogs are accepted in the two courtyard rooms.

the tower. Though other rooms are more simply decorated, they all come with complimentary water and sweets, along with posh toiletries in the bathrooms.

Because it's a dog-friendly hotel, visiting pooches are welcome in the two courtyard rooms, one of which is a large triple. It really is dog-walking heaven around here, too. Surrounded by woods and parkland with views of the River Eden, Crosby Lodge is only a few minutes' walk from the Hadrian's Wall footpath, while Birdoswald, one of the best-preserved Roman forts along the wall, is just six miles away. The Lake District isn't far either.

And in the middle of this countryside idyll, you also get the benefits of being just ten minutes' drive from Carlisle and very close to the M6.

Fingals Hotel, Devon

A duck taking a dip in the swimming pool, a folly in the garden and some

eccentric decor are all part of the charm of this quirky former farmhouse

Richard Johnston was running a restaurant in London when he fell in love with this once dilapidated 17th-century farmhouse in a lush valley next to the River Dart. Now, more than 20 years after he let out his first room, Fingals has established a reputation as a rather quirky place to stay (comedian Vic Reeves affectionately described it as 'bonkers'). The clock in the bar says 'Oneish, twoish, threeish' and you may find the odd duck waddling around the hotel or taking a dip in the swimming pool. The decor is very eclectic, with modern sculptures dotted around the garden, an old-fashioned, working telephone in the bar and a mixture of contemporary and traditional art adorning the walls.

If ever there was a small hotel that's ideal for a relaxed gathering of family or friends, this is it, largely because Richard already runs it like a country house party, where most guests prefer to eat together round a long farmhouse table in the oak-panelled dining room.

It's a laid-back kind of place where the good-natured staff make you feel at home as soon as you walk in the door. Don't expect to check in at a formal reception: room keys are collected at the bar where you can help yourself to drinks and keep your own tab. Breakfast is an equally relaxed affair and only finishes after the last guests have emerged.

Among the 11 bedrooms is a traditional four-poster room (although this isn't just any bed – it comes from whisky magnate Johnny Walker's house in Kilmarnock) and a loft-style family room with twin beds on a mezzanine level and Beryl Cook prints. There's also a brightly painted folly – a tiny mill house with an upstairs lounge, wood-burning stove and balcony overlooking a stream.

Eating is a big part of the Fingals' experience, where French chef, Eric, rustles up four-course menus with a Gallic flavour.

When you're not eating or sleeping you could be sitting in front of a roaring fire in the lounge's original inglenook fireplace or watching a DVD or video on one of the sofas in the mini cinema. There's also a library, snooker room with table

football and ping pong, heated indoor pool, hot tub, sauna and mini-gym (but don't expect to find the latest state-of-the-art equipment here: the exercise bike looks like an antique).

In fine weather, play croquet on the lawn, have a game of tennis on the grass court or sit and read a book on the decked terrace overlooking the stream.

There's plenty to do outside the hotel's grounds, too; Fingals' idyllic location close to the River Dart is hard to beat. Go sailing, fishing or canoeing on the river (you can even venture out in Fingals' own rowing boat) or take the ferry from nearby Dittisham to Dartmouth.

Meanwhile, arty, new age Totnes is a 20-minute drive away and there are plenty of sandy beaches within easy reach.

FINGALS HOTEL
at a glance

Richard and Sheila Johnston
Coombe, Dittisham, Nr Dartmouth, Devon TQ6 OJA
01803 722398, www.fingals.co.uk

Sleeps: 24-33. Up to 24 in Fingals in 11 ensuite bedrooms (one family room, eight doubles and two twins) plus possible use of The Barn and The Mill House sleeping an extra four and five.

Dining: 22 around one table or two lots of 16 in two adjoining dining rooms. Catered on a half-board basis with four-course meals from £27.50pp. Menus might include homemade venison terrine, grilled duck breast with lime and sweet chilli sauce, Grand Marnier crème brulée and cheese. Wine from £3.50 a glass or £13 a bottle.

Other facilities: indoor heated pool, sauna, Jacuzzi, mini-gym, grass tennis court, mini-cinema, table tennis, snooker, croquet and bikes. Massages can also be arranged.

Children: two cots and two highchairs. High tea at £7.50pp.

Wedding licence: no but receptions for up to 140.

Local attractions/things to do: take the scenic Dittisham to Dartmouth ferry (March to October); numerous sandy beaches within 45 minutes' drive; canoeing, fishing and boat trips on the Dart. The gardens at Greenway, home of Agatha Christie, are nearby. Arty, new age Totnes is a 20-minute drive away.

Transport: trains from London Paddington take three hours to Totnes, which is seven miles from Fingals. London is about three and a half hours' drive.

Price: from £110 B&B per room per night. Minimum number of guests for exclusive use: 22.

Note: well-behaved dogs allowed by arrangement. Fingals is closed from January 2 to Easter.

Ladyburn, Ayrshire

Roses and flowers of all shades grace the gardens of this intimate 17th-century dower house, which makes the perfect setting for a relaxing break

Come to Ladyburn in the summer to see the multitude of roses bathing the gardens in colour as well as climbing trees and trellises. There are so many roses at this small country house that the garden may soon gain the status of holding the national collection of ramblers – for the non-green-fingered, that means it has at least 75 per cent of all varieties of the plant.

When the roses aren't in bloom, there's still plenty to see. The garden is also awash with colour in the spring, with daffodils, crocus and rhododendrons. Even in winter, the frost clinging to the tree branches is scenic.

Jane Hepburn, who runs Ladyburn with her daughter, Catriona, has packed plenty into the five-acre plot, with a Celtic Cross formed by box hedges, an azalea walk, a pond and even a burn with its own Pooh-sticks bridge. The vegetable plot, dubbed Mr McGregor's Garden, comes with its own palette of colours – purple brussel sprouts, red French beans and a range of different coloured tomatoes.

Everything seems to flourish in this garden, helped by the Gulf Stream on Scotland's east coast (the sea is eight miles away).

As you'd expect, this pretty white house in one of Scotland's lesser-known corners is full of fresh flowers, while the home-grown vegetables are used by Jane in the delicious meals she cooks. Using locally sourced meat and seafood, she can turn her hand to most dishes – think mint and pea soup and roast gigot of local lamb. But the most requests she receives are for nursery puddings such as spotted dick, bread-and-butter pudding and semolina, as well as her homemade ice cream.

This wonderful comfort food is served up in the high-ceilinged Georgian dining room, which along with the drawing room holding pale sofas and antiques, was added to the original 17th-century dower house. There's also a snug library with an open fire, the only place guests can smoke.

There's a chintzy feel to the place, particularly upstairs in the bedrooms, where you'll find lots of floral furnishings, with fluffy loo-seat covers in the bathrooms. As well as a large selection of beds – an antique four-poster, French half-tester and a colonial bed – the rooms also have lots of thoughtful extras such as handmade soaps bundled up with dried flowers and complimentary chocolates and fruit.

If you've got children, you can book into the granny flat with its own entrance, as well as an interconnecting door. The flat is filled with modern pine furniture, which means you won't be worried about little hands scratching the antiques.

One of the beauties of Ladyburn is its size, which makes it perfect for an intimate house party. Seemingly in the middle of nowhere, this quaint family house almost invites you to relax. And just because it's small doesn't mean there isn't room for a party – they've had several country dancing sets strutting their stuff in the dining room, with a piper to boot.

But you need to remember that it's still a family home, and the family only goes to bed when you do, so you're unlikely to find yourselves climbing the stairs to bed much past midnight.

When you get there, you'll find a top-notch turndown service far better than in most hotels, with bathrooms cleaned, clothes hung up, lighting dimmed and in the winter, hot-water bottles slipped under the covers.

The only thing that's missing are rose petals scattered on the bed.

LADYBURN
at a glance

Jane and Catriona Hepburn
By Maybole, Ayrshire, Scotland KA19 7SG
01655 740585, www.ladyburn.co.uk

Sleeps: 12-16. Up to 12 can sleep in the main house in six rooms (four doubles, two twins, all with ensuite or dedicated bathrooms). There is also a granny flat sleeping four in one double, one twin and with one bathroom.

Dining: 20 at a single table, 40 at separate tables and 60 in a party tent. Catered on a half-board basis. A typical three-course dinner might include cheese soufflé with asparagus and cream source, roast gigot of lamb, and spotted dick. House wine £16.95 a bottle or corkage charged.

Other facilities: croquet.

Children: children's menu and beds, baby monitors.

Wedding licence: for up to 60 in the drawing room, or in the gardens.

Local attractions/things to do: Turnberry golf course is about 20 minutes away and Troon and Prestwick are within 45 minutes' drive. The National Trust for Scotland's Culzean Castle is nearby, and there is walking, horse riding, plus visits to other famous Scottish gardens. Salmon, trout and sea fishing nearby. The Trossachs National Park and Loch Lomond are just over an hour's drive. Horse racing at Ayr is 15 miles away.

Transport: Glasgow is an hour away, Prestwick airport (served by Ryanair) is 25 minutes' drive.

Price: from £1,250 B&B for the property per night, dinners from £32.50pp. Tea, coffee and squash are complimentary.

Note: smoking is only allowed in the library.

Farlam Hall, Cumbria

A traditional Victorian atmosphere reigns at this chintzy but unpretentious family-run country house that's earned a reputation for its gastronomy

When the Stevenson and Quinion families bought this Victorian creeper-clad house in 1975 and opened it as a hotel just a week later, there was only one bathroom, no heating, and all the rooms had electricity meters. Thirty years on and the conditions have changed considerably. The years of hard work have paid off with the creation of an unpretentious country house that feels very little like a hotel.

With just 12 rooms Farlam Hall has succeeded in maintaining the atmosphere of a large Victorian family home – just as it was when it was owned by local industrialists, the Thompsons.

As you'd expect, there's a lot of chintzy decor, accentuated by gilt mirrors over ornate fireplaces, high ceilings and bow windows letting in plenty of light. Even the downstairs loos live up to their names as 'powder rooms', a pink door opening on to a space for ladies to do their makeup.

The drawing room with its patterned wallpaper

and window seat overlooking the grounds is particularly reminiscent of days gone by when ladies would sit together on a cluster of sofas and gossip. There's also enough seating for everyone in the pink hallway, which doubles as a second sitting room.

The bedrooms vary considerably in size. The best in the house is one of two on the ground floor, and comes with an ornate four-poster in red and gold and large windows overlooking the garden. Apart from one room in the converted stables, the rest of the bedrooms are on the first floor, one with a bathroom that's big enough to be a bedroom, others with separate seating areas. All come with complimentary mineral water, fluffy bathrobes and posh toiletries along with bowls of fruit, chocolate and sugared almonds.

Don't stock up on the nibbles too much – the hotel is part of the prestigious Relais & Châteaux chain, renowned for its high standard of food, and

FARLAM HALL
at a glance

Helen Stevenson or Lynne Quinion
Brampton, Cumbria CA8 2NG
016977 46234, www.farlamhall.co.uk

Sleeps: 24 in 12 rooms (six doubles, six twins), all ensuite. One of the rooms is in the stables.

Dining: up to 40 can be seated at several tables. Catered on a half-board basis. A four-course meal might include warm English asparagus with herb hollandaise and medallion of local beef fillet with fried onions and a pink peppercorn sauce. There is an English cheese board with apple, grapes and celery and a choice of homemade ice cream. There's also an extensive vegetarian menu. Drinks at hotel rates.

Other facilities: a paddock is available for visiting horses. Everything from a piano to a piper can be arranged.

Children: no cots or highchairs but children's menu can be prepared. There is a lake in the garden.

Wedding licence: no. Small receptions for up to 40.

Local attractions/things to do: Hadrian's Wall is just four miles from the house, and there are plenty of country walks. Carlisle with its castle, cathedral and museum, is a 15-minute drive – pleasure flights can be taken from the airport. Three golf courses are within seven miles. There is also horse riding, fishing and cycling.

Transport: trains from London Euston to Carlisle, a 20-minute drive away, take four and a half hours. By car, the journey takes five hours. Two large or four small helicopters can land in the grounds at no extra charge.

Price: from £2,000-£5,000 per night for the whole property on a half-board basis. There is a minimum hire of two nights.

has won plenty of other gastronomic accolades. Dinner is served in the regal dining room decorated in yellow and blue with a fireplace at either end.

Both the food and location less than 20 minutes from the M6 make Farlam Hall a favourite stopping-off point for motorists on their way to Scotland. But it's worth more than a quick visit, being just four miles from Hadrian's Wall and surrounded by stunning countryside.

The 12-acre grounds are home to an ornamental lake and copper beech and cedar trees. At one time, the Thompson family had the experimental track from George Stephenson's The Rocket running through the gardens. Now, you can keep your own pony there, if it doesn't mind sharing the grounds with several rare-breed sheep and llamas.

It's just another feature that makes Farlam Hall different from your run-of-the-mill hotel.

Charlton House, Somerset

Sumptuous furnishings, a Michelin-starred restaurant and staff who greet you by name: just what you'd expect from a hotel run by Mulberry's founder

Given that Charlton House's owner is none other than Roger Saul, founder of Mulberry, it's no surprise to find this country-house hotel is stuffed full of sumptuous fabrics. There is a sprinkling of other labels, but the interior mostly doubles as a showcase for the company's designs with the original staircase from the Bond Street store and a signature bear in every bedroom.

It's an opulent look, particularly in the spacious drawing rooms, with their clusters of sofas and chairs upholstered in a mix of tweeds, silks, tapestries, leather and suede.

'I was fed up with the minimalist look,' says Roger. 'For me, hotels should be about pampering and the exotic. There should be theatre involved and lots of surprises.'

And drama is exactly what he's created in this 17th-century stone manor in the heart of the rolling Somerset countryside. Nowhere is this more evident than in the dining room, with a dramatic red and gilt opera box framing the entrance, and an inner section with maroon-coloured walls and specially designed kaftan chairs with hoods.

Though Saul says his inspiration came from India, it looks more Moroccan by candlelight. By day, the adjoining conservatory part of the dining room with its bay windows and glass ceiling is wonderfully light with lots of white, billowy curtains.

As you'd expect in a Michelin-starred restaurant, the food is not only beautifully presented, but is also top quality, with chef Simon Crannage using the best West Country produce. Many of the ingredients come from Roger's own farm, Sharpham Park, which is organic and specialises in rare-breed produce. Thus, duo of Sharpham lamb, braised and roast, might appear on the menu after a starter of foie gras with ginger beer jelly. The vegetarian selection is also particularly good.

While Charlton House is a hotel – and a very luxurious one at that – there's a relaxed feel to it. On arrival, staff come out and greet you by name and everywhere you look are mementoes from Roger's travels with his wife, Monty. In the hallway, with its dark wood floor and model of a hot-air balloon doubling as a light, you'll also find family photographs, racing memorabilia, antiques and other curios.

Although the hotel has a spa, which is exotic and intimate with a wide range of products, this is the only part of Charlton House you won't be able to have on an exclusive basis; the spa's members are free to come and go, and can also use the small heated indoor/outdoor pool.

However, the hotel does have an alternative, more private place for massages – two of its bedrooms convert into spa rooms where couples can enjoy treatments together. The Hayloft room is particularly suited to this, as it also boasts an upstairs bathroom with huge roll-top bath and projector television on the wall – a great place to relax.

All the bedrooms at Charlton are individual, some with enormous four-posters and flat-screen TVs, while others are smaller and more intimate, although they may have a private courtyard leading on to the garden as recompense. All come with a mix of wonderfully rich fabrics.

Of course, all this luxury does come at a price – it isn't cheap – but Charlton House is the perfect retreat for Mulberry fans. And should you get withdrawal symptoms on your way home, pop into the design house's factory just up the road for some discounted lines.

CHARLTON HOUSE
at a glance

Vanessa Willetts, special events manager
Shepton Mallet, Near Bath, Somerset BA4 4PR
01749 347344, www.charltonhouse.com

Sleeps: 52 in 25 rooms (16 doubles, eight double/twins and one suite with a double and a twin), all ensuite.

Dining: 60 can sit at one long table. Catered with a three-course dinner, for example, starting with breast of pigeon with celeriac remoulade, roast organic salmon fillet with lentils and foie gras and a tasting plate of green apple desserts. Dinner £50pp. Lunch from £20pp.

Other facilities: croquet, tennis court, spa (note the latter is not exclusive use). One bedroom doubles as a cinema screening room.

Children: cots, highchairs, children's menu, toy box and DVDs. Note that children under the age of 16 are not allowed in the spa.

Wedding licence: for up to 95 in the orangery, with dining for 60 or 120 in a marquee in the walled garden. Wedding arrangement fee £250, wedding room and marquee hire £2,000-£5,000.

Local attractions/things to do: Cheddar Gorge is 16 miles away, while Bath is just 18 miles. As well as the Somerset countryside, there are plenty of historic buildings within a 25-mile radius, including Longleat with its safari park, Sherborne Abbey and Stourhead House. There are also numerous golf courses nearby.

Transport: trains take 90 minutes from London Paddington to Castle Cary, about ten minutes' drive away. Three hours' drive by car from London.

Price: one night's B&B for the hotel from £15,000.

Note: dogs are permitted in one of the bedrooms.

Fairyhill, West Glamorgan

Enjoy a gastronomic meal using the best local produce at this relaxed 18th-century pad, which is set in some of Wales' most stunning countryside

Not many hotels have the right ambience for a house party – they're usually too big and sterile to create that special feel. Somehow Fairyhill manages to pull it off. This 18th-century creeper-covered house with just eight bedrooms on the stunning Gower Peninsula prides itself on its unstuffy, relaxed atmosphere.

One of its biggest attractions is the food, which has gained three AA rosettes and prompts lunch guests to heap praise in the visitors' book. Stay the night and you can wake up to a gastronomic breakfast including dry-cured Welsh bacon, pork sausages and the local seaweed delicacy, laver bread.

In the evening, much is made of local produce including lamb, beef, venison and cheese in the modern Welsh dinner menu, with many of the vegetables and fruit coming from the hotel's walled garden. The kitchen also makes its own

biscuits, bread, marmalade and chutney. And there's an extensive wine list (the owners run their own retail wine business).

The cosy bar with its log fire and a smart lounge holding an ornate fireplace, fresh flowers, and lots of magazines, make the perfect venues for before- and after-dinner drinks. If it's warm, there are doors leading on to the terrace, which overlooks the manicured lawns and mature woodland dotted with modern sculptures. The 24-acre estate has a trout stream and a lake inhabited by a family of friendly ducks.

As well as taking a walk in the extensive grounds or playing croquet on the lawn, you can treat yourself to some beauty therapy in the hotel's treatment room; choose from aromatherapy, Swedish massage, Indian head massage, reflexology and reiki healing.

After being pampered, retire to one of eight

Paul Davies or Andrew Hetherington
Reynoldston, Gower, Swansea, West Glamorgan,
Wales SA3 1BS
01792 390139, www.fairyhill.net

Sleeps: 16 in eight doubles, all of which are ensuite. There are three standard, three principal and two deluxe rooms.

Dining: dining room seats up to 40 at five round tables. Catered on a half-board basis. Meals might include slow-cooked spiced belly pork with a tartlet of spiced apple chutney, Welsh beef, and a banana crème brulée. Lunch from £14.95.

Other facilities: treatment room where guests can enjoy massages, reflexology and reiki healing. There is also a croquet lawn.

Children: over eight welcome.

Wedding licence: no but receptions for up to 40.

Local attractions/things to do: walking, cycling and surfing at Llangennith and Rhossili, as well as golf on the Gower Peninsula – there are three courses within 25 minutes' drive. The Brecon Beacons National Park – great for outdoor pursuits such as mountain biking and walking – is about an hour's drive.

Transport: trains from London Paddington to Swansea, which is 25 minutes' drive away, take about three hours. London is about three and a half hours' drive.

Price: half board from £2,450 per night for 16 (including £500 for exclusive use) between Sunday and Thursday or £2,650 for Fridays and Saturdays. Mid-week winter deals may be available.

spacious bedrooms, each of which has a TV, DVD and CD player as well as Penhaligon toiletries in the modern white bathrooms.

However, the decor in a few of the bedrooms may not be to everyone's taste with shiny bedspreads and matching headboards in greens and yellows. One of the two deluxe rooms has a much more contemporary feel, decorated in creams and beiges.

If you do want to explore a little further than the hotel grounds, you're in the perfect place. The Gower Peninsula is in an Area of Outstanding Natural Beauty with rugged coastline and long, sandy beaches that make it a surfer's and walker's paradise. Rhossili, with its three-mile stretch of sand, is only a few miles down the road and there are three golf courses within 25 minutes' drive. One is Machynys, where Fairyhill's owners have opened a bar and brasserie – just in case you fancy some more fine fare.

The Samling, Cumbria

House parties have been the lifeblood of The Samling since it opened under the current ownership in 1999 on a hill overlooking Lake Windermere. Originally wholly dedicated to group bookings, this 11-room hotel now accepts individual guests as well, but priority is still given to those who want to take over the whole property – individuals can't book any further ahead than three months, which means there's plenty of availability for groups.

It's no surprise, then, to find that The Samling's machinery is incredibly well oiled when it comes to throwing a good house party. If you want organised activities, a team of efficient staff

can lay on anything from fly-fishing lessons and a casino evening to a champagne cruise on the lake followed by fireworks. Send the children on a supervised outdoor treasure hunt while you enjoy a beauty treatment in your room or a quiet read in the tartan-checked library.

Or if you prefer to do your own thing, head out of the front door on a ramble through some of Britain's best scenery, starting in the hotel's own 67 acres of woodland, fields and landscaped gardens.

The Samling prides itself on being different from the typical country-house hotel with all the associated chintz and snootiness. Instead, the

Expect top-class service and fine food when you stay at this chic all-inclusive country hotel that was created with house parties in mind

decor is funky and metropolitan, with stylish sofas made for sprawling on, a minimalist wood-floored dining room and plenty of unfussy richly coloured textiles.

It's all very easy going, with no check-in desks or bars. Drinks materialise by your side in the light-filled wood-panelled drawing room as you sink into a chair around the fire – a superb place for afternoon tea – while a delicious array of canapés will appear in the evening. An all-inclusive pricing system also means you don't need to worry about signing for every cup of tea or gin and tonic (and you're not just confined to house wine – there's a range of 20 reds and 20 whites).

Don't be put off by the initial price to take over The Samling; it actually works out as very good value for money, particularly as the restaurant is Michelin starred. It certainly deserves the accolade – expect well-presented dishes with a strong French bias, incorporating foie gras, pigeon and St-Jacques. A typical evening menu might start with seared foie gras with ceps followed by loin of venison with black pudding ravioli. Round it all off with red-wine ice cream.

After such magnificent fare, it's good to be able to spoil yourself and linger in bed for breakfast the next day, which can be anything from a cuppa to

the full English fry up with the very best local produce (the Cumbrian sausages and bacon are particularly good).

The rooms aren't the type you'd want to leave in a hurry, anyway – all are beautifully furnished, often featuring stone walls and timber and with luxurious fabrics, comfortable beds and their own seating areas.

You'll want to dawdle in the bathrooms too, with two-person baths, walk-in showers (one an antique rainshower bath reputed to have belonged to Winston Churchill), candles and lots of Molton Brown toiletries.

No wonder celebs feel spoiled here, with Posh and Becks and Tom Cruise having visited.

Cruise stayed in the main house, where Wordsworth went to pay his rent, and where five of the rooms are located; the others are in the estate's cottages.

All but two of the rooms have lake views, and what views they are, with the morning mist rolling back over the water to reveal a whole artist's palette of blues. Fall asleep at night with the blinds up in your room and when you wake you'll be greeted by a scene straight out of a postcard.

But the best way to appreciate the vista is from the hot tub in the gardens, sinking back into the water as the sun sets, then wallowing by candlelight under the night sky.

THE SAMLING *at a glance*

Nigel Parkin, general manager
Ambleside Road, Windermere, Cumbria LA23 1HR
015394 31922, www.thesamling.com

Sleeps: 22 in 11 rooms (nine doubles, two double/twins), all ensuite and all but two with lake views. Five are in the main house with the rest in nearby cottages.

Dining: 22 around one long table in the dining room. Full board, with tea and all drinks and alcohol included. A typical dinner might include seared foie gras with ceps, loin of venison with black pudding ravioli, and red wine ice cream.

Other facilities: hot tub with view over Lake Windermere, croquet, and in-room beauty therapist.

Children: highchairs, cots, early evening meals. Children's activities, such as a treasure hunt in the grounds, can be arranged.

Wedding licence: for up to 50 in the barn with a disco and dancing, 35 in the drawing room or dining room. Larger numbers for receptions can be accommodated in a marquee in the grounds.

Local attractions/things to do: walking, sailing, fishing and all the other activities associated with the Lake District. Other pursuits such as clay-pigeon shooting, mountain biking, quad biking, horse riding, and ballooning can be arranged.

Transport: trains from London Euston to Windermere, less than 10 minutes' drive away, take almost four hours. Car journeys take four and a half hours.

Price: £5,500 per night for the property plus VAT, including all meals (with afternoon tea) and drinks within reason. Minimum hire of two nights if one is a Saturday.

Langar Hall, Nottinghamshire

As the childhood residence of charismatic owner/manager Imogen Skirving,

this idyllic rural retreat still has the feel of a home rather than a hotel

Fashion designer Sir Paul Smith liked the view from his bedroom at Langar so much that he recreated it pictorially in his shop in Hong Kong. That's no surprise when you see the view, down the sloping lawn through the trees to medieval fish ponds stocked with carp, a rural retreat in the Vale of Belvoir, midway between Nottingham and Grantham.

Nottingham-born Sir Paul is a regular visitor at Langar, where the bar is named after him and a collection of his photographs adorn the walls. He's not the only celeb to have discovered the charms of this country-house hotel, which has hosted musician Jools Holland, Coronation Street actress Sarah Lancashire (who got married here) and the late romantic novelist, Barbara Cartland, who has a bedroom named after her (it's pink, but not so kitsch as to be decked out in reams of flowing pink satin, with her books stacked high on the dresser).

Don't think celebrities visit Langar because it's posh; the attraction is not a Regency elegance but the home-from-home feel given to the hall by its charismatic owner, Imogen Skirving, who grew up here. Built in 1837 on the site of a much more elaborate building with colonnaded portico, the Langar of today has an unassuming mustard-coloured exterior that gives it an almost rustic look.

Although there's a front desk and a friendly team of Eastern European staff, Langar isn't really like a hotel at all, with dust on the top of the grandfather clock in the hall and slightly worn carpets (although they are due to be replaced). As well as an oil painting of a younger Imogen at the top of the stairs, her father's dressing room is now the sitting room of a suite, and the house's old dresser is still used to hold linen.

The pillared dining room was created from the old entrance hall. Here, you can sit down to English dishes of local produce including stilton from the Vale of Belvoir, homegrown vegetables and homemade ice cream.

The food is popular with the locals, which means if you want to take over Langar exclusively, including the restaurant, the price is quite steep, at more than £8,000 for two nights. You can cut this in half by taking a private dining room – the Indian Room with its swirly wallpaper and wooden floor – along the flagstone corridor, but that means you'll also have to share the public rooms, including a new conservatory, which can be reached via the white drawing room, and the darkly furnished library with its heraldic engravings.

Either way, you get to take over every one of Langar's nine bedrooms, all highly individualistic and decorated by Imogen (with a little help from Sir Paul). Some are quite chintzy, with four-posters or half-testers, and there's also a chalet in the garden for love birds. Perhaps the most romantic room is Bohemia, formerly the studio where Imogen's father painted. With exposed beams in the ceiling and walls, it now holds an enormous bed, the old beams forming part of its four posts. In the adjacent bathroom, love phrases are stencilled on the wall and you can look up from the bath through the skylight to the tower of an 11th-century church (you can also hear the bells) next door.

The church is so close that its graveyard merges into Langar's garden, leading to much talk of ghosts. The spirit of Imogen's father is reported to have appeared in the house on several occasions, and there was a lot of talk of paranormal activity after some building work revealed a mass grave of people thought to have been killed in the English Civil War. There's nothing to worry about now, though – the place has been blessed and the ghosts apparently put to rest.

LANGAR HALL
at a glance

Pascal Bouyssounouse, party organiser
Langar, Nottinghamshire NG13 9HG
01949 860559, www.langarhall.co.uk

Sleeps: 20 in ten rooms (six doubles, four double/twins) all ensuite). One suite has a sofa bed.

Dining: 30 at individual tables, 50 banqueting style in the main dining room and 22 in the Indian Room. Catered on a half-board basis. Three-course meals might include Timbale of Dorset crab, saddle of Langar park lamb with rosemary and garlic and chocolate tartlet with raspberries and lavender ice.

Other facilities: croquet and private fishing for carp.

Children: cots, highchairs and toys. A play area includes a trampoline, swings and slide. Ponds in the garden.

Wedding licence: for 30 in the Indian Room, 45 in the dining room and up to 150 in a marquee on the lawn. Facility fee including a meal for 40 guests and exclusive use of the house on weekdays and Sundays costs £6,000-£6,500. Extra guests £45pp, house wine from £14.50.

Local attractions/things to do: Belvoir Castle, the National Trust's Belton House and Nottingham are all nearby. Within 40 minutes' drive are Chatsworth and the Peak District National Park, the Elizabethan Burghley House, NT's Calke Abbey and Lincoln Cathedral. There is also parachuting, go-karting and golf.

Transport: trains from London King's Cross take 75 minutes to Grantham, which is about 12 miles from Langar. The drive to London takes two and a half hours.

Price: £8,950 for 20 people staying on a Friday and Saturday night, including breakfast and two dinners. Drinks are extra at hotel rates. This price decreases to £4,000 for the weekend if guests eat in the private dining room and have exclusive use of the study but the main restaurant is open to the public.

Note: dogs on lead by arrangement.

Northcote Manor, Lancashire

People flock to this Victorian red-brick house for its Michelin-starred

restaurant which specialises in regional dishes with a modern twist

If food is your thing, you can't do much better than take over a hotel with a one-Michelin star restaurant for that special meal. In the heart of Lancashire, this one specialises in regional dishes, often with an interesting twist – you may well find Southport shrimp organic porridge or even Lancashire cheese ice cream on the menu.

Chef and co-owner Nigel Haworth, who trained in Switzerland and worked at Gleneagles, wanted to come back to his roots and create regional dishes with a modern flavour using lots of fish, local game and organic salad and herbs from the garden. Thus you'll find signature dishes such as black pudding with pink trout and Lancashire hotpot cooked in the traditional way – Northcote is one of the only Michelin-starred restaurants in Great Britain with an Aga.

While Nigel looks after the kitchen, co-owner Craig Bancroft is responsible for the extensive wine list and front-of-house operations, making sure that everything runs smoothly. He takes great pride in getting things right, particularly for house parties. 'I'll go to London to meet people so they can be sure they get exactly what they want,' he says.

Craig and Nigel call this a restaurant with rooms but the red-brick Victorian manor house nine miles from the M6 is a lot more than that. It feels like a cross between a country-house hotel with its well-padded chairs, open fires and a sprinkling of antiques, and a gentleman's club, complete with leather Chesterfields, oak panelling and stained glass. As well as a welcoming drawing room, there's also a bright, modern room called the Terrace where weddings are held.

The restaurant is very contemporary, decorated in pastels with an array of colourful chairs and modern art hanging on the walls.

Craig Bancroft
Northcote Road, Langho, Blackburn,
Lancashire BB6 8BE
01254 240555, www.northcotemanor.com

Sleeps: 28 in 14 ensuite rooms (nine doubles, five double/twins).

Dining: up to 90 people in the dining room at individual tables. If only 28 are eating, a single table is possible. Half board – a seven-course meal might include a plate of tiny Lancashire delicacies including black pudding, pan seared foie gras with slow-cooked pork belly, garden leek and potato soup, roast wild sea bass with asparagus and chive fondue, cornfed duckling with duck straws, queen of pudding soufflé with lemon and crème fraiche ice cream plus a selection of cheeses.

Other facilities: beauty therapy can be arranged in the rooms.

Wedding licence: for up to 40 guests in the main dining room or Terrace room. No facility fee for exclusive use.

Children: children's menu, highchairs and extra beds.

Local attractions/things to do: clay-pigeon shooting, golf, walking in the Trough of Bowland, premiership football clubs at Bolton and Blackburn. Blackpool and Manchester, the Lake District and Yorkshire Dales are within an hour's drive.

Transport: trains take almost three hours from London Euston to Preston, which is 19 miles from Northcote Manor. By car, the journey from London takes almost four hours. Helicopter landing pad in grounds.

Price: from £5,500 for the hotel per night on a Sunday to £8,500 on a Saturday, based on guests arriving at 2pm, afternoon tea, champagne reception with canapés, seven-course dinner with unlimited alcohol and soft drinks, and breakfast the following morning before leaving at 11.30am. Extra dinner guests pay £70pp.

There's also plenty of space for dancing in this pleasant room.

A striking oak staircase leads to the upstairs bedrooms, one with a four-poster and all a good size with equally spacious bathrooms. All of the bedrooms – some on the ground floor – are undergoing refurbishment to give them a more modern take on the country-house look.

There aren't a massive list of attractions on your doorstep, though if you whiz off in the car, you can be in the Lake District, Yorkshire Dales or Blackpool and Manchester within an hour.

Eating is what it's all about here, and you can do that to your heart's content. Should you tire of Michelin-starred fare and yearn for something simpler, Northcote Manor has the answer to that too. Stroll down the road to the local pub, The Three Fishes, which the dynamic duo Craig and Nigel also own.

White Moss House, Cumbria

Stay in the heart of Wordsworth country amid spectacular scenery at this

small and friendly hotel that has a reputation for its gastronomic fare

People come to this tiny hotel at the northern end of Rydal Water between Grasmere and Windermere not only for its superb location, but also for its food.

Although owners Sue and Peter Dixon have no formal training in the restaurant business, they have built up quite a reputation for their gastronomy. Using locally sourced, organic food whenever possible, Peter, a Master Chef of Great Britain, serves up modern British fare in the low-ceilinged dining room with its large stone fireplace and polished tables.

You get the full five courses here, always finishing with a choice of desserts including a traditional English pudding followed by a selection of British cheeses. You might find yourself eating your way through leek and lovage soup, soufflé of haddock and halibut, guinea fowl braised in dry cider and an old-fashioned pudding before moving on to tackle the cheeses. At breakfast the next day, you'll get the full works too, with White Moss' own Cumbrian cooked breakfast, including black pudding and vine tomatoes, or fresh kipper that's been locally smoked.

After devouring such wonderful fare you'll find there are plenty of opportunities for burning off those extra calories. Step out of the front door and you're in the middle of some great walking country with stunning views. 'What we love about it here is that we can go out of the front door and choose any one of ten different directions to walk in,' says Peter.

This is real Wordsworth country, with Dove Cottage, where the poet lived, a mile's walk away at Grasmere, and his later home, Rydal Mount, just half a mile south along the lake.

The poet was a frequent visitor to White Moss House, which at that time consisted of three separate cottages built for quarry workers in 1730. Wordsworth bought the properties for his son, and shortly afterwards, they were knocked into one. Then the main house was added in the second half of the 19th century before the poet's family sold it in the 1930s.

The Dixons know that the sitting room with its large window-seat area and lots of easy chairs was added in 1860, because they discovered the date etched into the plaster when they peeled back several generations of wallpaper during redecoration.

The decor very much reflects the different ages of the house – while the older part is all oak panelling and grandfather clocks, the Victorian side is more floral with patterned carpets.

The floral theme continues upstairs in some of the bedrooms, added to with perhaps a Victorian bed with queen canopy and the odd frilled dressing table.

There's a slight disadvantage in that the ensuite bathrooms are tiny, along with two of the five bedrooms. But that doesn't seem to matter when you're confronted with sweeping views of the rolling Cumbrian hills from practically every window.

The view is better still from the rooms at Brockstone, a cottage just up the hill that is reached by crossing White Moss's pretty garden, followed by a ten-minute walk up a steep footpath by the side of a dry stone wall (you can also get there by road).

The cottage, which has its own kitchen, is more simply decorated than the hotel, but there is a whirlpool bath to soak weary limbs after a hard day's walking. After wallowing in it, sit on the small patio and listen to the stream burbling down the hillside as you gaze out across Rydal Water to the sublime views of Loughrigg Terrace and the Langdales.

WHITE MOSS HOUSE
at a glance

Sue and Peter Dixon
Rydal Water, Grasmere, Cumbria LA22 9SE
015394 35295, www.whitemoss.com

Sleeps: 14. Up to ten in the house in five rooms (two doubles, three double/twins, all ensuite), and four in the cottage a short walk up the hill (one twin room, one four poster).

Dining: 12-18 at either individual tables or one large one. Catered on a half-board basis. A typical five-course meal might include leek and lovage soup, soufflé of haddock and halibut, guinea fowl braised in dry cider, an old-fashioned dessert such as Guardsman's Pudding, and cheese. Alcohol at restaurant rates.

Other facilities: the hotel has membership of a gym and pool about ten minutes' drive away.

Children: travel cots but no highchairs. There is a stream at Brockstone Cottage.

Wedding licence: no

Local attractions/things to do: all the outdoor activities of the Lake District are on the doorstep, from walking to sailing. Visit Wordsworth's house at Grasmere, a 20-minute walk away, as well as his later home Rydal Mount, only a few minutes' walk along the lake. Beatrix Potter's home is also nearby.

Transport: trains from London Euston to Windermere, some 20 minutes from the hotel, take almost four hours. The same journey by car takes about four and a half hours.

Price: small rooms and cottage from £77pp per night, large rooms from £94pp, half board. Minimum stay two nights.

Manor Houses & Rectories

The Old Rectory, Dorset

There's an eclectic mix of modern art, antiques and original features in this spacious Georgian vicarage set in the pretty village of Symondsbury

There's a Bohemian feel to this Georgian rectory that's seen a whole host of artists, musicians and writers from Thomas Hardy to Mick Jagger grace its elegantly proportioned rooms.

Much of the modern artwork from its former days as a residential arts school in the 1980s still adorns the walls while the library is crammed with specialist art books. A sculptor, now also the on-site handyman, lives in the summerhouse and his work is dotted around the grounds.

While not an artist herself, owner Ann Barnes says her house is her art. She's certainly done a good job on it, preserving lots of original features such as flagstone floors, fireplaces, baize door coverings and a stunning oak staircase spanning three floors. She's also created an eclectic interior using pieces collected from her travels – an antique French wooden boat bed, Central Asian rugs and camel-bone mirrors from Morocco. Four

of the eleven bedrooms have super king-size sleigh beds and unusual bedside tables made from yew, which were crafted by Ann's father.

There's no shortage of space for these treasures: this is one of the largest rectories in England, doubling in size in 1810 with the addition of two wings, one of which was the servants' quarters where Ann lives today.

Much more prosperous than today's average clergyman, the original rector had plenty of servants, carriages and a fine cellar. He also had some great rooms for entertaining his guests: a dining room with crystal chandeliers and ornate fireplace and a drawing room, now home to a grand piano and lots of sofas. Another piano sits in the library next to a quarter-size billiard table.

The kitchen – the original butler's pantry – is small but well equipped with lots of mod cons. And if you want more informal dining, a separate

Ann Barnes
Symondsbury, Bridport, Dorset DT6 6HF
01308 422575, www.symondsbury.biz

Sleeps: 22 adults plus three children in 11 rooms (eight doubles and three twins). Two bathrooms and two shower rooms.

Dining: table seats up to 24. Self catering but a local caterer specialising in organic local produce can prepare anything from a Mediterranean buffet from £12pp to a five-course meal with canapés and champagne from £35pp.

Other facilities: library with quarter-size billiard table and croquet.

Children: no cots, two highchairs.

Wedding licence: no but receptions for up to 50.

Local attractions/things to do: sandy beaches at Lyme Regis and West Bay, small coves at Eype and Chideock – all within 15 minutes' drive. Bridport, a few miles away, has street markets on Wednesdays and Saturdays, and Thomas Hardy's Dorchester is 25 minutes away. Horse riding, sailing, diving, fishing, fossil hunting, hang gliding, walking and clay-pigeon shooting are all available nearby.

Transport: trains from London Waterloo to Dorchester, about 25 minutes' drive away, take two and a half hours. London is approximately three hours by car.

Price: two or three-night self-catering weekends (based on 18 people) cost £95pp year round. Week-long breaks cost from £150pp, except school holidays, which are from £170pp per week and Christmas and New Year weeks (min 20 people) from £220pp. The rectory can be hired for a minimum of 14/18/20 people depending on the time of year.

Note: live music and DJs can be arranged. No loud music after midnight, no fireworks, no pets.

breakfast room seats 16 along a wooden table.

You don't have to eat your own culinary creations. A great local caterer (ex Moro and The River Café) specialising in organic local produce can organise anything from a Mediterranean buffet to a four-course gastronomic feast. If the weather's fine, have pre-dinner drinks on the south-facing verandah while watching fellow house guests play croquet on the lawn. It's all terribly English, but then so is the village of Symondsbury, where even the pub is thatched.

If there is a downside to the Old Rectory, it's the lack of ensuite facilities, with just four shower and bathrooms for a group of 22. One of these bathrooms has a roll-top bath in the middle of the room so bathers can admire the views of local landmark Colmer's Hill. As you'd expect from a former art school, the same scene is captured in a charcoal drawing on the wall.

Goddards, Surrey

Architecture buffs will love this early example of Edwin Lutyens' work,

which comes with an impressive dining hall as well as a bowling alley

Forgive the pun, but it's easy to be bowled over by this architecturally stunning house designed by Edwin Lutyens that comes complete with its own 100-year-old skittle alley.

This unusual feature was commissioned by Frederick Mirrielees, a wealthy businessman who wanted to build a holiday home for gentlewomen of 'reduced means', and who regarded skittles as a suitable pastime for such ladies. After the house was built, Lutyens returned to enjoy a game with three nurses and two old governesses all of whom, he said, loved the house and 'invariably weep when they leave it'.

Today the lucky holidaymakers who get to stay in this characterful house, now on lease to The Landmark Trust from the Lutyens Trust, can still use the original heavy wooden balls for a quick game or full-blown tournament.

Regarded as one of Lutyens' most important early works, Goddards was designed in his traditional Surrey style using local materials such as stone, brick and oak. It has distinctive tall

chimneys made from layers of thin bricks, which are also used to form the mullions, windowsills and fireplaces in the bedrooms.

Everywhere you look in this house, you discover more of Lutyens' great attention to detail, from the decorative ironwork locks to the horse bells that called the ladies to their meals. A date stone engraved with MCM above the front door was the kind of play on words Lutyens loved. It marked the date the building was finished – 1900 – but was also the initials of Mirrielees' daughter.

Lutyens' first symmetrical building, the house had two cottages linked by an upper and lower common room where the ladies could socialise and eat together. The lower common room is now an impressive dining hall where the working fireplace with its brick arches, stone corbelling and keystone is the focal point of the room. Oil paintings of the architect's family, mostly the work of his father, Charles, line one wall and there's a solid oak dining table.

Landmark Trust buildings aren't renowned for

GODDARDS *at a glance*

Bookable through The Landmark Trust
Abinger, Dorking, Surrey RH5 6JH
01628 825925, www.landmarktrust.org.uk

Sleeps: 12 in eight rooms (one double with ensuite bathroom, three twins and four singles). One shower room and two other bathrooms.

Dining: table comfortably seats 12. Self catering but local catering can be arranged – anything from cold and hot buffets and barbecues to elaborate four-course dinners. Prices from £45pp for a three-course meal including staff but excluding drinks.

Other facilities: skittle alley, croquet, deckchairs.

Children: cots but no highchairs. There is a large enclosed garden.

Wedding licence: no. Receptions are not allowed.

Local attractions/things to do: Goddards is set in great walking country and is near pretty villages such as Shere and Coldharbour, the highest village in Surrey. London is 50 minutes by train from Dorking, five miles away. The cathedral city of Guildford with good shops is closer, at 20 minutes' drive away.

Transport: trains from London Waterloo take about 50 minutes to Dorking, which is five miles away. London is about one hour's drive away.

Price: from £1,386 for the whole property for a three-night self-catering weekend and £1,972 for a week.

Note: dogs, smoking and single-sex groups allowed. Part of the ground floor and the garden are open to the public by appointment only on Wednesday afternoons, from the Wednesday after Easter to the last Wednesday in October.

their mod cons – none of them have TVs or videos – but Goddards' kitchen is surprisingly well equipped with two dishwashers, a modern six-hob double oven and two fridges and a freezer.

That's more than enough to cater for the 12 people the house sleeps. The bedrooms are simple but classic, and one even has an ensuite bathroom with a toilet on a plinth allowing great views of the gardens.

The pretty courtyard garden was planted by Gertrude Jekyll. There are also lawns ideal for croquet and orchards bursting with rhododendrons and lilac trees.

You might, though, have a problem with passers by coming through the gardens; this architectural stunner of a house attracts lots of interest, and some of the curious walk up to the front door and ask for an impromptu tour. There's no obligation to show them around; and you can tell them to return on Wednesday afternoons between Easter and October, when the gardens and part of the ground floor are open to the public.

The Old Rectory, Suffolk

Escape to the Suffolk coast where the fresh sea air will stir up an appetite for the local produce served up in this beautifully furnished Georgian property

This elegant Georgian house oozes warmth and charm, helped by the fact that Michael and Sally Ball used to be in the hotel business and love hosting house parties.

Sally also has a flair for interior design, evident in the stylish drawing room with its plush sofas, silk cushions, ornate carved wooden fireplace, piano and a smattering of smart coffee-table books. Even the downstairs cloakroom with its Cath Kidston wallpaper has not been overlooked, while the hallway is decorated with Far Eastern artefacts collected when the couple lived in Hong Kong.

In the drawing room, help yourself to a drink from the honesty bar and sink into a sofa, tinkle the ivories or just admire the views of the gardens from the south-facing picture windows.

The dining room is equally welcoming with its wooden floors, rugs, plum silk curtains and an open fireplace that creates a cosy atmosphere on winter evenings. In summer the lofty, double-height conservatory overlooking the lawns and orchards makes the perfect setting for a meal.

Wherever you eat, you'll find that much is made of local, seasonal produce in the carefully crafted menus (Sally includes cooking in her repertoire). In summer tuck into the Suffolk Platter: locally smoked salmon and trout, Peasenhall ham and pickles; all laid out on a big wooden board and accompanied by fresh breads

and homemade soup. Dinner might feature starters such as butternut squash soup with coriander, Oriental duck salad or locally smoked salmon. This could be followed by rack of lamb or fillet of beef with seasonal vegetables, rounded off with chocolate mousse tart or tiramasu cheesecake. Wash it all down with one of 36 carefully selected wines from the well-stocked cellar.

Breakfast is an equally gastronomic affair. Try the award-winning local sausages along with eggs from neighbouring farms; homemade quince, plum jams and marmalade; yoghurts and organic muesli.

The eight ensuite bedrooms are mostly country-house style with one contemporary room: very Kelly Hoppen with its taupes and chocolate browns complemented by Oriental furniture and art. Another has a Victorian fireplace and gargantuan cast-iron, roll-top bath. Two of the double rooms, which are located in the grounds in a small cottage and the Coach House, also come with sofa beds, making them ideal for

families. There's also a more secluded, light-filled room up a private winding staircase in the main house with wonderful views over the acres of tranquil gardens.

There's plenty to do here. The Balls host numerous pheasant and partridge shooting parties (where lots of red meat, claret and port are consumed) and the odd hen party where they can arrange for a local beauty therapist to come and pamper you.

Head out for the day and you can be on the Suffolk coast, with lots of coastal and woodland walks, within minutes. Also nearby is the Anglo-Saxon royal cemetery with its low grassy burial mounds at Sutton Hoo, and Snape Maltings, a collection of granaries and malthouses converted into galleries, restaurants and a concert hall beside the River Alde.

You don't have to go to a concert there to enjoy one, though. Back at the rectory, entertainment from a harpist to a live band can be organised. Some house-party guests have even been known to bring their own guitars.

THE OLD RECTORY
at a glance

Sally and Michael Ball
Campsea Ashe, Woodbridge, Suffolk IP13 OPU
01728 746524, www.theoldrectorysuffolk.com

Sleeps: 16 plus up to six children on sofa beds in eight ensuite rooms (six doubles and two double/twins). One double is rather small and probably best as a single.

Dining: 26 in the dining room around one table, 40 in the conservatory and 140 in a marquee in the garden. Catered on a B&B basis but dinner can be arranged. Three-course menus from £24pp might include butternut squash soup with coriander, rack of lamb and chocolate mousse tart. Wine from £13 a bottle.

Other facilities: table tennis, croquet, trampoline and swing.

Children: one highchair and two cots. High tea available.

Wedding licence: no but receptions for up to 40 in the house and up to 140 in a marquee in the garden. No facility fee.

Local attractions/things to do: the Suffolk coast with the seaside towns of Southwold and Aldeburgh is minutes away. So too is Snape Maltings, a collection of granaries and malthouses converted into shops, galleries and restaurants, as well as the Anglo-Saxon burial ground of Sutton Hoo. Constable country is within an easy drive. Shooting (pheasant and partridge) and golf.

Transport: Wickham Market station is a few minutes' walk: trains to Ipswich take about 25 minutes and then an hour to London Liverpool Street. One hour from the M25.

Price: doubles from £95 per room including breakfast.

Note: entertainment can be arranged including a harpist, kids' entertainer and live bands. Dogs allowed in Garden Cottage and Coach House. No smoking.

Gerbestone Manor, Somerset

Go back in history to a time with priests' holes, timbered ceilings and

heavy wooden furniture but still enjoy all the modern comforts

It's easy to imagine King Henry VIII sitting down to dinner in the oak-panelled dining room here, casting a gnawed chicken leg into the huge fireplace. Although Gerbestone dates back well before Henry's time to the 13th century, with numerous additions after he died, it's very much in the Tudor style, with lots of timbered ceilings, heavy wooden doors and even a priest's hole.

What makes Gerbestone even more special is that it's one of the few properties with this much character to be available for self-catering rental. In the middle of the rolling Somerset countryside, it gives you the opportunity to play at being lord or lady of your very own manor.

Go the whole hog and book a medieval banquet, a three-course meal for a special occasion, or just order some fresh croissants to be delivered for breakfast – all kinds of catering can be arranged.

Or concoct something for yourself in the spacious, well-equipped kitchen with an Aga, lots of fridge space (there's even a drinks fridge), plus a herb garden and barbecue area just outside the back door.

It's a far cry from the original kitchen, in what is now the main sitting room, where meat was cooked on a spit in the enormous fireplace, now home to a wood-burning stove. Today the room has more of a shabby-chic feel with a timbered ceiling, old sofas and bookcases. Next door is a smaller sitting room which doubles as a TV room with videos, games and books, and a simply decorated twin bedroom ideal for those with limited mobility, although it's not ensuite.

Most of the bedrooms are on the first floor, up a wooden staircase and along a timbered hallway. Two are very special, with oodles of space and impressive four-posters while the rest are smaller

GERBESTONE MANOR
at a glance

Brian Lord
Wellington, Somerset TA21 9PJ
0870 7524501, www.gerbestonemanor.com

Sleeps: 24 in 12 rooms (two four-posters, seven double/twins, one twin, one triple, one single). There are eight bathrooms.

Dining: up to 40 can dine at interlocking or separate tables. Self catering although local caterers can do everything from deliver croissants for breakfast to three-course meals such as roasted pepper tarts with dolce latte, rack of lamb with a herb crust and plum crumble tart from £37.50pp.

Other facilities: heated outdoor swimming pool, sauna, tennis, croquet, coarse and fly fishing on the lake.

Children: cot, highchair, enclosed garden. Note that the grounds hold both a pool and a lake.

Wedding licence: no.

Local attractions/things to do: walking in the Somerset hills. Taunton is about three miles away and it's a 40-minute drive to the coast. Exmoor National Park and Dunster Castle near Minehead are also within an easy drive. Numerous nearby gardens include Bicton Park Botanical Gardens and East Lambrook Manor Gardens.

Transport: trains from London Paddington to Taunton, three miles away, take two hours. Driving takes about three hours from London.

Price: from £2,490 for the manor for two nights' self-catering midweek or three-night weekends from £3,990. Six nights from £5,490. Prices don't change according to the season. An extra 10% is charged for use of the pool in the summer months.

Note: smoking allowed on the ground floor only. No hen or stag parties.

with features such as half-timbered walls or oak floors. More winding stairs lead to an atmospheric attic with beamed eaves and three rooms that are perfect for children.

From the bedrooms, you can appreciate the views over the surrounding countryside – Gerbestone is at the foot of the wooded slopes of the Blackdown Hills that are great for walking (although it's also just three minutes from the M5, so you can sometimes hear the traffic from outside).

Not that you have to venture out of the grounds to get some exercise. The manor has 15 acres of gardens and woodland to explore, including a two-acre lake with a rowing boat that can be used for fishing, a tennis court and a heated swimming pool (you'll have to pay extra to use it). There's even a sauna and a room with gym equipment for the fitness conscious. You certainly didn't get that in Henry VIII's day.

Wortham Manor, Devon

When you're not marvelling at the architectural details of this Tudor house,

you'll find plenty to do in the Dartmoor National Park on your doorstep

Medieval banquets, complete with hired jugglers, minstrels and a pig roasting on a spit, are all the rage among guests who stay at this 15th-century manor house. You can understand why when you see the dining hall's Gothic oak-beamed ceiling, huge stone fireplace and flagstone floor, which make it perfect for this kind of celebration.

There are plenty of other features to admire, from the intricately decorated granite porch to the foliage and fruit carved in the parlour's wood-panelled ceiling, plus a magnificent arch-braced roof in the master bedroom.

Built by an old Devon family, Wortham Manor has remained largely unchanged since the Tudor era, slipping into genteel decay over the centuries. Its architectural importance was only recognised in the 1940s when renovations began under a new owner – one of his first jobs was uncovering the dining hall's original oak-carved ceiling with the help of German prisoners of war.

The manor is now owned by The Landmark Trust, a building preservation charity whose aim is to restore and rent out interesting properties around Britain. The slight downside to this is that one of the aims of restoration is to maintain the character of the buildings, preventing little of the original layouts to be altered. At Wortham, this means guests sleeping in one of the double bedrooms have to walk through a twin room, which might be suitable for families but isn't ideal for groups of friends.

Another feature of Landmark properties is that they are generally simply furnished and renowned for having few mod cons – none have TVs or microwaves, for instance.

Most guests like this but if you really can't cope without a TV, you can always bring your own. One group staying at the manor also came armed with a DVD, video, laptops, four dogs and a cat.

Thankfully you won't have to resort to washing up by hand for 15 people every day during your stay. Landmark makes a point of kitting out its larger properties with dishwashers, freezers and washing machines. Wortham has two of pretty much everything: dishwashers, fridges, toasters, kettles and cafetières – as well as a utility room off the large farmhouse kitchen with a washing machine, tumble dryer and deep freeze. There's also a modern six-hob double gas oven in the farmhouse kitchen, which has a large breakfast table.

There shouldn't be too much of a queue for the shower, either, with two ensuite and three further bathrooms. All are brilliant white, though they don't come with the latest contemporary suites and power showers – you may find the odd archaic hand-held shower attachment that slips on to the taps. But then you probably won't be worrying too much about such fripperies when you're revelling in all this architectural splendour.

Flick through the pages of the well-thumbed visitors' book to find plenty of recommendations for local pubs and restaurants. Near the Devon/Cornwall border on the edge of Dartmoor National Park, the manor also has plenty of activities nearby. The park's spectacular Lydford Gorge, the world-renowned Eden Project, and the fishing village of Padstow as well as Plymouth and Exeter are all within an easy drive.

Kids will love the steam railway at Launceston and there's a great local watersports centre offering everything from sailing to water skiing. The local farmer might even let your children help with the lambing.

At Wortham, the visitors' book also provides clues to help find the much-talked-about secret door. Go on the hunt for this, and you might be lucky enough to discover another one of the manor's architectural treasures.

WORTHAM MANOR
at a glance

Bookable through The Landmark Trust
Lifton, Devon PL16 0ED
01628 825925, www.landmarktrust.org.uk

Sleeps: 15 in eight bedrooms (two doubles, five twins and one single). Two ensuite bathrooms, one shared between two rooms, and two further bathrooms.

Dining: 15 people can be seated around the table along two long benches. Self catering but catering can be arranged. Cold buffets with a selection of desserts start at about £12 a head with three-course meals starting at £15pp plus waiting staff costs.

Other facilities: deckchairs. Note that there are no televisions or microwaves in the manor.

Children: two travel cots but no highchairs. Enclosed garden. Large millpond close by.

Wedding licence: no. No receptions are allowed.

Local attractions/things to do: the manor is on the edge of Dartmoor National Park, with the spectacular Lydford Gorge and opportunities for horse riding and walking. Sailing, windsurfing and canoeing are available at the Roadford Lake Watersports Centre nearby. The Eden Project, fishing village of Padstow and steam railway at Launceston are all within easy reach.

Transport: nearest mainline train station at Exeter St Davids (fastest journey time to London about two hours) or Plymouth (from three hours 15 minutes), both within 50 minutes' drive.

Price: from £1,508 in total for a three-night weekend and £1,879 for a week, self catering.

Note: the number of people staying must not exceed the number advertised. Dogs allowed. Smoking allowed. Single-sex groups accepted.

The Old Rectory, Norfolk

Party to your heart's content in this isolated manor in the middle of the countryside, then discover the area's beaches, pretty villages and pubs

When Anne Boleyn was accused of treason her daughter Elizabeth sought sanctuary in St Mary's church next door to this Georgian manor house, parts of which date back to the 14th century. It's not hard to see why the local Shelton family, who had close connections with the Boleyn family, chose this tiny hamlet in the heart of rural Norfolk to hide the young princess.

Shelton is still a hamlet surrounded by acres of open countryside. It's also perfectly positioned for the best that East Anglia has to offer: long sandy beaches, pretty villages and gastro pubs.

One great advantage of the Old Rectory's remote location is that you can make as much noise as you want, making it ideal for raucous hen and stag parties. It's also a suitably spooky setting for murder-mystery weekends, which are very popular.

Whatever your raison d'être, you'll find a manor house that's used to catering for large groups. You can arrange for a home-cooked meal to be waiting for you on your arrival or a local cordon-bleu cook to prepare a gastronomic feast. And you can pre-order wine and champagne at wholesale prices from a selection chosen by wine expert Liz Morcom.

The dining room off the small farmhouse kitchen is quite snug for 18 people, although the whole group can fit comfortably around a long table, parts of which fold down when it's not in use. The kitchen is rather rustic with a small table and Gothic windows overlooking the gardens. All the other paraphernalia required for catering and housekeeping – a dishwasher, fridge, freezer and washing machine – are housed in the scullery and a half cellar next door.

The two other reception rooms are also quite compact, although there is enough seating for

Kirsty Bourne or Peter Golphin, booking managers
Shelton, Norwich, Norfolk NR15 2SD
01508 530529, www.sheltonrectory.com

Sleeps: 16 (+2) in ten bedrooms (three doubles, one with ensuite shower; five twins, one with 2ft 6" beds most suitable for children; and two singles). Two family bathrooms. Note that rooms and the corridor on the top floor have sloping walls and low ceilings.

Dining: 18 around the table. Self catering but a local cordon-bleu caterer can arrange anything from a buffet to a three-course meal with canapés. Three courses from £18pp. Wine and champagne can be pre-ordered at wholesale prices from the Old Rectory's sister company, Shelton Wines.

Other facilities: mini football and pool tables in one of the twin rooms. Exercise bike. BBQ.

Children: two cots, one highchair. Two unfenced ponds.

Wedding licence: you can get married at the Tudor church next door. Marquees in the garden for up to 500 people (a wedding facility fee will be charged – price on application).

Local attractions/things to do: Norwich is 14 miles away, Norfolk Broads' Waveney Valley is only 15 minutes' drive while the north Norfolk coast is just over an hour. The pretty seaside Suffolk towns of Southwold and Aldeburgh are also around an hour's drive. Children's attractions include Banham Zoo and the Bressingham Steam Museum and Gardens near Diss. Horse riding, golf and hot-air ballooning.

Transport: nearest mainline train station at Norwich or Diss — both 14 miles away (trains to London take two hours). London is about two and a half hours' drive.

Price: from £1,219 for a three-night self-catering break and £1,624 for a week for the whole property.

Note: pets by arrangement but not in bedrooms. No smoking. Single-sex groups welcome.

everyone if you split yourselves between the library and the drawing room with its gilt mirror over the fireplace and smart chairs. Not that it's a problem when kids make up the party; they'll no doubt be playing upstairs in one of the bedrooms that doubles as a games room with table football and mini pool, or exploring the four-acre grounds with two ponds.

One of the best things about this house is the large number of twin rooms that make it ideal for families or a gaggle of close friends, although there are only three bathrooms.

There are some doubles, including a lovely room with an iron four-poster bed and shuttered windows overlooking the gardens. These make the perfect setting for a wedding marquee, especially as the vicar of the Tudor church where the young Elizabeth sought sanctuary now marries people from outside the parish.

Symondsbury Manor, Dorset

There's more than enough space in the enormous living room here to entertain in style - all you need do is fill it with family and friends

The crowning glory of this Tudor manor house in the pretty Dorset village of Symondsbury is a 60ft south-facing living room: the ideal entertaining space for a gaggle of friends or an extended family.

Filled with pieces of contemporary art (owner Peter Hitchin is an art dealer and collector), the spacious room has plenty of light streaming in from skylights in the ceiling. A long dining table dominates one end while at the other is a lounge area with wood-burning stove, sofas and ethnic rugs. On warm summer evenings throw open the doors and spill out on to landscaped gardens, play croquet on the lawn or have a barbecue.

An atmospheric oak-panelled room is also great for sociable gatherings with a huge ornate stone fireplace, grandfather clock and door leading to the garden. If you hire a DJ or live band you can strut your stuff on the wooden floors.

While the living areas in the west wing of this house (Peter and his family live in the other half)

are spot on, this isn't the place to come if you want stylish bedrooms with ensuite bathrooms and power showers. There are only three bathrooms and all of them could do with updating.

That said, some of the bedrooms are lovely and rather quirky, particularly in the range of beds offered, from ornate iron to French antique. There's a gilt four-poster in one room while a large theatrical-looking black bed is the centrepiece in a tiny room off the sitting room. A charming twin room with colourfully painted beds on the ground floor has its own entrance making it ideal for the less mobile.

The remaining bedrooms, however, are a bit bare and probably best suited to children, who aren't so bothered by mismatched duvets and sparse furniture (some opt to sleep on mattresses in the loft area).

That's not the case in the country-style kitchen, which is well-equipped with a four-oven Aga, small table, dishwasher, microwave, large

SYMONDSBURY MANOR
at a glance

Peter Hitchin
Bridport, Dorset DT6 6HD
01308 456288, www.symondsbury.com

Sleeps: 21 in 11 rooms (six doubles, four twins and one single). An extra single bed is in one of the double rooms. Three bathrooms.

Dining: 21 can be seated around the table. Self catering but a local catering company specialising in organic local produce can prepare anything from a Mediterranean buffet from £12pp to a five-course celebratory meal with canapés and champagne from £35pp.

Other facilities: BBQ and croquet.

Children: no cots or highchairs.

Wedding licence: no but receptions for up to 80 in the sitting room. Marquees for up to 100.

Local attractions/things to do: seaside resort of Lyme Regis, twice weekly markets in Bridport and Thomas Hardy's Dorchester are all within 30 minutes' drive. Good beaches at nearby Eype, Chideock, West Bay and Lyme Regis.

Transport: trains from London Waterloo take two and a half hours to Dorchester, which is 25 minutes' drive away. London is approximately three hours' drive.

Price: two-night self-catering weekends £100pp year round and week-long holidays £170pp except July, August, Easter and half-term when the price rises to £210pp. Central heating and electricity cost £50 for a weekend and £90 for a week. The manor can be booked for parties of 16 and above. The 18th-century wood-panelled room, which is suitable for a disco or band, costs an extra £200 to hire.

Note: one dog allowed. Symondsbury Manor can arrange anything from pianists to jazz quartets. No smoking.

fridge, freezer and separate pantry.

If you can't stand cooking and want someone else to do the work, you're in the perfect spot. West Dorset has gained a bit of a foodie reputation, partly due to TV chef Hugh Fearnley-Whittingstall who set up a restaurant – where Peter's son is a chef – in a converted barn at River Cottage HQ, only one and a half miles down the road. He sells his wares at the monthly farmers' market in Bridport where you can pick up lots of other goodies. A local caterer can also serve up anything from a delicious Mediterranean buffet to a four-course meal with champagne and canapés.

As well as being in gastronomic heaven, Symondsbury Manor is less than two miles from the sea and a stone's throw to the pub in this charming village with its yellow-stone thatched cottages and church. It's also close to the Jurassic Coast, a World Heritage Site, and there are some great sandy beaches within an easy drive.

Unusual

Eilean Shona, Argyll

Just as Sir Richard Branson owns an island – Necker in the Caribbean – so does his younger sister, Vanessa. Hers, though, is a paradise island of a different kind, full of rugged, wild beauty; Scotland at its scenic best.

It may be a long way from anywhere (and three hours from the nearest airport) but the views of untamed mountains and glens, lochs and burns on the hour-long car journey from Fort William alone are worth it. Finally, at the entrance to Loch Moidart – the area from where Bonnie Prince Charlie set off on his ill-fated Jacobite uprising in the 18th century – and beyond the ruined castle of Tioram, you glimpse Eilean Shona, midway between the islands of Mull and Skye.

It's then a five-minute boat ride to reach this Neverland of wild coastline, sandy beaches and belt of woodland surmounted by fern and heather-covered hills. At two and a half miles by one and a half, it's a comfortable size – just big enough to get lost in but not so big that you'll be lost for long.

It's no surprise that the views are wonderful from the rooms of Eilean Shona House, built in the late 18th century and considerably enlarged a hundred years later by the celebrated Edinburgh architect Sir Robert Lorimer. When you're not gazing out of the windows, there's plenty to look at inside, where the decoration, along the lines of a contemporary art gallery in some rooms, inspires either violent love or hatred.

The dining room's walls are a mass of different colours, like bright splodges on an artist's palette. Modern Scottish artwork by Callum Colvin and Alan Davie hangs throughout the house. And a sculpture of an African woman made from a fallen tree on the beach stands proudly in an alcove in the neo-Gothic stairwell. The island's trees were also used to create one bed's intricate headboard, while driftwood has been entwined to make the four poles of a tester bed.

That's not to say there aren't traditional elements in the house – leather chairs from the House of Lords in a small nook off the hallway, an enormous period four-poster with cream silk tumbling down from the canopy in the master bedroom, huge old roll-top baths (one is a 1920s Art Deco original, but unfortunately comes with a stain in it) and a baby grand piano in the classic Victorian drawing room, with its low-back tartan sofas.

There's also a wonderful snooker room with wooden floors, a snooker table built at the house in 1897, and a raised sofa by the wall that looks somewhat bizarre but is the perfect height from which to survey the game.

It's an eclectic, shabby-chic style, where you can happily let the children run around without being too concerned about sticky fingers damaging antiques. You don't need to worry about finding enough to entertain them, either, even if there isn't a television. There's a well-

stocked playroom and a rocking horse but most children will find that exploring the island is the best game; they can run wild in safety as long as they don't go down to the pontoon alone, where the water is deep. Managers Marie and Ian Lewis, who live in their own house on Eilean Shona, have two youngsters of their own, plus a collection of quacking ducks, and stress how child friendly the island is – a paradise of fresh air and freedom. When you can lure the children in from the big outdoors at the end of the day, high tea will be waiting for them in the kitchen.

Marie cooks all the food, which is Scottish with a Mediterranean twist, all sourced locally, and where possible, organic. Seafood is obviously good, with the island's own oysters, plus lots of fresh fish and mussels. But so too is the Aberdeen Angus beef, the local lamb and the island's venison. And there's freshly baked bread every day. Bring your own alcohol or order it before you arrive – here, you don't have to worry about paying restaurant prices for booze.

You won't have a problem working up an appetite either. Trek up the 870ft deer-trodden hill for panoramic views over the Hebrides, take an hour-long stroll to the sandy cove on the south west corner of the island (some people choose to get married here), or head off in a canoe with a picnic to one of the neighbouring deserted islands, thought to have been the inspiration behind JM Barrie's play, *Marie Rose*. Swimming and boating fanatics will really be in their element, and there's also plenty of flora and fauna, including a fine collection of azaleas and rhododendrons in the gardens.

With so much to do on the island, many previous guests, who have hired cars intending to explore the south west coast, end up leaving them parked in a layby next to the boat launch for the duration of their stay. And you can't blame them.

As JM Barrie, *Peter Pan*'s author, wrote about Eilean Shona: 'We have mountains and lochs and boats and tennis and billiards, and most of the Western islands of Scotland lying at our feet.' Now that really is paradise.

EILEAN SHONA
at a glance

Marie and Inn Lewis, managers
Acharacle, Argyll, Scotland PH36 4LR
01967 431249, www.eileanshona.com

Sleeps: 19-23 in eight rooms (five doubles, one single, two children's rooms with four bunks each). There are two ensuite bathrooms plus another three bathrooms and a shower room. An additional four people can sleep in the bothy next door, which has one double and one twin sharing a bathroom.

Dining: 22 at one table. The house is rented on a full-board basis. Three-course dinners might include the island's own oysters, roast leg of Eilean Shona venison and chocolate nemesis. Alcohol is BYO.

Other facilities: tennis, snooker, boats – Canadian canoes, rowing boats and motor boats. Note that there is no television.

Children: very child friendly, with lots of freedom and space. Cots, highchairs and children's menu.

Wedding licence: on the beach or in the house. Maximum 22.

Local attractions/things to do: hill walking on the island, fishing from boats or river fishing on the mainland, picnic lunches on other deserted islands, boating, and swimming off the beach.

Transport: the sleeper train from London Euston goes to Fort William, just over an hour away (about £50 in a taxi). Glasgow is about three and a half hours away, Inverness about three hours.

Price: adults £140pp per night, children 2-16 £70 each. Minimum rental £4,000 for three nights, £7,000 for a week, on a full-board basis.

Note: although Eilean Shona is available year round, the weather can be bleak outside the summer.

Three Choirs, Gloucestershire

This has to be the ultimate house-party venue for wine buffs: an English

vineyard complete with its own winery for touring, sampling and enjoying

Sitting on the shaded terrace of this vineyard's restaurant overlooking the undulating 70-acre estate on a warm summer's evening you could almost believe you were in Tuscany, not Gloucestershire.

Growing grapes in this part of Britain is not new – the Romans were doing it 2,000 years ago – but the art was almost lost following the Reformation and the abolition of the monasteries, where most of England's wine was made.

After years in the winemaking doldrums, England is now following other cool-climate countries such as New Zealand in gaining a reputation for producing good-quality vintages. And Three Choirs – the second largest vineyard in Britain – makes some of the best.

Three Choirs' micro-climate of low rainfall, warm temperatures and free-draining sandstone soil produces award-winning wines praised by critics such as Oz Clark and Malcolm Gluck. Sixteen different varieties of white and red wine are produced on the estate, which also has its

own mini brewery, famous for its award-winning Whittington's Cats Whiskers.

The vineyard has developed such a strong reputation for its wine that people come from all over Britain (and indeed the world) to tour the estate and visit the winery. In the height of summer there could be as many as 600 visitors a day, although by 5pm everyone – except you and your party – has to leave.

Named after the annual choral festival which alternates between Gloucester, Hereford and Worcester, Three Choirs is more of a restaurant with rooms than a hotel. The eight bedrooms housed in a modern single-storey block aren't brimming over with character but are furnished to a high standard with king-sized beds, matching pale-wood furniture, flowery curtains, separate seating areas and power showers in the modern bathrooms. What they lack in period detail is more than compensated for by the panoramic views from each room's private patio.

There are more great views from the vine-

THREE CHOIRS *at a glance*

Thomas Shaw, managing director
Newent, Gloucestershire GL18 1LS
01531 890223, www.threechoirs.com

Sleeps: 16 (plus two single beds) in eight ensuite double/twin bedrooms. One room has disabled access.

Dining: catered on a half-board basis. The restaurant seats up to 65. A typical three-course menu might feature twice-baked goat's cheese soufflé with homemade tomato chutney, pan-fried organic lamb with a honey roast parsnip purée followed by sticky pear and ginger pudding with toffee sauce and clotted cream. House wine from £14 a bottle.

Other facilities: wine shop, vineyard tours.

Children: one cot and two highchairs.

Wedding licence: for 20 guests in the Leadon Room, which costs £700 to hire. Wedding receptions for a minimum of 65 people (with obligatory accommodation on Friday and Saturday night if it's a weekend event).

Local attractions/things to do: explore the cathedral cities of Gloucester, Hereford and Worcester. The spa town of Cheltenham and Forest of Dean are within an easy drive.

Transport: trains from London Paddington take just under two hours to Gloucester, ten miles away. The same journey by car takes about two hours.

Price: from £15,000 in total for the weekend (from Friday 5pm to Sunday 10am) including breakfast and dinner but excluding wine. This rate includes exclusive use of the restaurant. Alternatively, you could use the Leadon Room seating up to 20 for private dining and take over all eight rooms for a minimum of two nights. Dinner, bed and breakfast costs £165 per room per night at the weekend.

Note: no smoking.

covered terrace, the perfect place to sip an aperitif before enjoying a gastronomic treat. Much is made of local, seasonal produce in the modern British menu. Three Choirs also makes its own bread and ice cream using local organic milk and cream.

A typical meal might feature smoked salmon with caperberries, followed by fillet of award-winning Aubrey Allen Scottish beef. Accompany your sticky pear and ginger pudding with the estate's Late Harvest dessert wine before retiring to a lounge area for coffee in front of a log fire.

You can hire the services of a Master of Wine to talk you through the different vintages selected for your celebratory meal. The extensive wine list doesn't just feature the estate's own produce; it also includes other small producers throughout the world, which means you'll be able to sample many varieties not available in your local off-licence.

The pleasure doesn't have to stop when you leave – before heading home you can stock up with your newly discovered favourite tipple by the crateload.

Fenton Tower, East Lothian

There's more than a passing resemblance to a posh ski chalet inside this ancient defence tower, which also has some very unusual bathrooms

You get the best of both worlds at Fenton Tower – the romance of staying in a castle without any of the draughty old rooms. The interior of this 16th-century defence tower, which rises starkly from the surrounding lowland on a hillock of wind-whipped land, has been totally overhauled. From ruins, it has undergone an impressive metamorphosis at the hands of a team of architects, engineers and designers tackling the job with gusto and flair.

While the interior maintains the essence of the castle, with spiral staircases, fortified doors and lots of flagstones, it also has all the necessary conveniences of modern life. Think underfloor heating, WiFi internet access, a

communications room with computer, and water pressure that would have left the original owners marvelling.

The result is a harmonious mix of the old and the new. In the double-height Great Hall, for instance, you'll find a beamed ceiling, tapestries and oil paintings on the walls alongside fabric shutters and squishy sofas. Everything goes together – instead of a mix of antiques amassed by different generations of the same family, all of the pieces in Fenton Tower have been carefully sourced and selected to complement each other.

Details are carefully thought through, be they the special bathroom unguents from Greece, or

the game book recording recent shoots. Most of these extras are down to Kiwi manager Wayne Moran, who doubles up as a concierge and can arrange everything from restaurant bookings to golf reservations (there are 100 courses within 30 miles of the castle). Forgotten your clubs? Grab the ones in the hall for guests' use and practise your swing just outside the front door, aiming for the island in the lake.

Care is taken over the food, too, with meals such as scallops in pancetta, fillet of Scottish beef in Burgundy sauce and dark chocolate and rum truffle torte served on crockery bearing hand-painted pictures of the tower. Eat in the vaulted dining room (which comes with its resident suit of armour) seated around the large walnut refectory table on tartan-upholstered chairs. After dinner, head to the library with its flatscreen TV and open bar for a nightcap of whisky before tackling the spiral stairs for bed.

The bedrooms have all the style of luxury ski chalets, with contemporary fabrics and wooden ceilings, and even a four-poster in one and a half-tester in another. You get all the goodies here too – Fenton Tower bathrobes, a choice of sheets and blankets or duvets, and TVs, DVDs and cordless phones in every room.

In all this luxury, the bathrooms don't disappoint. Two of the larger rooms have been fitted out with huge claw-foot baths in which to wallow (one has an original shower unit at one end) while a third holds an enormous copper tub, the perfect size for two.

All the upstairs rooms come with views over the surrounding lowland, although the best panorama can be seen from the very top of the tower. From the double attic bedroom with its garret sitting room, a door leads on to the rooftop with its stunning view of the windswept countryside. It's an area that's definitely worth exploring, with miles of white-sand beaches, two nature reserves close by and Edinburgh just 20 miles up the road. But the best thing about a day of outdoor activities or culture is that you can return to Fenton Tower to play king of this very luxurious castle.

FENTON TOWER
at a glance

Wayne Moran, manager
Kingston, North Berwick, East Lothian,
Scotland EH39 5JH
01620 890089, www.fentontower.com

Sleeps: 12 in seven rooms (two doubles, two double/twins, one twin, one single and an optional extra single in the communications room) all with ensuite bathrooms apart from the communications room.

Dining: 14 around the refectory table, up to 22 with another table. Catered on a B&B basis, with dinner costing about £45 a head for three courses, and wine £11.75-£14.74. The meal might start with scallops in pancetta and move on to fillet of Scottish beef in Burgundy sauce before finishing with dark chocolate and rum truffle torte.

Other facilities: WiFi internet access, computer, area to practise golf.

Children: the spiral staircases are hazardous for younger children and there is a lake in the grounds.

Wedding licence: for up to 22 people seated in the Great Hall, larger numbers in a marquee.

Local attractions/things to do: the Museum of Flight, which houses Concorde, is nearby, and the Pencaitland whisky distillery is 20 minutes away. Golfers can choose from 100 courses within 30 miles of the castle, including Muirfield just three miles away, host of the 2002 British Open. Shooting, clay-pigeon shooting, horse riding and fishing can be arranged. There are plenty of white-sand beaches nearby.

Transport: Edinburgh is 20 miles away. Fenton Tower can arrange car hire or transfers.

Price: from £1,400 per night for the property, including breakfast, or £350 per room.

Polhawn Fort, Cornwall

Cross over the working drawbridge to the granite-faced battlements of this

isolated 19th-century fort, perched on a cliff overlooking Whitsand Bay

The description 'with sea views' fails to do justice to the panorama that greets you from this isolated stronghold on the Rame Peninsula. On a clear day, you can see for miles over the ocean, with a maritime vista from every room, bar the kitchen.

In the 80ft Napoleonic Hall, dominated by four huge, arched and vaulted casements, your eyes are immediately drawn to where the cannon would once have pointed: out of the windows towards the sea. There's an even better view from the windows of the Waterloo bedroom at the far end of the fort. One of two four-poster rooms used as a bridal suite, it also shares the same stunning barrel-vaulted red-brick ceiling as two other bedrooms on the same floor.

Commissioned by Prime Minister Lord Palmerston in the 19th century to help protect Plymouth naval base from the French, the fort quickly became known as one of Palmerston's Follies when no such attack materialised. You'll find lots of reminders of Polhawn's military past.

One of the bedrooms was formerly an ammunition store and has four slit windows that would have been used as the musketry slots. The boiler room used to be a magazine where gunpowder and explosives were stored, and was later used as a prison for errant British soldiers during the early part of the First World War. Their graffiti is still visible today.

It couldn't have been much fun being a soldier here; the risk of explosions from accidental sparks was high during the fort's early years. Every evening one unfortunate 'volunteer' had to don slippers and take off all metal from his uniform before heading off to light the oil lamps in the glass-fronted cupboards in the lower corridors of the fort.

Today's modern conveniences have had to be fitted into the original layout of this grade-II listed building. The two single rooms share an unusual tiny bathroom under the stairs that's so narrow you have to step into the bath from the tap end.

Kathy Deakin, manager
Rame Head, Torpoint, Cornwall PL10 1LL
01752 822864, www.polhawnfort.com

Sleeps: 14 (+6) in eight bedrooms (six ensuite doubles and two singles sharing a bathroom). Six single beds can be moved into the double rooms. An extra ten mattresses are available free of charge, but come with no bedding.

Dining: up to 130 at round or long tables. Self-catering but meals can be organised, including buffets, spit roasts and banquets. Three-course menus start at about £28pp. A typical meal might feature a cheese, smoked bacon and chive tartlet, leg of lamb with red wine jus and individual summer puddings with a berry coulis.

Other facilities: tennis court, croquet, private beach and BBQ.

Children: two travel cots and three highchairs available. Baby gates on main stairs, if needed. Babysitting can be arranged.

Wedding licence: ceremonies in the Napoleonic Hall (up to 130) and the Emperor Suite (maximum 45) next door. Up to 130 for a reception. An extra £650 will be charged for ceremonies/receptions of more than 90.

Local attractions/things to do: walking along the South West Coast Path, horse riding, sailing, fishing and windsurfing. The Eden Project and Dartmoor National Park are both about an hour's drive away.

Transport: Plymouth is a 45-minute drive via ferry. Trains from Plymouth to London Paddington take a minimum of three hours 15 minutes. London is a four-hour drive.

Price: from £2,595 for a mid-week, four-night break, for the whole property on a self-catering basis.

Note: wheelchair access is possible via a ramp from the car park to the fort. Pets allowed.

Some of the other ensuite bathrooms are a bit dated with corner baths in pinks and greens and hand-held showers.

Not surprisingly, the fort's spectacular location makes it popular for weddings. The bride and groom often write their names in the sand in the private cove directly below the fort, which is also used for summer barbecues. The Napoleonic Hall is a great location for a large reception with a log fire and sofas at one end and a large dining and dancing area at the other.

Even if you're not getting married the setting is wonderful. A large expanse of lawn overlooking the cliff edge is perfect for pre-dinner drinks and a spot of croquet. You can also enjoy one of the most scenic games of tennis you've ever had on the tennis court. You don't have to go far to reach the coastal path; it's just behind the fort. In an Area of Outstanding Natural Beauty on the farther reaches of Mount Edgcumbe Country Park, Polhawn's location is hard to beat.

Isle of Eriska, Argyll

Seals and otters swim in the waters surrounding the island, badgers visit

the hotel terrace nightly and you might be lucky and spot a golden eagle

You don't have to worry about getting a ferry or plane to this private island on Scotland's west coast – it's just across a rickety bridge, which could have come straight out of the tale of *The Three Billy Goats Gruff*.

Although there's only a small strip of water separating the 300-acre Isle of Eriska from the mainland, it's a world apart from the fast pace of everyday life. This is a real wildlife haven – grey seals and otters swim in the surrounding waters and badgers visit the hotel terrace nightly for refreshment. If you follow the island trails lined with shaggy Highland cattle, you might even see a golden eagle soaring above.

Naturally, the great outdoors is a big draw on Eriska, where distant islands form a spectacular backdrop to the six-hole golf course, and a multitude of activities such as sailing and fishing are right on the doorstep. You can even go deer stalking on a nearby 30,000-acre private estate. And you don't need to remember all your gear – for hikers, there are rows of wellington boots lined up by the front door.

That's just one of the many extra touches that make you feel special here. Though it's a hotel, it really doesn't feel like one. One of the Buchanan-Smith family, which owns the island, is always on hand and makes a point of greeting arriving guests – if it's not Beppo or his brother, then chances are it's an elderly gentleman who cheerfully introduces himself as 'Mr B, Beppo's father'.

Since buying the island, named after 10th-century Viking invader Erik the Red, in the 1970s, the family has converted the Big House in the centre – a perfect example of Scottish Baronial architecture – into an extremely well-run hotel.

It's all very much like attending a country house party of yesteryear – people still dress for dinner before descending the wooden staircase (complete with tapestries and stags heads) to the atmospheric oak-panelled hall with its open fire and ticking clock. There's a library bar with book-lined walls and leather chairs, a drawing room with sofa after squishy sofa, and a piano room with a sprung floor that's perfect for dancing.

The formal but friendly atmosphere extends into the dining room, where the wood panelling and ornate ceiling-work make a perfect setting for the delicious food, carefully crafted with a heavy French influence (it's well worth saving room for pudding here). Not that you have to eat in the dining room – there's also the conservatory (a good place for children to eat) and a more modern restaurant by the spa, whose verandah overlooks the golf course.

The spa itself is a huge bonus to staying on Eriska, and comes with a 17m ozone pool, sauna, steam room and plenty of treatments on offer. Real aficionados might like to bag one of the nearby spa suites, with their modern decor, plus a conservatory and outdoor Jacuzzi – don't worry about the midges, as there are strategically placed zappers in the gardens.

There's also a two-bedroom cottage in the grounds with a spacious upstairs living area done up in modern furnishings and a small kitchenette.

Otherwise, the bedrooms are all in the Big House and are traditionally decorated with wood-panelled walls and dressing tables, often with fabulous views over the island to the water.

There are lots of thoughtful extras too, such as books and fruit, Molton Brown toiletries and bathrobes, plus a hot-water bottle slipped between the sheets in the cold winter months. Which just goes to show that not all islands are cut off from civilisation.

ISLE OF ERISKA
at a glance

Beppo Buchanan-Smith
Ledaig, Oban, Argyll, Scotland PA37 1SD
01631 720371, www.eriska-hotel.co.uk

Sleeps: 32-42 in 17 rooms (15 double/twins with sofa beds and two singles), all ensuite. There is a two-bedroom cottage in the grounds as well as three one-bedroom spa suites.

Dining: 44 at a series of tables in the dining room. Catered on a half-board basis. Dinner might include a shellfish mousseline with scallops and asparagus, vine tomato and coriander soup, breast of duck, bitter chocolate and kirsch pudding, cheese and coffee with petit fours.

Other facilities: six-hole golf course, 17m indoor heated swimming pool and spa with gym, plus croquet and tennis.

Children: cots, highchairs and children's menu. Children under five cannot use the pool and those aged 5-15 can only use the pool from 10am-5pm.

Wedding licence: for 50 in the conservatory and up to 120 in a marquee in the grounds.

Local attractions/things to do: walking, sailing, fishing and clay-pigeon shooting on the island. Deer stalking on a 30,000-acre private estate can be arranged. Visit the nearby Isles of Mull and Iona and the Oban whisky distillery.

Transport: Glasgow and Edinburgh are both two hours' drive away; transfers can be arranged for about £100. The sleeper train leaves London King's Cross for Fort William, which is 40 minutes from the island.

Price: from £10,000 for the whole property for two nights' half board (minimum of two nights).

The Royal Scotsman, Mid Lothian

They say it's better to travel than arrive; do it in style as you glide through the Scottish highlands in one of Britain's most handsome locomotives

Proof positive that a party can be a moving experience, The Royal Scotsman, a luxurious train that gently rides the rails through some spectacularly scenic areas of Scotland, can be hired privately for up to seven nights. The longer the party, the more of the country you'll see.

Though constantly changing views might be one of the main attractions of a party aboard a rolling train, it's the plush interior that would make The Royal Scotsman a more likely choice of venue than, say, the 12.22 from St Pancras. The train is not, as many assume, powered by steam; its locomotive is diesel and its nine burgundy carriages relatively new, with the exception of the Victory dining car, which dates back to 1945.

The style, however, is distinctly fin de siècle and displays a forensic level of attention to detail – think Titanic, the Raj or Paris in the 1910s, when some people really did travel only by private train, and you will get some idea of what is achieved here. There's miles of marquetry and mahogany-panelled walls, hung with Victorian prints and Venetian glass lightholders. Where there's a brass to be shone, it shines, the flowers are fresh, and old-fashioned ceiling fans whirr quietly, to ward off any hint of stuffiness. It's also virtuously low-tech: there are no TVs, minibars or radios.

At the back of the train, the Observation Car is a civilised, if narrow, drawing room, with groups of sofas and chairs in tartan upholstery, a bar and a verandah which allows you to feel the wind in your hair as you trundle along at a steady 40mph.

The sleeping cabins succeed in jigsawing an impressive amount elegantly into a small space – reminiscent of a Tardis, but of the distinctly luxurious variety. If you are two to a cabin, a bit of time and space management is required when it comes to dressing or showering, but you'll find everything you need. Each cabin has an ensuite shower room, with a surprisingly powerful shower

and racks of upmarket unguents. The rooms have two single beds – not bunks – with thick mattresses, high-gauge sheets and little brass reading lights attached to the wall. The dressing table doubles as a desk complete with writing paper; there's wardrobe space for two; and again, everything is wood panelled and immaculately finished in brass or chrome, even down to the tiebacks.

Dining is important in The Royal Scotsman scheme – the train could be stationary or snaking over the Glenfinnan Viaduct as you eat your Kyle of Lochalsh scallops. A pair of talented chefs produce immaculate meals for the whole party, using the freshest Scottish produce, from a kitchen the size of a snooker table. A lot of care, and a surprising amount of innovation has also gone into the wine list.

There are two dining spaces: Raven, which also doubles as a library, can be configured to seat 20 around a big table, but Victory can only do intimate tables of two or four up to a total of 16, with seats that have been reupholstered in suitably retro fabric.

Service is discreet and tireless. You almost can't get from one end of a corridor to the other without someone offering you a drink or a canapé, or whisking into your room to make up the bed. Nothing is too much trouble. As with any private house party, the bar is always open, and no one bothers with measures.

The tour host – a key figure – will tell you, if you so desire, more about the sights you see out of the window, how long it takes to get to Bridge of Orchy and who built Mount Stuart on the Isle of Bute. There's nothing he doesn't know about this luxurious train, its routes and the numerous side excursions that can be organised along the way.

The train is stationary at night, allowing you to sleep properly. Then wake to some glorious view as it moves off very slowly in the morning.

All in all, one gets the feeling that only Hercule Poirot is missing.

THE ROYAL SCOTSMAN
at a glance

Les Maitland, commercial manager
46a Constitution Street, Edinburgh, Mid Lothian
Scotland EH6 6RS
0131 555 1344, www.royalscotsman.com

Sleeps: 36, in 16 twins and four single state cabins, all ensuite.

Dining: 36, with 20 in one carriage and 16 in the other. All meals and drinks are included, and the chef will discuss menus and timings, which can depend on the train schedule. Anything from a cold buffet to a four-course black-tie dinner can be arranged. A typical dinner might feature poached Scottish lobster with a fricassée of broad beans, peas and pancetta followed by fillet of Black Gold Beef with celeriac purée and morels and baked custard tart with nutmeg crème chantilly.

Other facilities: after-dinner entertainment such as a Highland Jacobite warrior in traditional Plaid dress who talks about what life was like in the 18th century.

Children: highchairs and cots available on request.

Wedding licence: if the train is stationary and in the Highland region. There are no double beds, however.

Local attractions/things to do: The Royal Scotsman can create itineraries around many themes, including golf, fishing, shooting and heritage. A standard trip incorporates numerous side outings, using the Royal Scotsman coach. These could include a trip to see Ballindalloch Castle, hosted by the lady laird; a walk on the beach at Morar; a private tour of Mount Stuart on the Isle of Bute; or a seal-spotting trip at Plockton.

Transport: all journeys start and end at Edinburgh Waverley Station, although this is negotiable.

Price: from £24,100 per night for 36 people (VAT not applicable) including meals, drinks and off-train visits.

Note: the train operates seasonally, generally from April to October.

BIG HOUSE PARTY
index of properties

GROUP SIZE

Note that where a venue is mentioned in more than one category, it can accommodate groups of different sizes. Extra beds may be available for children.

12-15

Barnacre Cottages, Lancashire
Berkeley House, Gloucestershire
Bruern Cottages, Oxfordshire
Combermere Abbey Cottages,
    Shropshire
Cotswold Cottages, Gloucestershire
Crosby Lodge, Cumbria
Dove House, Dorset
Drumkilbo House, Perthshire
Farlam Hall, Cumbria
Fell House, Cumbria
Fenton Tower, East Lothian
Ford Abbey, Herefordshire
Frogg Manor, Cheshire
Glenmorangie House, Ross-shire
Goddards, Surrey
Grove House, Gloucestershire
Harburn House, West Lothian
Kentchurch Court, Herefordshire
Ladyburn, Ayrshire
Langar Hall, Nottinghamshire
The Lodge, Argyll
Lower Farm Barns, Norfolk
Mains of Taymouth Cottages,
    Perthshire
Mansefield House, Argyll
Maunsel House, Somerset
Muncaster Castle, Cumbria
Old Kilmun House, Argyll
The Old Rectory, Dorset
Peek House, Devon
Polhawn Fort, Cornwall
The Riverside, Cornwall
The Samling, Cumbria
Skipton Hall, Yorkshire
Tresillian House, Cornwall
Trevor Hall, Denbighshire
Upper Court, Gloucestershire
Upper Rectory Farm Cottages,
    Warwickshire
Westover Hall Hotel, Hampshire
White Heron Cottages,
    Herefordshire

White Lodge Farm, Norfolk
White Moss House, Cumbria
Wintonhill Farmhouse, East Lothian
Wortham Manor, Devon

16-25

Augill Castle, Cumbria
Barnacre Cottages, Lancashire
Berkeley House, Gloucestershire
Blanch House, East Sussex
Bruern Cottages, Oxfordshire
Carnell, Ayrshire
Cliff Barns, Norfolk
Combermere Abbey Cottages,
    Shropshire
Cotswold Cottages, Gloucestershire
Dove House, Dorset
Drynachan Lodge, Inverness-shire
Duns Castle, Berwickshire
Eastnor Castle, Herefordshire
Eilean Shona, Argyll
Fairyhill, West Glamorgan
Fingals Hotel, Devon
Ford Abbey, Herefordshire
Gerbestone Manor, Somerset
Grove House, Gloucestershire
Kentchurch Court, Herefordshire
Llanfendigaid, Gwynedd
Llwynin Farmhouse, Powys
Lower Farm Barns, Norfolk
Mains of Taymouth Cottages,
    Perthshire
Manderston, Berwickshire
Muncaster Castle, Cumbria
Myres Castle, Fife
The Old Neptune Inn, Suffolk
The Old Rectory, Dorset
The Old Rectory, Norfolk
The Old Rectory, Suffolk
Plas Glansevin, Dyfed
Polhawn Fort, Cornwall
Symondsbury Manor, Dorset
Three Choirs, Gloucestershire
Toft Hall, Staffordshire
Tregawne, Cornwall
Upper Court, Gloucestershire
Upper Rectory Farm Cottages,
    Warwickshire
Wedderburn Castle, Berwickshire
The Well House, Cornwall
White Heron Cottages,

    Herefordshire
White Lodge Farm, Norfolk
Willows and Beeches, Powys
Wintonhill Farmhouse, East Lothian

26-40

Blair, Ayrshire
Bruern Cottages, Oxfordshire
Buckland House, Devon
Combermere Abbey Cottages,
    Shropshire
Drumkilbo House, Perthshire
Drynachan Lodge, Inverness-shire
Duns Castle, Berwickshire
Eastnor Castle, Herefordshire
Glenapp Castle, Ayrshire
Harburn House, West Lothian
Fingals Hotel, Devon
Isle of Eriska, Argyll
Leeds Castle, Kent
Muncaster Castle, Cumbria
Northcote Manor, Lancashire
Plas Glansevin, Dyfed
The Royal Scotsman, Mid Lothian
Upper Rectory Farm Cottages,
    Warwickshire
Willows and Beeches, Powys

41-68

Castle Ashby, Northamptonshire
Charlton House, Somerset
Combermere Abbey Cottages,
    Shropshire
Drynachan Lodge, Inverness-shire
Duns Castle, Berwickshire
Isle of Eriska, Argyll
Leeds Castle, Kent
Lower Farm Barns, Norfolk
Pelham House, East Sussex
Plas Glansevin, Dyfed

PRICE
£

Barnacre Cottages, Lancashire
Berkeley House, Gloucestershire
Buckland House, Devon
Fell House, Cumbria
Grove House, Gloucestershire
Kentchurch Court, Herefordshire
Llanfendigaid, Gwynedd
Llwynin Farmhouse, Powys

BIG HOUSE PARTY
cross references

Mansefield House, Argyll
Muncaster Castle, Cumbria
Old Kilmun House, Argyll
The Old Rectory, Dorset
The Old Rectory, Norfolk
The Old Rectory, Suffolk
The Riverside, Cornwall
Tregawne, Cornwall
Upper Rectory Farm Cottages,
    Warwickshire
White Lodge Farm, Norfolk
Wintonhill Farmhouse, East Lothian

££

Blanch House, East Sussex
Cotswold Cottages, Gloucestershire
Crosby Lodge, Cumbria
Dove House, Dorset
Drumkilbo House, Perthshire
Eilean Shona, Argyll
Fairyhill, West Glamorgan
Farlam Hall, Cumbria
Fingals Hotel, Devon
Ford Abbey, Herefordshire
Frogg Manor, Cheshire
Gerbestone Manor, Somerset
Goddards, Surrey
Ladyburn, Ayrshire
Lower Farm Barns, Norfolk
Mains of Taymouth Cottages,
    Perthshire
The Old Neptune Inn, Suffolk
Peek House, Devon
Pelham House, East Sussex
Plas Glansevin, Dyfed
Skipton Hall, Yorkshire
Symondsbury Manor, Dorset
Toft Hall, Staffordshire
Tresillian House, Cornwall
Trevor Hall, Denbighshire
Upper Court, Gloucestershire
The Well House, Cornwall
White Heron Cottages,
    Herefordshire
White Moss House, Cumbria
Willows and Beeches, Powys
Wortham Manor, Devon

£££

Augill Castle, Cumbria
Blair, Ayrshire

Bruern Cottages, Oxfordshire
Carnell, Ayrshire
Cliff Barns, Norfolk
Combermere Abbey Cottages,
    Shropshire
Drynachan Lodge, Inverness-shire
Duns Castle, Berwickshire
Eastnor Castle, Herefordshire
Fenton Tower, East Lothian
Glenmorangie House, Ross-shire
Harburn House, West Lothian
Isle of Eriska, Argyll
The Lodge, Argyll
Manderston, Berwickshire
Maunsel House, Somerset
Northcote Manor, Lancashire
Polhawn Fort, Cornwall
Westover Hall Hotel, Hampshire

££££

Castle Ashby, Northamptonshire
Charlton House, Somerset
Glenapp Castle, Ayrshire
Langar Hall, Nottinghamshire
Leeds Castle, Kent
Myres Castle, Fife
The Royal Scotsman, Mid Lothian
The Samling, Cumbria
Three Choirs, Gloucestershire
Wedderburn Castle, Berwickshire

CATERED VENUES

Augill Castle, Cumbria
Blair, Ayrshire
Blanch House, East Sussex
Carnell, Ayrshire
Castle Ashby, Northamptonshire
Charlton House, Somerset
Crosby Lodge, Cumbria
Drumkilbo House, Perthshire
Drynachan Lodge, Inverness-shire
Duns Castle, Berwickshire
Eastnor Castle, Herefordshire
Eilean Shona, Argyll
Fairyhill, West Glamorgan
Farlam Hall, Cumbria
Fenton Tower, East Lothian
Fingals Hotel, Devon
Ford Abbey, Herefordshire
Frogg Manor, Cheshire
Glenapp Castle, Ayrshire

Glenmorangie House, Ross-shire
Grove House, Gloucestershire
Harburn House, West Lothian
Isle of Eriska, Argyll
Kentchurch Court, Herefordshire
Ladyburn, Ayrshire
Langar Hall, Nottinghamshire
Leeds Castle, Kent
The Lodge, Argyll
Manderston, Berwickshire
Maunsel House, Somerset
Myres Castle, Fife
Northcote Manor, Lancashire
The Old Rectory, Suffolk
Pelham House, East Sussex
The Riverside, Cornwall
The Royal Scotsman, Mid Lothian
The Samling, Cumbria
Three Choirs, Gloucestershire
Tregawne, Cornwall
Upper Court, Gloucestershire
Wedderburn Castle, Berwickshire
The Well House, Cornwall
Westover Hall Hotel, Hampshire
White Moss House, Cumbria
Willows and Beeches, Powys
    (during shooting season)

SELF-CATERING VENUES

(but catering can be arranged)
Augill Castle, Cumbria
Barnacre Cottages, Lancashire
Berkeley House, Gloucestershire
Blair, Ayrshire
Bruern Cottages, Oxfordshire
Buckland House, Devon
Cliff Barns, Norfolk
Combermere Abbey Cottages,
    Shropshire
Cotswold Cottages, Gloucestershire
Dove House, Dorset
Fell House, Cumbria
Gerbestone Manor, Somerset
Goddards, Surrey
Grove House, Gloucestershire
Harburn House, West Lothian
Llanfendigaid, Gwynedd
Llwynin Farmhouse, Powys
Lower Farm Barns, Norfolk
Mains of Taymouth Cottages,
    Perthshire

Mansefield House, Argyll
Maunsel House, Somerset
Muncaster Castle, Cumbria
Old Kilmun House, Argyll
The Old Neptune Inn, Suffolk
The Old Rectory, Dorset
The Old Rectory, Norfolk
Peek House, Devon
Plas Glansevin, Dyfed
Polhawn Fort, Cornwall
Skipton Hall, Yorkshire
Symondsbury Manor, Dorset
Toft Hall, Staffordshire
Tresillian House, Cornwall
Trevor Hall, Denbighshire
Upper Court, Gloucestershire
Upper Rectory Farm Cottages,
    Warwickshire
White Heron Cottages,
    Herefordshire
White Lodge Farm, Norfolk
Willows and Beeches, Powys
    (between February and
    September)
Wintonhill Farmhouse, East Lothian
Wortham Manor, Devon

WEDDING LICENCE

Augill Castle, Cumbria
Blair, Ayrshire
Blanch House, East Sussex
Carnell, Ayrshire
Castle Ashby, Northamptonshire
Charlton House, Somerset
Cliff Barns, Norfolk
Combermere Abbey Cottages,
    Shropshire
Crosby Lodge, Cumbria
Drumkilbo House, Perthshire
Drynachan Lodge, Inverness-shire
Duns Castle, Berwickshire
Eastnor Castle, Herefordshire
Eilean Shona, Argyll
Fenton Tower, East Lothian
Ford Abbey, Herefordshire
Frogg Manor, Cheshire
Glenapp Castle, Ayrshire
Glenmorangie House, Ross-shire
Harburn House, West Lothian
Isle of Eriska, Argyll
Ladyburn, Ayrshire

Leeds Castle, Kent
The Lodge, Argyll
Manderston, Berwickshire
Maunsel House, Somerset
Muncaster Castle, Cumbria
Myres Castle, Fife
Northcote Manor, Lancashire
Pelham House, East Sussex
Polhawn Fort, Cornwall
The Royal Scotsman, Mid Lothian
The Samling, Cumbria
Three Choirs, Gloucestershire
Upper Court, Gloucestershire
Wedderburn Castle, Berwickshire
Westover Hall Hotel, Hampshire
Wintonhill Farmhouse, East Lothian

HEN AND STAG PARTIES

(at owner's discretion – deposit may
be required)
Bruern Cottages, Oxfordshire
Cliff Barns, Norfolk (hens only)
Cotswold Cottages, Gloucestershire
Goddards, Surrey
Grove House, Gloucestershire
Kentchurch Court, Herefordshire
Llanfendigaid, Gwynedd
Old Kilmun House, Argyll
The Old Neptune Inn, Suffolk
    (hens only)
The Old Rectory, Norfolk
Plas Glansevin, Dyfed
Trevor Hall, Denbighshire
Upper Court, Gloucestershire
    (hens only)
White Heron Cottages,
    Herefordshire
Wintonhill Farmhouse, East Lothian
Wortham Manor, Devon

GOOD FOR CHILDREN

Barnacre Cottages, Lancashire
Bruern Cottages, Oxfordshire
Buckland House, Devon
Combermere Abbey Cottages,
    Shropshire
Dove House, Dorset
Eilean Shona, Argyll
Llanfendigaid, Gwynedd
Llwynin Farmhouse, Powys
Old Kilmun House, Argyll

Peek House, Devon
Plas Glansevin, Dyfed
Toft Hall, Staffordshire
Trevor Hall, Denbighshire
Upper Court, Gloucestershire
    (only allowed in cottages)
White Lodge Farm, Norfolk

GOOD FOR SHOOTING

Buckland House, Devon
Carnell, Ayrshire
Castle Ashby, Northamptonshire
Cotswold Cottages, Gloucestershire
Drynachan Lodge, Inverness-shire
Duns Castle, Berwickshire
Harburn House, West Lothian
Isle of Eriska, Argyll
Kentchurch Court, Herefordshire
Myres Castle, Fife
The Old Rectory, Suffolk
Tregawne, Cornwall
Upper Court, Gloucestershire
The Well House, Cornwall
Willows and Beeches, Powys
Wintonhill Farmhouse, East Lothian

GOOD FOR GOLF

Blair, Ayrshire
Carnell, Ayrshire
Drumkilbo House, Perthshire
Drynachan Lodge, Inverness-shire
Fairyhill, West Glamorgan
Farlam Hall, Cumbria
Fenton Tower, East Lothian
Glenapp Castle, Ayrshire
Harburn House, West Lothian
Isle of Eriska, Argyll
Ladyburn, Ayrshire
Llanfendigaid, Gwynedd
Mains of Taymouth Cottages,
    Perthshire
Myres Castle, Fife
Old Kilmun House, Argyll
Plas Glansevin, Dyfed
Tregawne, Cornwall
The Well House, Cornwall
White Lodge Farm, Norfolk
Wintonhill Farmhouse, East Lothian

BIG HOUSE PARTY
cross references

GOURMET STAYS
Charlton House, Somerset
  (one Michelin star)
Fairyhill, West Glamorgan
  (three AA rosettes)
Farlam Hall, Cumbria
  (Relais & Châteaux member)
Glenapp Castle, Ayrshire
  (Relais & Châteaux member
  and three AA rosettes)
Northcote Manor, Lancashire
  (one Michelin star)
The Samling, Cumbria
  (one Michelin star)
The Well House, Cornwall
  (three AA rosettes)

GOOD FOR FISHING
Castle Ashby, Northamptonshire
Combermere Abbey Cottages,
  Shropshire
Cotswold Cottages, Gloucestershire
Eilean Shona, Argyll
Ford Abbey, Herefordshire
Gerbestone Manor, Somerset
Glenmorangie House, Ross-shire
Harburn House, West Lothian
Isle of Eriska, Argyll
Kentchurch Court, Herefordshire
Ladyburn, Ayrshire
Langar Hall, Nottinghamshire
Llwynin Farmhouse, Powys
The Lodge, Argyll
Mains of Taymouth Cottages,
  Perthshire
Mansefield House, Argyll
Old Kilmun House, Argyll
Peek House, Devon
Plas Glansevin, Dyfed
The Samling, Cumbria
The Well House, Cornwall
Willows and Beeches, Powys

PROPERTIES WITH
SWIMMING POOLS
Blair, Ayrshire
Bruern Cottages, Oxfordshire
Buckland House, Devon
Castle Ashby, Northamptonshire
Charlton House, Somerset
Dove House, Dorset

Drumkilbo House, Perthshire
Fingals Hotel, Devon
Ford Abbey, Herefordshire
Gerbestone Manor, Somerset
Grove House, Gloucestershire
Isle of Eriska, Argyll
Llanfendigaid, Gwynedd
Plas Glansevin, Dyfed
Tregawne, Cornwall
Upper Court, Gloucestershire
The Well House, Cornwall
White Heron Cottages,
  Herefordshire

PROPERTIES WITH BOATS
Eilean Shona, Argyll
Harburn House, West Lothian
Isle of Eriska, Argyll
The Lodge, Argyll
The Riverside, Cornwall
Upper Court, Gloucestershire

PROPERTIES WITH
TENNIS COURTS
Augill Castle, Cumbria
Barnacre Cottages, Lancashire
Blair, Ayrshire
Bruern Cottages, Oxfordshire
Carnell, Ayrshire
Castle Ashby, Northamptonshire
Charlton House, Somerset
Combermere Abbey Cottages,
  Shropshire
Dove House, Dorset
Duns Castle, Berwickshire
Fingals Hotel, Devon (grass court)
Frogg Manor, Cheshire
Gerbestone Manor, Somerset
Glenapp Castle, Ayrshire
Harburn House, West Lothian
Isle of Eriska, Argyll
Mains of Taymouth Cottages,
  Perthshire
Manderston, Berwickshire
Myres Castle, Fife
Polhawn Fort, Cornwall
Upper Court, Gloucestershire
The Well House, Cornwall

WHEELCHAIR ACCESS
(full and approved wheelchair
facilities)
Bruern Cottages, Oxfordshire
Charlton House, Somerset
Ford Abbey, Herefordshire
Frogg Manor, Cheshire
Glenapp Castle, Ayrshire
Isle of Eriska, Argyll
Pelham House, East Sussex

LIMITED MOBILITY
(with downstairs
bedroom/bathroom)
Barnacre Cottages, Lancashire
Cliff Barns, Norfolk
Combermere Abbey Cottages,
  Shropshire
Cotswold Cottages, Gloucestershire
Crosby Lodge, Cumbria
Dove House, Dorset
Drumkilbo House, Perthshire
Eastnor Castle, Herefordshire
Eilean Shona, Argyll
Farlam Hall, Cumbria
Fell House, Cumbria
Fingals Hotel, Devon
Glenmorangie House, Ross-shire
Grove House, Gloucestershire
Harburn House, West Lothian
Ladyburn, Ayrshire
Lower Farm Barns, Norfolk
Mansefield House, Argyll
Maunsel House, Somerset
Myres Castle, Fife
The Old Neptune Inn, Suffolk
The Old Rectory, Suffolk
Peek House, Devon
Plas Glansevin, Dyfed
Skipton Hall, Yorkshire
Symondsbury Manor, Dorset
Three Choirs, Gloucestershire
Upper Court, Gloucestershire
Wedderburn Castle, Berwickshire
The Well House, Cornwall
White Heron Cottages,
  Herefordshire
White Lodge Farm, Norfolk
Willows and Beeches, Powys
Wortham Manor, Devon

Many people have been involved in the production of this book, but special thanks should go to Darren Southern, our incredibly patient designer from em Creative and his wife Katy. Also to Charles Arnold, Hugh Brune and Carol Farley from Portfolio, our book distributor, for their encouragement right from the start. Also to our skilled proof readers Chlöe Bryan-Brown and David Pollard from Redaktiv Editorial Services. We are also very grateful for the technical support given by Tessa and Derek. Particular thanks, though, should go to our husbands, François and Matt. Our parents, Maureen and Patrick and Margaret and John, also proved to be incredibly supportive, along with the rest of our family and friends. Finally, a special thank you should go to Liz's father-in-law Pete, whose chauffering and babysitting skills were second to none.

Photographic acknowledgements

Barnacre Cottages – Andy Hockridge
Berkeley House – Chris Drake/
    Red Cover.com
Blair – Tom Gibson
Cliff Barns – Kate Esherby
Cotswold Cottages – James Meyer
Crosby Lodge – Malcolm Farrer,
    Institute of the Arts
Eastnor Castle – Archie Miles
Eilean Shona – Angus Bremner
Goddards – Martin Charles/
    James Morris/Landmark Trust
Harburn House – Helena Bayler/Mike Welch
Kentchurch Court – Jim Hellier
Ladyburn – John Boyd-Brent/Annie and Felix
Langar Hall – Richard Prescott
Llanfendigaid – Chris Wright Photography
The Lodge – Iain Hopkins
Llwynin Farmhouse – David Coates
Lower Farm Barns – Chris Wright
Photography

Manderston – Skyscan, Jennie Collins,
    LB Chapell, Tom Scott and Fritz Von
    Schulenberg
Mansefield House – John Boyd-Brent
Maunsel House – Western Daily Press
Muncaster Castle – Brian Sherwen
The Old Neptune Inn, Suffolk – Chris Lee
The Old Rectory, Dorset – Petrina Photos
The Riverside – Andrew Beasley/
    Cornwall Tourist Board
Skipton Hall – Peter Horton
Trevor Hall – Peter Sion Evans
Upper Court – Hamish Herford
Westover Hall Hotel – Jim Pascoe
White Heron Cottages – Nigel Hudson
Wintonhill Farmhouse – Jenny Collins
Wortham Manor – Ross Hoddinott/
    Landmark Trust

Front cover
Clockwise, from top left, Duns Castle, Upper Court (Hamish Herford), The Old Rectory, Dorset (Petrina Photos) and Sherriffs/White Heron Cottages (Nigel Hudson).

Back cover
Blandfords, Cotswold Cottages (James Meyer)

Preface
Top left, Sherriffs/White Heron Cottages (Nigel Hudson), the rest were taken at The Old Rectory, Suffolk.

The Royal Scotsman piece in the Unusual chapter was written by Kate Patrick.

None of the properties paid to be in this book. However, to offset production costs, each one agreed to buy 15 copies at the retail price. Each property had to be inspected and meet strict criteria – when they didn't measure up, we didn't include them. None of the entries saw their write up before we went to press.